American Men of Letters.

EDITED BY

CHARLES DUDLEY WARNER.

" Thou wert the morning star among the living,
  Ere thy fair light had fled:
Now, having died, thou art as Hesperus, giving
  New splendor to the dead."

The Riverside Press, Cambridge:
Electrotyped and Printed by H. O. Houghton & Co.

R. Waldo Emerson

NOTE.

My thanks are due to the members of Mr. Emerson's family, and the other friends who kindly assisted me by lending interesting letters and furnishing valuable information.

The Index, carefully made by Mr. J. H. Wiggin, was revised and somewhat abridged by myself.

OLIVER WENDELL HOLMES.

Boston, *November* 25, 1884.

CONTENTS.

CHAPTER IV.

1833–1838. ÆT. 30–35.

CHAPTER V.

1838–1843. ÆT. 35–40.

CHAPTER IX.

1858–1863. Æt. 55–60.

CHAPTER X.

1863–1868. Æt. 60–65.

CHAPTER XI.

1868–1873. Æt. 65–70.

CHAPTER XII.

1873–1878. ÆT. 70–75.

CHAPTER XIII.

1878–1882. ÆT. 75–79.

CHAPTER XIV.

CHAPTER XV.

CHAPTER XVI.

EMERSON. — A RETROSPECT.

INTRODUCTION.

"I HAVE the feeling that every man's biography is at his own expense. He furnishes not only the facts, but the report. I mean that all biography is autobiography. It is only what he tells of himself that comes to be known and believed."

So writes the man whose life we are to pass in review, and it is certainly as true of him as of any author we could name. He delineates himself so perfectly in his various writings that the careful reader sees his nature just as it was in all its essentials, and has little more to learn than those human accidents which individualize him in space and time. About all these accidents we have a natural and pardonable curiosity. We wish to know of what race he came, what were the conditions into which he was born, what educational and social influences helped to mould his character, and what new elements Nature added to make him Ralph Waldo Emerson.

He himself believes in the hereditary transmission of certain characteristics. Though Nature appears capricious, he says, "Some qualities she carefully fixes and transmits, but some, and those the finer, she exhales with the breath of the individual, as too costly to perpetuate. But I notice also that they may become fixed and permanent in any stock, by painting and repainting them on every individual, until at last Nature adopts them and bakes them in her porcelain."

We have in New England a certain number of families who constitute what may be called the Academic Races. Their names have been on college catalogues for generation after generation. They have filled the learned professions, more especially the ministry, from the old colonial days to our own time. If aptitudes for the acquisition of knowledge can be bred into a family as the qualities the sportsman wants in his dog are developed in pointers and setters, we know what we may expect of a descendant of one of the Academic Races. Other things being equal, he will take more naturally, more easily, to his books. His features will be more pliable, his voice will be more flexible, his whole nature more plastic than those of the youth with less favoring antecedents. The gift of genius is never to be reckoned upon beforehand, any more than a choice new variety of pear or peach in a seedling; it is always a surprise, but it is born with great advantages when the stock from which it springs has been long under cultivation.

These thoughts suggest themselves in looking back at the striking record of the family made historic by the birth of Ralph Waldo Emerson. It was remarkable for the long succession of clergymen in its genealogy, and for the large number of college graduates it counted on its rolls.

A genealogical table is very apt to illustrate the "survival of the fittest," — in the estimate of the descendants. It is inclined to remember and record those ancestors who do most honor to the living heirs of the family name and traditions. As every man may count two grandfathers, four great-grandfathers, eight great-great-grandfathers, and so on, a few generations give him a good chance for selection. If he adds his distinguished grandmothers, he may double the number of personages to choose from. The great-grandfathers of Mr. Emerson at the sixth remove were thirty-two in number, unless the list was shortened by intermarriage of relatives. One of these, from whom the name descended, was Thomas Emerson of Ipswich, who furnished the staff of life to the people of that wonderfully interesting old town and its neighborhood.

His son, the Reverend Joseph Emerson, minister of the town of Mendon, Massachusetts, married Elizabeth, daughter of the Reverend Edward Bulkeley, who succeeded his father, the Reverend Peter Bulkeley, as Minister of Concord, Massachusetts.

Peter Bulkeley was therefore one of Emerson's sixty-four grandfathers at the seventh remove. We know the tenacity of certain family characteristics through long lines of descent, and it is not impossible that any one of a hundred and twenty-eight grandparents, if indeed the full number existed in spite of family admixtures, may have transmitted his or her distinguishing traits through a series of lives that cover more than two centuries, to our own contemporary. Inherited qualities move along their several paths not unlike the pieces in the game of chess. Sometimes the character of the son can be traced directly to that of the father or of the mother, as the pawn's move carries him from one square to the next. Sometimes a series of distinguished fathers follows in a line, or a succession of superior mothers, as the black or white bishop sweeps the board on his own color. Sometimes the distinguishing characters pass from one sex to the other indifferently, as the castle strides over the black and white squares. Sometimes an uncle or aunt lives over again in a nephew or niece, as if the knight's move were repeated on the squares of human individuality. It is not impossible, then, that some of the qualities we mark in Emerson may have come from the remote ancestor whose name figures with distinction in the early history of New England.

The Reverend Peter Bulkeley is honorably commemorated among the worthies consigned to immortality in that precious and entertaining medley of fact and fancy, enlivened by a wilderness of quotations at first or second hand, the *Magnalia Christi Americana*, of the Reverend Cotton Mather. The old chronicler tells his story so much better than any one can tell it for him that he must be allowed to speak for himself in a few extracts, transferred with all their typographical idiosyncrasies from the London-printed folio of 1702.

"He was descended of an Honourable Family in *Bedfordshire.* — He was born at *Woodhil* (or *Odel*) in *Bedfordshire, January* 31st, 1582.

"His *Education* was answerable unto his *Original ;* it was *Learned,* it was *Genteel,* and, which was the top of all, it was very *Pious :* At length it made him a *Batchellor* of *Divinity,* and a Fellow of Saint *John's* Colledge in Cambridge. ——

"When he came abroad into the World, a good benefice befel him, added unto the estate of a Gentleman, left him by his Father ; whom he succeeded in his Ministry, at the place of his Nativity : Which one would imagine *Temptations* enough to keep him out of a *Wilderness*."

But he could not conscientiously conform to the ceremonies of the English Church, and so,—

"When Sir *Nathaniel Brent* was Arch-Bishop *Laud's* General, as Arch-Bishop *Laud* was *another's*, Complaints were made against Mr. *Bulkly*, for his Non-Conformity, and he was therefore Silenced.

"To *New-England* he therefore came, in the Year 1635 ; and there having been for a while, at *Cambridge*, he carried a good Number of Planters with him, up further into the *Woods*, where they gathered the *Twelfth Church*, then formed in the Colony, and call'd the Town by the Name of *Concord*.

"Here he *buried* a great Estate, while he *raised* one still, for almost every Person whom he employed in the Affairs of his Husbandry.—

"He was a most excellent *Scholar*, a very-*well read* Person, and one, who in his advice to young Students, gave Demonstrations, that he knew what would go to make a *Scholar*. But it being essential unto a *Scholar* to love a *Scholar*, so did he ; and in Token thereof, endowed the Library of *Harvard-*Colledge with no small part of his own.

"And he was therewithal a most exalted *Christian* — " In his Ministry he was another *Farel*, *Quo nemo tonuit fortius* — And the observance which his own People had for him, was also paid him from all sorts of People throughout the Land ; but especially from the Ministers of the Country, who would still address him as a *Father*, a *Prophet*, a *Counsellor*, on all occasions."

These extracts may not quite satisfy the exacting reader, who must be referred to the old folio from which they were taken, where he will receive the following counsel : —

" If then any Person would know what Mr. *Peter Bulkly* was, let him read his Judicious and Savory Treatise of the *Gospel Covenant*, which has passed through several Editions, with much Acceptance among the People of God." It must be added that " he had a competently good Stroke at Latin Poetry ; and even in his Old Age, affected sometimes to improve it. Many of his Composure are yet in our Hands."

It is pleasant to believe that some of the qualities of this distinguished scholar and Christian were reproduced in the descendant whose life we are studying. At his death in 1659 he was succeeded, as was mentioned, by his son Edward, whose daughter became the wife of the Reverend Joseph Emerson, the minister of Mendon who, when that village was destroyed by the Indians, removed to Concord, where he died in the year 1680. This is the first connection of the name

of Emerson with Concord, with which it has
since been so long associated.

Edward Emerson, son of the first and father
of the second Reverend Joseph Emerson, though
not a minister, was the next thing to being one,
for on his gravestone he is thus recorded : " Mr.
Edward Emerson, sometime Deacon of the first
church in Newbury." He was noted for the
virtue of patience, and it is a family tradition
that he never complained but once, when he
said mildly to his daughter that her dumplings
were somewhat harder than needful, — " *but not
often.*" This same Edward was the only break
in the line of ministers who descended from
Thomas of Ipswich. He is remembered in the
family as having been " a merchant in Charles-
town."

Their son, the second Reverend Joseph Emerson, Minister of Malden for nearly half a century, married Mary, the daughter of the Reverend Samuel Moody, — Father Moody, — of
York, Maine. Three of his sons were ministers,
and one of these, William, was pastor of the
church at Concord at the period of the outbreak
of the Revolutionary War.

As the successive generations narrow down
towards the individual whose life we are recalling, the character of his progenitors becomes
more and more important and interesting to the

biographer. The Reverend William Emerson, grandfather of Ralph Waldo, was an excellent and popular preacher and an ardent and devoted patriot. He preached resistance to tyrants from the pulpit, he encouraged his townsmen and their allies to make a stand against the soldiers who had marched upon their peaceful village, and would have taken a part in the Fight at the Bridge, which he saw from his own house, had not the friends around him prevented his quitting his doorstep. He left Concord in 1776 to join the army at Ticonderoga, was taken with fever, was advised to return to Concord and set out on the journey, but died on his way. His wife was the daughter of the Reverend Daniel Bliss, his predecessor in the pulpit at Concord. This was another very noticeable personage in the line of Emerson's ancestors. His merits and abilities are described at great length on his tombstone in the Concord burial-ground. There is no reason to doubt that his epitaph was composed by one who knew him well. But the slabs which record the excellences of our New England clergymen of the past generations are so crowded with virtues that the reader can hardly help inquiring whether a sharp bargain was not driven with the stonecutter, like that which the good Vicar of Wakefield arranged with the portrait-painter. He was to represent

Sophia as a shepherdess, it will be remembered, with as many sheep as he could afford to put in for nothing.

William Emerson left four children, a son bearing the same name, and three daughters, one of whom, Mary Moody Emerson, is well remembered as pictured for us by her nephew, Ralph Waldo. His widow became the wife of the Reverend Ezra Ripley, Doctor of Divinity, and his successor as Minister at Concord.

The Reverend William Emerson, the second of that name and profession, and the father of Ralph Waldo Emerson, was born in the year 1769, and graduated at Harvard College in 1789. He was settled as Minister in the town of Harvard in the year 1792, and in 1799 became Minister of the First Church in Boston. In 1796 he married Ruth Haskins of Boston. He died in 1811, leaving five sons, of whom Ralph Waldo was the second.

The interest which attaches itself to the immediate parentage of a man like Emerson leads us to inquire particularly about the characteristics of the Reverend William Emerson so far as we can learn them from his own writings and from the record of his contemporaries.

The Reverend Dr. Sprague's valuable and well-known work, " Annals of the American Pulpit," contains three letters from which we learn some of his leading characteristics. Dr. Pierce of Brookline, the faithful chronicler of his time, speaks of his pulpit talents as extraordinary, but thinks there was not a perfect sympathy between him and the people of the quiet little town of Harvard, while he was highly acceptable in the pulpits of the metropolis. In personal appearance he was attractive; his voice was melodious, his utterance distinct, his manner agreeable. "He was a faithful and generous friend and knew how to forgive an enemy. — In his theological views perhaps he went farther on the liberal side than most of his brethren with whom he was associated. — He was, however, perfectly tolerant towards those who differed from him most widely."

Dr. Charles Lowell, another brother minister, says of him, "Mr. Emerson was a handsome man, rather tall, with a fair complexion, his cheeks slightly tinted, his motions easy, graceful, and gentlemanlike, his manners bland and pleasant. He was an honest man, and expressed himself decidedly and emphatically, but never bluntly or vulgarly. — Mr. Emerson was a man of good sense. His conversation was edifying and useful; never foolish or undignified. — In his theological opinions he was, to say the least, far from having any sympathy with Calvinism. I have not supposed that he was, like Dr. Freeman, a Humanitarian, though he may have been so."

There was no honester chronicler than our clerical Pepys, good, hearty, sweet-souled, fact-loving Dr. John Pierce of Brookline, who knew the dates of birth and death of the graduates of Harvard, starred and unstarred, better, one is tempted to say (*Hibernice*), than they did themselves. There was not a nobler gentleman in charge of any Boston parish than Dr. Charles Lowell. But after the pulpit has said what it thinks of the pulpit, it is well to listen to what the pews have to say about it.

This is what the late Mr. George Ticknor said in an article in the "Christian Examiner" for September, 1849.

" Mr. Emerson, transplanted to the First Church in Boston six years before Mr. Buckminster's settlement, possessed, on the contrary, a graceful and dignified style of speaking, which was by no means without its attraction, but he 1 the fervor that could rouse the masses, and the original resources that could command the few."

As to his religious beliefs, Emerson writes to Dr. Sprague as follows: " I did not find in any manuscript or printed sermons that I looked at, any very explicit statement of opinion on the question between Calvinists and Socinians. He inclines obviously to what is ethical and universal in Christianity; very little to the personal and historical. — I think I observe in his writings, as in the writings of Unitarians down to a recent date, a studied reserve on the subject of the nature and offices of Jesus. They had not made up their own minds on it. It was a mystery to them, and they let it remain so."

Mr. William Emerson left, published, fifteen Sermons and Discourses, an Oration pronounced at Boston on the Fourth of July, 1802, a Collection of Psalms and Hymns, an Historical Sketch of the First Church in Boston, besides his contributions to the "Monthly Anthology," of which he was the Editor.

Ruth Haskins, the wife of William and the mother of Ralph Waldo Emerson, is spoken of by the late Dr. Frothingham, in an article in the "Christian Examiner," as a woman "of great patience and fortitude, of the serenest trust in God, of a discerning spirit, and a most courteous bearing, one who knew how to guide the affairs of her own house, as long as she was responsible for that, with the sweetest authority, and knew how to give the least trouble and the greatest happiness after that authority was resigned. Both her mind and her character were of a superior order, and they set their stamp upon manners of peculiar softness and natural

grace and quiet dignity. Her sensible and
kindly speech was always as good as the best
instruction; her smile, though it was ever ready,
was a reward."

The Reverend Dr. Furness of Philadelphia,
who grew up with her son, says, " Waldo bore a
strong resemblance to his father ; the other children resembled their mother."

Such was the descent of Ralph Waldo Emerson. If the ideas of parents survive as impressions or tendencies in their descendants, no man
had a better right to an inheritance of theological instincts than this representative of a long
line of ministers. The same trains of thought
and feeling might naturally gain in force from
another association of near family relationship,
though not of blood. After the death of the
first William Emerson, the Concord minister,
his widow, Mr. Emerson's grandmother, married, as has been mentioned, his successor, Dr.
Ezra Ripley. The grandson spent much time in
the family of Dr. Ripley, whose character he
has drawn with exquisite felicity in a sketch
read before The Social Circle of Concord, and
published in the " Atlantic Monthly " for November, 1883. Mr. Emerson says of him :
" He was identified with the ideas and forms of
the New England Church, which expired about
the same time with him, so that he and his

coevals seemed the rear guard of the great camp and army of the Puritans, which, however in its last days declining into formalism, in the heyday of its strength had planted and liberated America. . . . The same faith made what was strong and what was weak in Dr. Ripley." It would be hard to find a more perfect sketch of character than Mr. Emerson's living picture of Dr. Ripley. I myself remember him as a comely little old gentleman, but he was not so communicative in a strange household as his clerical brethren, smiling John Foster of Brighton and chatty Jonathan Homer of Newton. Mr. Emerson says, " He was a natural gentleman; no dandy, but courtly, hospitable, manly, and public-spirited; his nature social, his house open to all men. — His brow was serene and open to his visitor, for he loved men, and he had no studies, no occupations, which company could interrupt. His friends were his study, and to see them loosened his talents and his tongue. In his house dwelt order and prudence and plenty. There was no waste and no stint. He was open-handed and just and generous. Ingratitude and meanness in his beneficiaries did not wear out his compassion ; he bore the insult, and the next day his basket for the beggar, his horse and chaise for the cripple, were at their door." How like Goldsmith's good Dr. Prim-

rose ! I do not know any writing of Mr. Emerson which brings out more fully his sense of
humor, — of the picturesque in character, —
and as a piece of composition, continuous, fluid,
transparent, with a playful ripple here and
there, it is admirable and delightful.

Another of his early companionships must
have exercised a still more powerful influence on
his character, — that of his aunt, Mary Moody
Emerson. He gave an account of her in a paper
read before the Woman's Club several years ago,
and published in the " Atlantic Monthly " for
December, 1883. Far more of Mr. Emerson is
to be found in this aunt of his than in any other
of his relations in the ascending series, with
whose history we are acquainted. Her story is
an interesting one, but for that I must refer the
reader to the article mentioned. Her character
and intellectual traits are what we are most concerned with. "Her early reading was Milton,
Young, Akenside, Samuel Clarke, Jonathan
Edwards, and always the Bible. Later, Plato,
Plotinus, Marcus Antoninus, Stewart, Coleridge, Herder, Locke, Madam De Staël, Channing, Mackintosh, Byron. Nobody can read in
her manuscript, or recall the conversation of
old-school people, without seeing that Milton
and Young had a religious authority in their
minds, and nowise the slight merely entertain-

ing quality of modern bards. And Plato, Aristotle, Plotinus, — how venerable and organic as Nature they are in her mind ! "

There are many sentences cited by Mr. Emerson which remind us very strongly of his own writings. Such a passage as the following might have come from his Essay, " Nature," but it was written when her nephew was only four years old.

" Malden, 1807, September. — The rapture of feeling I would part from for days devoted to higher discipline. But when Nature beams with such excess of beauty, when the heart thrills with hope in its Author, — feels it is related to Him more than by any ties of creation, — it exults, too fondly, perhaps, for a state of trial. But in dead of night, nearer morning, when the eastern stars glow, or appear to glow, with more indescribable lustre, a lustre which penetrates the spirits with wonder and curiosity, — then, however awed, who can fear ? " — " A few pulsations of created beings, a few successions of acts, a few lamps held out in the firmament, enable us to talk of Time, make epochs, write histories, — to do more, — to date the revelations of God to man. But these lamps are held to measure out some of the moments of eternity, to divide the history of God's operations in the birth and death of nations, of worlds. It is a goodly name for our notions of breathing, suffering, enjoying, acting. We personify it. We call it by every name of fleeting, dreaming, vaporing imagery.

Yet it is nothing. We exist in eternity. Dissolve the body and the night is gone; the stars are extinguished, and we measure duration by the number of our thoughts, by the activity of reason, the discovery of truths, the acquirement of virtue, the approval of God."

Miss Mary Emerson showed something of the same feeling towards natural science which may be noted in her nephews Waldo and Charles. After speaking of "the poor old earth's chaotic state, brought so near in its long and gloomy transmutings by the geologist," she says: —

"Yet its youthful charms, as decked by the hand of Moses' Cosmogony, will linger about the heart, while Poetry succumbs to science." — "And the bare bones of this poor embryo earth may give the idea of the Infinite, far, far better than when dignified with arts and industry; its oceans, when beating the symbols of countless ages, than when covered with cargoes of war and oppression. How grand its preparation for souls, souls who were to feel the Divinity, before Science had dissected the emotions and applied its steely analysis to that state of being which recognizes neither psychology nor element." — Usefulness, if it requires action, seems less like existence than the desire of being absorbed in God, retaining consciousness. . . . Scorn trifles, lift your aims; do what you are afraid to do. Sublimity of character must come from sublimity of motive."

So far as hereditary and family influences can account for the character and intellect of Ralph Waldo Emerson, we could hardly ask for a better inborn inheritance, or better counsels and examples.

Having traced some of the distinguishing traits which belong by descent to Mr. Emerson to those who were before him, it is interesting to note how far they showed themselves in those of his own generation, his brothers. Of these I will mention two, one of whom I knew personally.

Edward Bliss Emerson, who graduated at Harvard College in 1824, three years after Ralph Waldo, held the first place in his class. He began the study of the law with Daniel Webster, but overworked himself and suffered a temporary disturbance of his reason. After this he made another attempt, but found his health unequal to the task and exiled himself to Porto Rico, where, in 1834, he died. Two poems preserve his memory, one that of Ralph Waldo, in which he addresses his memory, —

" Ah, brother of the brief but blazing star,"

the other his own " Last Farewell," written in 1832, whilst sailing out of Boston Harbor. The lines are unaffected and very touching, full of that deep affection which united the brothers in the closest intimacy, and of the tenderest love for the mother whom he was leaving to see no more.

I had in my early youth a key furnished me to some of the leading traits which were in due time to develop themselves in Emerson's character and intelligence. As on the wall of some great artist's studio one may find unfinished sketches which he recognizes as the first growing conceptions of pictures painted in after years, so we see that Nature often sketches, as it were, a living portrait, which she leaves in its rudimentary condition, perhaps for the reason that earth has no colors which can worthily fill in an outline too perfect for humanity. The sketch is left in its consummate incompleteness because this mortal life is not rich enough to carry out the Divine idea.

Such an unfinished but unmatched outline is that which I find in the long portrait-gallery of memory, recalled by the name of Charles Chauncy Emerson. Save for a few brief glimpses of another, almost lost among my life's early shadows, this youth was the most angelic adolescent my eyes ever beheld. Remembering what well-filtered blood it was that ran in the veins of the race from which he was descended, those who knew him in life might well say with Dryden, —

" If by traduction came thy mind
    Our wonder is the less to find
    A soul so charming from a stock so good."

His image is with me in its immortal youth as
when, almost fifty years ago, I spoke of him in
these lines, which I may venture to quote from
myself, since others have quoted them before me.

Thou calm, chaste scholar ! I can see thee now,
The first young laurels on thy pallid brow,
O'er thy slight figure floating lightly down
In graceful folds the academic gown,
On thy curled lip the classic lines that taught
How nice the mind that sculptured them with thought,
And triumph glistening in the clear blue eye,
Too bright to live, — but O, too fair to die.

Being about seven years younger than Waldo, he
must have received much of his intellectual and
moral guidance at his elder brother's hands. I
told the story at a meeting of our Historical
Society of Charles Emerson's coming into my
study, — this was probably in 1826 or 1827, —
taking up Hazlitt's "British Poets" and turning
at once to a poem of Marvell's, which he read
with his entrancing voice and manner. The
influence of this poet is plain to every reader in
some of Emerson's poems, and Charles' liking
for him was very probably caught from Waldo.
  When Charles was nearly through college, a
periodical called "The Harvard Register" was

published by students and recent graduates. Three articles were contributed by him to this periodical. Two of them have the titles " Conversation," " Friendship." His quotations are from Horace and Juvenal, Plato, Plutarch, Bacon, Jeremy Taylor, Shakespeare, and Scott. There are passages in these Essays which remind one strongly of his brother, the Lecturer of twenty-five or thirty years later. Take this as an example : —

" Men and mind are my studies. I need no observatory high in air to aid my perceptions or enlarge my prospect. I do not want a costly apparatus to give pomp to my pursuit or to disguise its inutility. I do not desire to travel and see foreign lands and learn all knowledge and speak with all tongues, before I am prepared for my employment. I have merely to go out of my door; nay, I may stay at home at my chambers, and I shall have enough to do and enjoy."

The feeling of this sentence shows itself constantly in Emerson's poems. He finds his inspiration in the objects about him, the forest in which he walks; the sheet of water which the hermit of a couple of seasons made famous; the lazy Musketaquid; the titmouse that mocked his weakness in the bitter cold winter's day; the mountain that rose in the horizon; the lofty pines; the lowly flowers. All talked with him as brothers and sisters, and he with them as of his own household.

The same lofty idea of friendship which we find in the man in his maturity, we recognize in one of the Essays of the youth.

"All men of gifted intellect and fine genius," says Charles Emerson, "must entertain a noble idea of friendship. Our reverence we are constrained to yield where it is due, — to rank, merit, talents. But our affections we give not thus easily.

'The hand of Douglas is his own.'"

— "I am willing to lose an hour in gossip with persons whom good men hold cheap. All this I will do out of regard to the decent conventions of polite life. But my friends I must know, and, knowing, I must love. There must be a daily beauty in their life that shall secure my constant attachment. I cannot stand upon the footing of ordinary acquaintance. Friendship is aristocratical — the affections which are prostituted to every suitor I will not accept."

Here are glimpses of what the youth was to be, of what the man who long outlived him became. Here is the dignity which commands reverence, — a dignity which, with all Ralph Waldo Emerson's sweetness of manner and expression, rose almost to majesty in his serene presence. There was something about Charles Emerson which lifted those he was with into a lofty and pure region of thought and feeling.

A vulgar soul stood abashed in his presence. I could never think of him in the presence of such, listening to a paltry sentiment or witnessing a mean action without recalling Milton's line,

" Back stepped those two fair angels half amazed,"

and thinking how he might well have been taken for a celestial messenger.

No doubt there is something of idealization in all these reminiscences, and of that exaggeration which belongs to the *laudator temporis acti.* But Charles Emerson was idolized in his own time by many in college and out of college. George Stillman Hillard was his rival. Neck and neck they ran the race for the enviable position of first scholar in the class of 1828, and when Hillard was announced as having the first part assigned to him, the excitement within the college walls, and to some extent outside of them, was like that when the telegraph proclaims the result of a Presidential election, — or the Winner of the Derby. But Hillard honestly admired his brilliant rival. " Who has a part with * * * * at this next exhibition ? " I asked him one day, as I met him in the college yard. " * * * * * * the Post," answered Hillard. " Why call him *the Post?* " said I. " He is a wooden creature," said Hillard. " Hear him and Charles Emerson translating from the Latin *Domus* *tota inflammata erat.* The Post will render the words, ' The whole house was on fire.' Charles Emerson will translate the sentence ' The entire edifice was wrapped in flames.' " It was natural enough that a young admirer should prefer the Bernini drapery of Charles Emerson's version to the simple nudity of " the Post's " rendering.

The nest is made ready long beforehand for the bird which is to be bred in it and to fly from it. The intellectual atmosphere into which a scholar is born, and from which he draws the breath of his early mental life, must be studied if we would hope to understand him thoroughly.

When the present century began, the elements, thrown into confusion by the long struggle for Independence, had not had time to arrange themselves in new combinations. The active intellects of the country had found enough to keep them busy in creating and organizing a new order of political and social life. Whatever purely literary talent existed was as yet in the nebular condition, a diffused luminous spot here and there, waiting to form centres of condensation.

Such a nebular spot had been brightening in and about Boston for a number of years, when,

in the year 1804, a small cluster of names became visible as representing a modest constellation of literary luminaries : John Thornton
Kirkland, afterwards President of Harvard University ; Joseph Stevens Buckminster ; John
Sylvester John Gardiner ; William Tudor ; Samuel Cooper Thacher ; William Emerson. These
were the chief stars of the new cluster, and their
light reached the world, or a small part of it,
as reflected from the pages of "The Monthly
Anthology," which very soon came under the
editorship of the Reverend William Emerson.

The father of Ralph Waldo Emerson may
be judged of in good measure by the associates
with whom he was thus connected. A brief
sketch of these friends and fellow-workers of his
may not be out of place, for these men made the
local sphere of thought into which Ralph Waldo
Emerson was born.

John Thornton Kirkland should have been
seen and heard as he is remembered by old graduates of Harvard, sitting in the ancient Presidential Chair, on Commencement Day, and calling in his penetrating but musical accents : " *Ex-
pectatur Oratio in Lingua Latina* " or " *Ver-
nacula*," if the " First Scholar " was about
to deliver the English oration. It was a presence not to be forgotten. His " shining morning face " was round as a baby's, and talked as

pleasantly as his voice did, with smiles for accents and dimples for punctuation. Mr. Ticknor speaks of his sermons as " full of intellectual wealth and practical wisdom, with sometimes a quaintness that bordered on humor." It was of him that the story was always told, — it may be as old as the invention of printing, — that he threw his sermons into a barrel, where they went to pieces and got mixed up, and that when he was going to preach he fished out what he thought would be about enough for a sermon, and patched the leaves together as he best might. The Reverend Dr. Lowell says : " He always found the right piece, and that was better than almost any of his brethren could have found in what they had written with twice the labor." Mr. Cabot, who knew all Emerson's literary habits, says he used to fish out the number of leaves he wanted for a lecture in somewhat the same way. Emerson's father, however, was very methodical, according to Dr. Lowell, and had " a place for everything, and everything in its place." Dr. Kirkland left little to be remembered by, and like many of the most interesting personalities we have met with, has become a very thin ghost to the grandchildren of his contemporaries.

Joseph Stevens Buckminster was the pulpit darling of his day, in Boston. The beauty of his person, the perfection of his oratory, the finish of his style, added to the sweetness of his character, made him one of those living idols which seem to be as necessary to Protestantism as images and pictures are to Romanism.

John Sylvester John Gardiner, once a pupil of the famous Dr. Parr, was then the leading Episcopal clergyman of Boston. Him I recon· struct from scattered hints I have met with as a scholarly, social man, with a sanguine temperament and the cheerful ways of a wholesome English parson, blest with a good constitution and a comfortable benefice. Mild Orthodoxy, ripened in Unitarian sunshine, is a very agreeable aspect of Christianity, and none was readier than Dr. Gardiner, if the voice of tradition may be trusted, to fraternize with his brothers of the liberal persuasion, and to make common cause with them in all that related to the interests of learning.

William Tudor was a chief connecting link between the period of the "Monthly Anthology," and that of the "North American Review," for he was a frequent contributor to the first of these periodicals, and he was the founder of the second. Edward Everett characterizes him, in speaking of his "Letters on the Eastern States," as a scholar and a gentleman, an impartial observer, a temperate champion, a liberal opponent, and a correct writer. Daniel Web·

ster bore similar testimony to his talents and
character.

Samuel Cooper Thacher was hardly twenty
years old when the " Anthology " was founded,
and died when he was only a little more than
thirty. He contributed largely to that periodical, besides publishing various controversial sermons, and writing the " Memoir of Buckminster."

There was no more brilliant circle than this in
any of our cities. There was none where so
much freedom of thought was united to so much
scholarship. The " Anthology " was the literary precursor of the " North American Review,"
and the theological herald of the " Christian
Examiner." Like all first beginnings it showed
many marks of immaturity. It mingled extracts
and original contributions, theology and medicine, with all manner of literary chips and shav-
ings. It had Magazine ways that smacked of
Sylvanus Urban ; leading articles with balanced
paragraphs which recalled the marching tramp
of Johnson ; translations that might have been
signed with the name of Creech, and Odes to
Sensibility, and the like, which recalled the
syrupy sweetness and languid trickle of Laura
Matilda's sentimentalities. It talked about " the
London Reviewers " with a kind of provincial
deference. It printed articles with quite too

much of the license of Swift and Prior for
the Magazines of to-day. But it had opinions
of its own, and would compare well enough with
the " Gentleman's Magazine," to say nothing
of " My Grandmother's Review, the British."
A writer in the third volume (1806) says: " A
taste for the belles lettres is rapidly spreading
in our country. I believe that, fifty years ago,
England had never seen a Miscellany or a
Review so well conducted as our ' Anthology,'
however superior such publications may now be
in that kingdom."

It is well worth one's while to look over the
volumes of the " Anthology " to see what our
fathers and grandfathers were thinking about,
and how they expressed themselves. The stiff-
ness of Puritanism was pretty well relaxed when
a Magazine conducted by clergymen could say
that " The child," — meaning the new periodical,
— " shall not be destitute of the manners of a
gentleman, nor a stranger to genteel amusements.
He shall attend Theatres, Museums, Balls, and
whatever polite diversions the town shall furnish." The reader of the " Anthology " will
find for his reward an improving discourse on
" Ambition," and a commendable schoolboy's
" theme " on " Inebriation." He will learn
something which may be for his advantage about
the " Anjou Cabbage," and may profit by a

" Remedy for Asthma." A controversy respecting the merits of Sir Richard Blackmore may
prove too little exciting at the present time, and
he can turn for relief to the epistle " Studiosus "
addresses to " Alcander." If the lines of " The
Minstrel " who hails, like Longfellow in later
years, from " The District of Main," fail to
satisfy him, he cannot accuse " R. T. Paine, Jr.,
Esq.," of tameness when he exclaims : —

> " Rise Columbia, brave and free,
> Poise the globe and bound the sea ! "

But the writers did not confine themselves to
native or even to English literature, for there is
a distinct mention of " Mr. Goethe's new novel,"
and an explicit reference to " Dante Aligheri, an
Italian bard." But let the smiling reader go a
little farther and he will find Mr. Buckminster's
most interesting account of the destruction of
Goldau. And in one of these same volumes
he will find the article, by Dr. Jacob Bigelow,
doubtless, which was the first hint of our rural
cemeteries, and foreshadowed that new era in
our underground civilization which is sweeten-
ing our atmospheric existence.

The late President Josiah Quincy, in his
" History of the Boston Athenæum," pays a
high tribute of respect to the memory and the
labors of the gentlemen who founded that institution and conducted the " Anthology." A lit-

erary journal had already been published in Boston, but very soon failed for want of patronage.
An enterprising firm of publishers, " being desirous that the work should be continued, applied
to the Reverend William Emerson, a clergyman of the place, distinguished for energy and
literary taste; and by his exertions several gentlemen of Boston and its vicinity, conspicuous
for talent and zealous for literature, were in-
duced to engage in conducting the work, and for
this purpose they formed themselves into a Society.   This Society was not completely organized
until the year 1805, when Dr. Gardiner was
elected President, and William Emerson Vice-
President. The Society thus formed maintained
its existence with reputation for about six years,
and issued ten octavo volumes from the press,
constituting one of the most lasting and honorable monuments of the literature of the period,
and may be considered as a true revival of polite learning in this country after that decay and
neglect which resulted from the distractions of
the Revolutionary War, and as forming an epoch
in the intellectual history of the United States.
Its records yet remain, an evidence that it was a
pleasant, active, high-principled association of
literary men, laboring harmoniously to elevate
the literary standard of the time, and with a
success which may well be regarded as remark-

able, considering the little sympathy they received from the community, and the many difficulties with which they had to struggle."

The publication of the "Anthology" began in 1804, when Mr. William Emerson was thirty-four years of age, and it ceased to be published in the year of his death, 1811. Ralph Waldo Emerson was eight years old at that time. His intellectual life began, we may say, while the somewhat obscure afterglow of the "Anthology" was in the western horizon of the New England sky.

The nebula which was to form a cluster about the "North American Review" did not take definite shape until 1815. There is no such memorial of the growth of American literature as is to be found in the first half century of that periodical. It is easy to find fault with it for uniform respectability and occasional dulness. But take the names of its contributors during its first fifty years from the literary record of that period, and we should have but a meagre list of mediocrities, saved from absolute poverty by the genius of two or three writers like Irving and Cooper. Strike out the names of Webster, Everett, Story, Sumner, and Cushing; of Bryant, Dana, Longfellow, and Lowell; of Prescott, Ticknor, Motley, Sparks, and Bancroft; of Verplanck, Hillard, and Whipple; of Stuart and

Robinson; of Norton, Palfrey, Peabody, and Bowen; and, lastly, that of Emerson himself, and how much American classic literature would be left for a new edition of "Miller's Retrospect"?

These were the writers who helped to make the "North American Review" what it was during the period of Emerson's youth and early manhood. These, and men like them, gave Boston its intellectual character. We may count as symbols the three hills of "this darling town of ours," as Emerson called it, and say that each had its beacon. Civil liberty lighted the torch on one summit, religious freedom caught the flame and shone from the second, and the lamp of the scholar has burned steadily on the third from the days when John Cotton preached his first sermon to those in which we are living.

The social religious influences of the first part of the century must not be forgotten. The two high-caste religions of that day were white-handed Unitarianism and ruffled-shirt Episcopalianism. What called itself "society" was chiefly distributed between them. Within less than fifty years a social revolution has taken place which has somewhat changed the relation between these and other worshipping bodies. This movement is the general withdrawal of the native New Englanders of both sexes from domestic service. A large part of the "hired help," — for the word servant was commonly repudiated, — worshipped, not with their employers, but at churches where few or no well-appointed carriages stood at the doors. The congregations that went chiefly from the drawing-room and those which were largely made up of dwellers in the culinary studio were naturally separated by a very distinct line of social cleavage. A certain exclusiveness and fastidiousness, not reminding us exactly of primitive Christianity, was the inevitable result. This must always be remembered in judging the men and women of that day and their immediate descendants, as much as the surviving prejudices of those whose parents were born subjects of King George in the days when loyalty to the crown was a virtue. The line of social separation was more marked, probably, in Boston, the headquarters of Unitarianism, than in the other large cities; and even at the present day our Jerusalem and Samaria, though they by no means refuse dealing with each other, do not exchange so many cards as they do checks and dollars. The exodus of those children of Israel from the house of bondage, as they chose to consider it, and their fusion with the mass of independent citizens, got rid of a class distinction which was felt even in the sanctuary. True religious equality is harder to es-

tablish than civil liberty. No man has done
more for spiritual republicanism than Emerson,
though he came from the daintiest sectarian circle of the time in the whole country.

Such were Emerson's intellectual and moral
parentage, nurture, and environment; such was
the atmosphere in which he grew up from youth
to manhood.

CHAPTER I.

Birthplace. — Boyhood. — College Life.

1803–1823.   To ÆT. 20.

RALPH WALDO EMERSON was born in Boston, Massachusetts, on the 25th of May, 1803.

He was the second of five sons; William, R. W., Edward Bliss, Robert Bulkeley, and Charles Chauncy.

His birthplace and that of our other illustrious Bostonian, Benjamin Franklin, were within a kite-string's distance of each other. When the baby philosopher of the last century was carried from Milk Street through the narrow passage long known as Bishop's Alley, now Hawley Street, he came out in Summer Street, very nearly opposite the spot where, at the beginning of this century, stood the parsonage of the First Church, the home of the Reverend William Emerson, its pastor, and the birthplace of his son, Ralph Waldo. The oblong quadrangle between Newbury, now Washington Street, Pond, now Bedford Street, Summer Street, and the open space called Church Green, where the New

South Church was afterwards erected, is represented on Bonner's maps of 1722 and 1769 as an almost blank area, not crossed or penetrated by a single passageway.

Even so late as less than half a century ago this region was still a most attractive little *rus in urbe.* The sunny gardens of the late Judge Charles Jackson and the late Mr. S. P. Gardner opened their flowers and ripened their fruits in the places now occupied by great warehouses and other massive edifices. The most aristocratic pears, the "Saint Michael," the "Brown Bury," found their natural homes in these sheltered enclosures. The fine old mansion of Judge William Prescott looked out upon these gardens. Some of us can well remember the window of his son's, the historian's, study, the light from which used every evening to glimmer through the leaves of the pear-trees while "The Conquest of Mexico" was achieving itself under difficulties hardly less formidable than those encountered by Cortes. It was a charmed region in which Emerson first drew his breath, and I am fortunate in having a communication from one who knew it and him longer than almost any other living person.

Mr. John Lowell Gardner, a college classmate and life-long friend of Mr. Emerson, has favored me with a letter which contains matters of interest concerning him never before given to the public. With his kind permission I have made some extracts and borrowed such facts as seemed especially worthy of note from his letter.

" I may be said to have known Emerson from the very beginning. A very low fence divided my father's estate in Summer Street from the field in which I remember the old wooden parsonage to have existed, — but this field, when we were very young, was to be covered by Chauncy Place Church and by the brick houses on Summer Street. Where the family removed to I do not remember, but I always knew the boys, William, Ralph, and perhaps Edward, and I again associated with Ralph at the Latin School, where we were instructed by Master Gould from 1815 to 1817, entering College in the latter year.

. . . I have no recollection of his relative rank as a scholar, but it was undoubtedly high, though not t' highest. He never was idle or a lounger, nor ' ever engage in frivolous ~~~~~~~~ his conduct w~ s- sible that t' but of regard an~ ~~~ ~~~~ ~~~ same manner and courtly hesitation in addressing you that you have known in him since. Still, he was not prominent in the class, and, but for what all the world has since known of him, his would not have been a conspicuous figure to his classmates in recalling College days.

" The fact that we were almost the only Latin

School fellows in the class, and the circumstance that
he was slow during the Freshman year to form new
acquaintances, brought us much together, and an
intimacy arose which continued through our College
life.   We were in the habit of taking long strolls together, often stopping for repose at distant points, as
at Mount Auburn, etc. . . . Emerson was not talk-
ative ; he never spoke for effect ; his utterances were
well weighed and very deliberately made, but there
was a certain flash when he uttered anything that
was more than usually worthy to be remembered.
He was so universally amiable and complying that
my evil spirit would sometimes instigate me to take
advantage of his gentleness and forbearance, but
nothing could disturb his equanimity.   All that was
wanting to render him an almost perfect character
was a few harsher traits and perhaps more masculine
vigor.

" On leaving College our paths in life were so remote from each other that we met very infrequently.
He soon became, as it were, public property, and I was
engrossed for many years in my commercial under-
takings.   All his course of life is known to many sur-
vivors. I am inclined to believe he had a most liberal
spirit. I remember that some years since, when it was
known that our classmate —— was reduced almost
to absolute want by the war, in which he lost his two
sons, Emerson exerted himself to raise a fund among
his classmates for his relief, and, there being very few
possible subscribers, made what I considered a noble
contribution, and this you may be sure was not from

any Southern sentiment on the part of Emerson. I send you herewith the two youthful productions of Emerson of which I spoke to you some time since."

The first of these is a prose Essay of four pages, written for a discussion in which the Professions of Divinity, Medicine, and Law were to be weighed against each other. Emerson had the Lawyer's side to advocate. It is a fair and sensible paper, not of special originality or brilliancy. His opening paragraph is worth citing, as showing the same instinct for truth which displayed itself in all his after writings and the conduct of his life.

" It is usual in advocating a favorite subject to appropriate all possible excellence, and endeavor to concentrate every doubtful auxiliary, that we may fortify to the utmost the theme of our attention. Such a design should be utterly disdained, except as far as is consistent with fairness ; and the sophistry of weak arguments being abandoned, a bold appeal should be made to the heart, for the tribute of honest conviction, with regard to the merits of the subject."

From many boys this might sound like well-meaning commonplace, but in the history of Mr. Emerson's life that " bold appeal to the heart," that " tribute of honest conviction," were made eloquent and real. The boy meant it when he said it. To carry out his law of sincerity and

self-trust the man had to sacrifice much that was
dear to him, but he did not flinch from his early
principles.

It must not be supposed that the blameless
youth was an ascetic in his College days. The
other old manuscript Mr. Gardner sends me is
marked " 'Song for Knights of Square Table,'
R. W. E."

There are twelve verses of this song, with a
chorus of two lines. The Muses and all the
deities, not forgetting Bacchus, were duly invited
to the festival.

> " Let the doors of Olympus be open for all
>   To descend and make merry in Chivalry's hall."
> .   .   .   .

Mr. Sanborn has kindly related to me several
circumstances told him by Emerson about his
early years.

The parsonage was situated at the corner of
Summer and what is now Chauncy streets. It
had a yard, and an orchard which Emerson said
was as large as Dr. Ripley's, which might have
been some two or three acres. Afterwards there
was a brick house looking on Summer Street, in
which Emerson the father lived. It was separated, Emerson said, by a brick wall from a
garden in which *pears grew* (a fact a boy is
likely to remember). Master Ralph Waldo used
to *sit on this wall*, — but we cannot believe he

ever got off it on the wrong side, unless politely asked to do so. On the occasion of some alarm the little boy was carried in his nightgown to a neighboring house.

After Reverend William Emerson's death Mrs. Emerson removed to a house in Beacon Street, where the Athenæum Building now stands. She kept some boarders, — among them Lemuel Shaw, afterwards Chief Justice of the State of Massachusetts. It was but a short distance to the Common, and Waldo and Charles used to drive their mother's cow there to pasture.

The Reverend Doctor Rufus Ellis, the much respected living successor of William Emerson as Minister of the First Church, says that R. W. Emerson must have been born in the old parsonage, as his father (who died when he was eight years old) lived but a very short time in " the new parsonage," which was, doubtless, the " brick house " above referred to.

We get a few glimpses of the boy from other sources. Mr. Cooke tells us that he entered the public grammar school at the age of eight years, and soon afterwards the Latin School. At the age of eleven he was turning Virgil into very readable English heroics. He loved the study of

Greek; was fond of reading history and given
to the frequent writing of verses. But he thinks
"the idle books under the bench at the Latin
School" were as profitable to him as his regular
studies.

Another glimpse of him is that given us by
Mr. Ireland from the "Boyhood Memories" of
Rufus Dawes. His old schoolmate speaks of
him as "a spiritual-looking boy in blue nankeen,
who seems to be about ten years old, — whose
image more than any other is still deeply stamped
upon my mind, as I then saw him and loved
him, I knew not why, and thought him so angelic and remarkable." That "blue nankeen"
sounds strangely, it may be, to the readers of this
later generation, but in the first quarter of the
century blue and yellow or buff-colored cotton
from China were a common summer clothing of
children. The places where the factories and
streets of the cities of Lowell and Lawrence
were to rise were then open fields and farms.
My recollection is that we did not think very
highly of ourselves when we were in blue nankeen,— a dull-colored fabric, too nearly of the
complexion of the slates on which we did our
ciphering.

Emerson was not particularly distinguished
in College. Having a near connection in the

same class as he, and being, as a Cambridge boy, generally familiar with the names of the more noted young men in College from the year when George Bancroft, Caleb Cushing, and Francis William Winthrop graduated until after I myself left College, I might have expected to hear something of a young man who afterwards became one of the great writers of his time. I do not recollect hearing of him except as keeping school for a short time in Cambridge, before he settled as a minister. His classmate, Mr. Josiah Quincy, writes thus of his college days : —

"Two only of my classmates can be fairly said to have got into history, although one of them, Charles W. Upham [the connection of mine referred to above] has written history very acceptably. Ralph Waldo Emerson and Robert W. Barnwell, for widely different reasons, have caused their names to be known to well-informed Americans. Of Emerson, I regret to say, there are few notices in my journals. Here is the sort of way in which I speak of the man who was to make so profound an impression upon the thought of his time. 'I went to the chapel to hear Emerson's dissertation : a very good one, but rather too long to give much pleasure to the hearers.' The fault, I suspect, was in the hearers ; and another fact which I have mentioned goes to confirm this belief. It seems that Emerson accepted the duty of delivering the Poem on Class Day, after seven others had been

asked who positively refused. So it appears that, in
the opinion of this critical class, the author of the
' Woodnotes ' and the ' Humble Bee ' ranked about
eighth in poetical ability. It can only be because the
works of the other five [seven] have been ' heroically
unwritten ' that a different impression has come to
prevail in the outside world. But if, according to the
measurement of undergraduates, Emerson's ability as
a poet was not conspicuous, it must also be admitted
that, in the judgment of persons old enough to know
better, he was not credited with that mastery of
weighty prose which the world has since accorded
him. In our senior year the higher classes competed
for the Boylston prizes for English composition. Emerson and I sent in our essays with the rest and were
fortunate enough to take the two prizes ; but — Alas
for the infallibility of academic decisions ! Emerson
received the second prize. I was of course much
pleased with the award of this intelligent committee,
and should have been still more gratified had they
mentioned that the man who was to be the most original and influential writer born in America was my un-
successful competitor. But Emerson, incubating over
deeper matters than were dreamt of in the established
philosophy of elegant letters, seems to have given no
sign of the power that was fashioning itself for leadership in a new time. He was quiet, unobtrusive, and
only a fair scholar according to the standard of the
College authorities. And this is really all I have to
say about my most distinguished classmate."

Barnwell, the first scholar in the class, delivered the Valedictory Oration, and Emerson the Poem. Neither of these performances was highly spoken of by Mr. Quincy.

I was surprised to find by one of the old Catalogues that Emerson roomed during a part of his College course with a young man whom I well remember, J. G. K. Gourdin. The two Gourdins, Robert and John Gaillard Keith, were dashing young fellows as I recollect them, belonging to Charleston, South Carolina. The " Southerners " were the reigning College *elegans* of that time, the *merveilleux*, the *mirliflores*, of their day. Their swallow-tail coats tapered to an arrow-point angle, and the prints of their little delicate calfskin boots in the snow were objects of great admiration to the village boys of the period. I cannot help wondering what brought Emerson and the showy, fascinating John Gourdin together as room-mates.

CHAPTER II.

1823–1828. Æt. 20–25.

Extract from a Letter to a Classmate. — School-Teaching. — Study of Divinity. — "Approbated" to Preach. — Visit to the South. — Preaching in Various Places.

WE get a few brief glimpses of Emerson during the years following his graduation. He writes in 1823 to a classmate who had gone from Harvard to Andover : —

"I am delighted to hear there is such a profound studying of German and Hebrew, Parkhurst and Jahn, and such other names as the memory aches to think of, on foot at Andover. Meantime, Unitarianism will not hide her honors ; as many hard names are taken, and as much theological mischief is planned, at Cambridge as at Andover. By the time this generation gets upon the stage, if the controversy will not have ceased, it will run such a tide that we shall hardly be able to speak to one another, and there will be a Guelf and Ghibelline quarrel, which cannot tell where the differences lie."

"You can form no conception how much one grovelling in the city needs the excitement and impulse of literary example. The sight of broad vellum-bound quartos, the very mention of Greek and German names, the glimpse of a dusty, tugging scholar, will wake you up to emulation for a month."

After leaving College, and while studying Divinity, Emerson employed a part of his time in giving instruction in several places successively.

Emerson's older brother William was teaching in Boston, and Ralph Waldo, after graduating, joined him in that occupation. In the year 1825 or 1826, he taught school also in Chelmsford, a town of Middlesex County, Massachusetts, a part of which helped to constitute the city of Lowell. One of his pupils in that school, the Honorable Josiah Gardiner Abbott, has favored me with the following account of his recollections : —

The school of which Mr. Emerson had the charge was an old-fashioned country "Academy." Mr. Emerson was probably studying for the ministry while teaching there. Judge Abbott remembers the impression he made on the boys. He was very grave, quiet, and very impressive in his appearance. There was something engaging, almost fascinating, about him ; he was never harsh or severe, always perfectly self-controlled, never punished except with words, but exercised complete command over the boys. His old pupil recalls the stately, measured way

4

in which, for some offence the little boy had committed, he turned on him, saying only these two words: " Oh, sad ! " That was enough, for he had the faculty of making the boys love him. One of his modes of instruction was to give the boys a piece of reading to carry home with them, — from some book like Plutarch's Lives, — and the next day to examine them and find out how much they retained from their reading. Judge Abbott remembers a peculiar look in his eyes, as if he saw something beyond what seemed to be in the field of vision. The whole impression left on this pupil's mind was such as no other teacher had ever produced upon him.

Mr. Emerson also kept a school for a short time at Cambridge, and among his pupils was Mr. John Holmes. His impressions seem to be very much like those of Judge Abbott.

My brother speaks of Mr. Emerson thus : —

" Calm, as not doubting the virtue residing in his sceptre. Rather stern in his very infrequent rebukes. Not inclined to win boys by a surface amiability, but kindly in explanation or advice. Every inch a king in his dominion. Looking back, he seems to me rather like a captive philosopher set to tending flocks ; resigned to his destiny, but not amused with its incongruities. He once recommended the use of rhyme as a cohesive for historical items."

In 1823, two years after graduating, Emerson

began studying for the ministry. He studied under the direction of Dr. Channing, attending some of the lectures in the Divinity School at Cambridge, though not enrolled as one of its regular students.

The teachings of that day were such as would now be called " old-fashioned Unitarianism." But no creed can be held to be a finality. From Edwards to Mayhew, from Mayhew to Channing, from Channing to Emerson, the passage is like that which leads from the highest lock of a canal to the ocean level. It is impossible for human nature to remain permanently shut up in the highest lock of Calvinism. If the gates are not opened, the mere leakage of belief or unbelief will before long fill the next compartment, and the freight of doctrine finds itself on the lower level of Arminianism, or Pelagianism, or even subsides to Arianism. From this level to that of Unitarianism the outlet is freer, and the subsidence more rapid. And from Unitarianism to Christian Theism, the passage is largely open for such as cannot accept the evidence of the supernatural in the history of the church.

There were many shades of belief in the liberal churches. If De Tocqueville's account of Unitarian preaching in Boston at the time of his visit is true, the Savoyard Vicar of Rousseau would have preached acceptably in some of our pulpits. In fact, the good Vicar might have been thought too conservative by some of our unharnessed theologians.

At the period when Emerson reached manhood, Unitarianism was the dominating form of belief in the more highly educated classes of both of the two great New England centres, the town of Boston and the University at Cambridge. President Kirkland was at the head of the College, Henry Ware was Professor of Theology, Andrews Norton of Sacred Literature, followed in 1830 by John Gorham Palfrey in the same office. James Freeman, Charles Lowell, and William Ellery Channing were preaching in Boston. I have mentioned already as a simple fact of local history, that the more exclusive social circles of Boston and Cambridge were chiefly connected with the Unitarian or Episcopalian churches. A Cambridge graduate of ambition and ability found an opening far from undesirable in a worldly point of view, in a profession which he was led to choose by higher motives. It was in the Unitarian pulpit that the brilliant talents of Buckminster and Everett had found a noble eminence from which their light could shine before men.

Descended from a long line of ministers, a man of spiritual nature, a reader of Plato, of Augustine, of Jeremy Taylor, full of hope for

his fellow-men, and longing to be of use to them,
conscious, undoubtedly, of a growing power of
thought, it was natural that Emerson should
turn from the task of a school-master to the
higher office of a preacher. It is hard to conceive of Emerson in either of the other so-called
learned professions. His devotion to truth for
its own sake and his feeling about science would
have kept him out of both those dusty high-
ways. His brother William had previously begun the study of Divinity, but found his mind
beset with doubts and difficulties, and had taken
to the profession of Law. It is not unlikely that
Mr. Emerson was more or less exercised with
the same questionings. He has said, speaking
of his instructors : " If they had examined me,
they probably would not have let me preach at
all." His eyes had given him trouble, so that
he had not taken notes of the lectures which he
heard in the Divinity School, which accounted for
his being excused from examination. In 1826,
after three years' study, he was " approbated to
preach " by the Middlesex Association of Ministers. His health obliging him to seek a southern climate, he went in the following winter to
South Carolina and Florida. During this absence he preached several times in Charleston
and other places. On his return from the South
he preached in New Bedford, in Northampton,

in Concord, and in Boston. His attractiveness
as a preacher, of which we shall have sufficient
evidence in a following chapter, led to his being
invited to share the duties of a much esteemed
and honored city clergyman, and the next position in which we find him is that of a settled
minister in Boston.

CHAPTER III.

1828–1833. ÆT. 25–30.

Settled as Colleague of Rev. Henry Ware. — Married to Ellen
Louisa Tucker. — Sermon at the Ordination of Rev. H. B.
Goodwin. — His Pastoral and Other Labors. — Emerson
and Father Taylor. — Death of Mrs. Emerson. — Differ-
ence of Opinion with some of his Parishioners. — Sermon
Explaining his Views. — Resignation of his Pastorate.

ON the 11th of March, 1829, Emerson was
ordained as colleague with the Reverend Henry
Ware, Minister of the Second Church in Boston.
In September of the same year he was married
to Miss Ellen Louisa Tucker. The resignation
of his colleague soon after his settlement threw
all the pastoral duties upon the young minister,
who seems to have performed them diligently
and acceptably. Mr. Conway gives the following brief account of his labors, and tells in the
same connection a story of Father Taylor too
good not to be repeated : —

" Emerson took an active interest in the public
affairs of Boston. He was on its School Board, and
was chosen chaplain of the State Senate. He invited
the anti-slavery lecturers into his church, and helped
philanthropists of other denominations in their work.

Father Taylor [the Methodist preacher to the sail-
ors], to whom Dickens gave an English fame, found
in him his most important supporter when establish-
ing the Seaman's Mission in Boston. This was told
me by Father Taylor himself in his old age. I happened to be in his company once, when he spoke
rather sternly about my leaving the Methodist Church;
but when I spoke of the part Emerson had in it, he
softened at once, and spoke with emotion of his great
friend. I have no doubt that if the good Father of
Boston Seamen was proud of any personal thing, it
was of the excellent answer he is said to have given
to some Methodists who objected to his friendship for
Emerson. Being a Unitarian, they insisted that he
must go to " — [the place which a divine of Charles the
Second's day said it was not good manners to mention
in church]. — " ' It does look so,' said Father Taylor,
' but I am sure of one thing : if Emerson goes to ' "
— [that place] — " ' he will change the climate there,
and emigration will set that way.' "

n 1830, Emerson took part in the services at
he ordination of the Reverend H. B. Goodwin
as Dr. Ripley's colleague. His address on giving
the right hand of fellowship was printed, but
is not included among his collected works.

The fair prospects with which Emerson began
his life as a settled minister were too soon darkened. In February, 1832, the wife of his youth,
who had been for some time in failing health,
died of consumption.

He had become troubled with doubts respecting a portion of his duties, and it was not in his nature to conceal these doubts from his people. On the 9th of September, 1832, he preached a sermon on the Lord's Supper, in which he announced unreservedly his conscientious scruples against administering that ordinance, and the grounds upon which those scruples were founded. This discourse, as his only printed sermon, and as one which heralded a movement in New England theology which has never stopped from that day to this, deserves some special notice. The sermon is in no sense "Emersonian" except in its directness, its sweet temper, and outspoken honesty. He argues from his comparison of texts in a perfectly sober, old-fashioned way, as his ancestor Peter Bulkeley might have done. It happened to that worthy forefather of Emerson that upon his "pressing a piece of *Charity* disagreeable to the will of the *Ruling Elder,* there was occasioned an unhappy *Discord* in the Church of *Concord;* which yet was at last healed, by their calling in the help of a *Council* and the *Ruling Elder's* Abdication." So says Cotton Mather. Whether zeal had grown cooler or charity grown warmer in Emerson's days we need not try to determine. The sermon was only a more formal declaration of views respecting the Lord's Supper, which he had previously made known in a conference with some of the most active members of his church. As a committee of the parish reported resolutions radically differing from his opinion on the subject, he preached this sermon and at the same time resigned his office. There was no "discord," there was no need of a "council." Nothing could be more friendly, more truly Christian, than the manner in which Mr. Emerson expressed himself in this parting discourse. All the kindness of his nature warms it throughout. He details the differences of opinion which have existed in the church with regard to the ordinance. He then argues from the language of the Evangelists that it was not intended to be a permanent institution. He takes up the statement of Paul in the Epistle to the Corinthians, which he thinks, all things considered, ought not to alter our opinion derived from the Evangelists. He does not think that we are to rely upon the opinions and practices of the primitive church. If that church believed the institution to be permanent, their belief does not settle the question for us. On every other subject, succeeding times have learned to form a judgment more in accordance with the spirit of Christianity than was the practice of the early ages.

"But, it is said, 'Admit that the rite was not designed to be perpetual.' What harm doth it?"

He proceeds to give reasons which show it to
be inexpedient to continue the observance of the
rite. It was treating that as authoritative which,
as he believed that he had shown from Scrip-
ture, was not so. It confused the idea of God
by transferring the worship of Him to Christ.
Christ is the Mediator only as the instructor of
man. In the least petition to God " the soul
stands alone with God, and Jesus is no more
present to your mind than your brother or child."
Again : —

" The use of the elements, however suitable to the
people and the modes of thought in the East, where
it originated, is foreign and unsuited to affect us.
The day of formal religion is past, and we are to seek
our well-being in the formation of the soul. The
Jewish was a religion of forms ; it was all body, it
had no life, and the Almighty God was pleased to
qualify and send forth a man to teach men that they
must serve him with the heart ; that only that life
was religious which was thoroughly good ; that sac
fice was smoke and forms were shadows. This
lived and died true to that purpose ; and w
blessed word and life before us, Christians must contend that it is a matter of vital importance, — really a duty to commemorate him by a certain form,
whether that form be acceptable to their understand-.
ing or not. Is not this to make vain the gift of God ?
Is not this to turn back the hand on the dial ? "

To these objections he adds the practical consideration that it brings those who do not partake of the communion service into an unfavorable relation with those who do.

The beautiful spirit of the man shows itself in all its noble sincerity in these words at the close of his argument: —

"Having said this, I have said all. I have no hostility to this institution; I am only stating my want of sympathy with it. Neither should I ever have obtruded this opinion upon other people, had I not been called by my office to administer it. That is the end of my opposition, that I am not interested in it. I am content that it stand to the end of the world if it please men and please Heaven, and I shall rejoice in all the good it produces."

He then announces that, as it is the prevailing opinion and feeling in our religious community that it is a part of a pastor's duties to administer this rite, he is about to resign the office which had been confided to him.

This is the only sermon of Mr. Emerson's ever published. It was impossible to hear or to read it without honoring the preacher for his truthfulness, and recognizing the force of his statement and reasoning. It was equally impossible that he could continue his ministrations over a congregation which held to the ordinance he wished to give up entirely. And thus it was, that with the most friendly feelings on both sides, Mr. Emerson left the pulpit of the Second Church and found himself obliged to make a beginning in a new career.

CHAPTER IV.

1833–1838. Æt. 30–35.

§ 1. In the year 1833 Mr. Emerson visited Europe for the first time. A great change had come over his life, and he needed the relief which a corresponding change of outward circumstances might afford him. A brief account of this visit is prefixed to the volume entitled "English Traits." He took a short tour, in which he visited Sicily, Italy, and France, and,

crossing from Boulogne, landed at the Tower
Stairs in London. He finds nothing in his Diary
to publish concerning visits to places. But he
saw a number of distinguished persons, of whom
he gives pleasant accounts, so singularly different in tone from the rough caricatures in which
Carlyle vented his spleen and caprice, that one
marvels how the two men could have talked ten
minutes together, or would wonder, had not one
been as imperturbable as the other was explosive.
Horatio Greenough and Walter Savage Landor
are the chief persons he speaks of as having met
upon the Continent. Of these he reports various opinions as delivered in conversation. He
mentions incidentally that he visited Professor
Amici, who showed him his microscopes " mag-
nifying (it was said) two thousand diameters."
Emerson hardly knew his privilege; he may
have been the first American to look through
an immersion lens with the famous Modena professor. Mr. Emerson says that his narrow and
desultory reading had inspired him with the
wish to see the faces of three or four writers,
Coleridge, Wordsworth, Landor, De Quincey,
Carlyle. His accounts of his interviews with
these distinguished persons are too condensed to
admit of further abbreviation. Goethe and
Scott, whom he would have liked to look upon,
were dead; Wellington he saw at Westminster

Abbey, at the funeral of Wilberforce. His impressions of each of the distinguished persons whom he visited should be looked at in the light of the general remark which follows : —

" The young scholar fancies it happiness enough to live with people who can give an inside to the world ; without reflecting that they are prisoners, too, of their own thought, and cannot apply themselves to yours. The conditions of literary success are almost destructive of the best social power, as they do not have that frolic liberty which only can encounter a companion on the best terms. It is probable you left some obscure comrade at a tavern, or in the farms, with right mother-wit, and equality to life, when you crossed sea and land to play bo-peep with celebrated scribes. I have, however, found writers superior to their books, and I cling to my first belief that a strong head will dispose fast enough of these impediments, and give one the satisfaction of reality, the sense of having been met, and a larger horizon."

Emerson carried a letter of introduction to a gentleman in Edinburgh, who, being unable to pay him all the desired attention, handed him over to Mr. Alexander Ireland, who has given a most interesting account of him as he appeared during that first visit to Europe. Mr. Ireland's presentation of Emerson as he heard him in the Scotch pulpit shows that he was not less impressive and attractive before an audience of strangers than among his own countrymen and countrywomen : —

"On Sunday, the 18th of August, 1833, I heard him deliver a discourse in the Unitarian Chapel, Young Street, Edinburgh, and I remember distinctly the effect which it produced on his hearers. It is almost needless to say that nothing like it had ever been heard by them before, and many of them did not know what to make of it. The originality of his thoughts, the consummate beauty of the language in which they were clothed, the calm dignity of his bearing, the absence of all oratorical effort, and the singular directness and simplicity of his manner, free from the least shadow of dogmatic assumption, made a deep impression on me. Not long before this I had listened to a wonderful sermon by Dr. Chalmers, whose force, and energy, and vehement, but rather turgid eloquence carried, for the moment, all before them, — his audience becoming like clay in the hands of the potter. But I must confess that the pregnant thoughts and serene self-possession of the young Boston minister had a greater charm for me than all the rhetorical splendors of Chalmers. His voice was the sweetest, the most winning and penetrating of any I ever heard ; nothing like it have I listened to since.

'That music in our hearts we bore
Long after it was heard no more.'"

Mr. George Gilfillan speaks of " the solemnity of his manner, and the earnest thought pervading his discourse."

5

As to the effect of his preaching on his American audiences, I find the following evidence in Mr. Cooke's diligently gathered collections. Mr. Sanborn says : —

"His pulpit eloquence was singularly attractive, though by no means equally so to all persons. In 1829, before the two friends had met, Bronson Alcott heard him preach in Dr. Channing's church on 'The Universality of the Moral Sentiment,' and was struck, as he said, with the youth of the preacher, the beauty of his elocution and the direct and sincere manner in which he addressed his hearers."

Mr. Charles Congdon, of New Bedford, well known as a popular writer, gives the following account of Emerson's preaching in his "Reminiscences." I borrow the quotation from Mr. Conway : —

"One day there came into our pulpit the most gracious of mortals, with a face all benignity, who gave out the first hymn and made the first prayer as an angel might have read and prayed. Our choir was a pretty good one, but its best was coarse and discordant after Emerson's voice. I remember of the sermon only that it had an indefinite charm of simplicity and wisdom, with occasional illustrations from nature, which were about the most delicate and dainty things of the kind which I had ever heard. I could understand them, if not the fresh philosophical novelties of the discourse."

Everywhere Emerson seems to have pleased his audiences. The Reverend Dr. Morison, formerly the much respected Unitarian minister of New Bedford, writes to me as follows : —

"After Dr. Dewey left New Bedford, Mr. Emerson preached there several months, greatly to the satisfaction and delight of those who heard him. The Society would have been glad to settle him as their minister, and he would have accepted a call, had it not been for some difference of opinion, I think, in regard to the communion service. Judge Warren, who was particularly his friend, and had at that time a leading influence in the parish, with all his admiration for Mr. Emerson, did not think he could well be the pastor of a Christian church, and so the matter was settled between him and his friend, without any action by the Society."

All this shows well enough that his preaching was eminently acceptable. But every one who has heard him lecture can form an idea of what he must have been as a preacher. In fact, we have all listened, probably, to many a passage from old sermons of his, — for he tells us he borrowed from those old sermons for his lectures, — without ever thinking of the pulpit from which they were first heard.

Among the stray glimpses we get of Emerson between the time when he quitted the pulpit of his church and that when he came before the public as a lecturer is this, which I owe to the kindness of Hon. Alexander H. Rice. In 1832 or 1833, probably the latter year, he, then a boy, with another boy, Thomas R. Gould, afterwards well known as a sculptor, being at the Episcopal church in Newton, found that Mr. Emerson was sitting in the pew behind them. Gould knew Mr. Emerson, and introduced young Rice to him, and they walked down the street together. As they went along, Emerson burst into a rhapsody over the Psalms of David, the sublimity of thought, and the poetic beauty of expression of which they are full, and spoke also with enthusiasm of the Te Deum as that grand old hymn which had come down through the ages, voicing the praises of generation after generation.

When they parted at the house of young Rice's father, Emerson invited the boys to come and see him at the Allen farm, in the afternoon. They came to a piece of woods, and, as they entered it, took their hats off. " Boys," said Emerson, " here we recognize the presence of the Universal Spirit. The breeze says to us in its own language, How d' ye do? How d' ye do? and we have already taken our hats off and are answering it with our own How d' ye do? How d' ye do? And all the waving branches of the trees, and all the flowers, and the field of corn yonder, and the singing brook, and the insect and the bird, — every living thing and things we call inanimate feel the same divine universal impulse while they join with us, and we with them, in the greeting which is the salutation of the Universal Spirit."

We perceive the same feeling which pervades many of Emerson's earlier Essays and much of his verse, in these long-treasured reminiscences of the poetical improvisation with which the two boys were thus unexpectedly favored. Governor Rice continues : —

"You know what a captivating charm there always was in Emerson's presence, but I can never tell you how this line of thought then impressed a country boy. I do not remember anything about the remain- der of that walk, nor of the after-incidents of that day, — I only remember that I went home wondering about that mystical dream of the Universal Spirit, and about what manner of man he was under whose influence I had for the first time come. . . .

"The interview left impressions that led me into new channels of thought which have been a life-long pleasure to me, and, I doubt not, taught me somewhat how to distinguish between mere theological dogma and genuine religion in the soul."

In the summer of 1834 Emerson became a resident of Concord, Massachusetts, the town of his forefathers, and the place destined to be his home for life. He first lived with his venerable connection, Dr. Ripley, in the dwelling made famous by Hawthorne as the "Old Manse." It is an old-fashioned gambrel-roofed house, standing close to the scene of the Fight on the banks of the river. It was built for the Reverend William Emerson, his grandfather. In one of the rooms of this house Emerson wrote "Nature," and in the same room, some years later, Hawthorne wrote "Mosses from an Old Manse."

The place in which Emerson passed the greater part of his life well deserves a special notice. Concord might sit for its portrait as an ideal New England town. If wanting in the variety of surface which many other towns can boast of, it has at least a vision of the distant summits of Monadnock and Wachusett. It has fine old woods, and noble elms to give dignity to its open spaces. Beautiful ponds, as they modestly call themselves, — one of which, Walden, is as well known in our literature as Windermere in that of Old England, — lie quietly in their clean basins. And through the green meadows runs, or rather lounges, a gentle, unsalted stream, like an English river, licking its grassy margin with a sort of bovine placidity and contentment. This is the Musketaquid, or Meadow River, which, after being joined by the more restless Assabet, still keeps its temper and flows peacefully along by and through other towns, to lose itself in the broad Merrimac. The names of these rivers tell us that Concord has an Indian history, and there is evidence that it was a favorite residence of the race which preceded our own. The native tribes knew as well as the white settlers where were pleasant streams and sweet springs, where corn grew tall in the mead-ows and fish bred fast in the unpolluted waters.

The place thus favored by nature can show a record worthy of its physical attractions. Its settlement under the lead of Emerson's ancestor, Peter Bulkeley, was effected in the midst of many difficulties, which the enterprise and self-sacrifice of that noble leader were successful in overcoming. On the banks of the Musketaquid was fired the first fatal shot of the " rebel " farmers. Emerson appeals to the Records of the town for two hundred years as illustrating the working of our American institutions and the character of the men of Concord : —

" If the good counsel prevailed, the sneaking coun-sel did not fail to be suggested ; freedom and virtue, if they triumphed, triumphed in a fair field. And so be it an everlasting testimony for them, and so much ground of assurance of man's capacity for self-government."

What names that plain New England town reckons in the roll of its inhabitants ! Stout Major Buttrick and his fellow-soldiers in the war

of Independence, and their worthy successors in
the war of Freedom; lawyers and statesmen like
Samuel Hoar and his descendants; ministers
like Peter Bulkeley, Daniel Bliss, and William
Emerson; and men of genius such as the idealist and poet whose inspiration has kindled so
many souls; as the romancer who has given an
atmosphere to the hard outlines of our stern
New England; as that unique individual, half
college-graduate and half Algonquin, the Robinson Crusoe of Walden Pond, who carried out a
school-boy whim to its full proportions, and told
the story of Nature in undress as only one who
had hidden in her bedroom could have told it.
I need not lengthen the catalogue by speaking
of the living, or mentioning the women whose
names have added to its distinction. It has long
been an intellectual centre such as no other
country town of our own land, if of any other,
could boast. Its groves, its streams, its houses,
are haunted by undying memories, and its hill-
sides and hollows are made holy by the dust that
is covered by their turf.

Such was the place which the advent of Emerson made the Delphi of New England and the
resort of many pilgrims from far-off regions.

On his return from Europe in the winter
of 1833–4, Mr. Emerson began to appear before the public as a lecturer. His first sub-

jects, "Water," and the "Relation of Man to
the Globe," were hardly such as we should have
expected from a scholar who had but a limited
acquaintance with physical and physiological
science. They were probably chosen as of a
popular character, easily treated in such a way
as to be intelligible and entertaining, and thus
answering the purpose of introducing him pleasantly to the new career he was contemplating.
These lectures are not included in his published
works, nor were they ever published, so far as I
know. He gave three lectures during the same
winter, relating the experiences of his recent tour
in Europe. Having made himself at home on the
platform, he ventured upon subjects more congen-
ial to his taste and habits of thought than some
of those earlier topics. In 1834 he lectured on
Michael Angelo, Milton, Luther, George Fox,
and Edmund Burke. The first two of these lectures, though not included in his collected works,
may be found in the "North American Review"
for 1837 and 1838. The germ of many of the
thoughts which he has expanded in prose and
verse may be found in these Essays.

The *Cosmos* of the Ancient Greeks, the *piu
nel' uno*, "The Many in One," appear in the
Essay on Michael Angelo as they also appear in
his "Nature." The last thought takes wings to
itself and rises in the little poem entitled "Each

and All." The " Rhodora," another brief poem, finds itself foreshadowed in the inquiry, " What is Beauty?" and its answer, " This great Whole the understanding cannot embrace. Beauty may be felt. It may be produced. But it cannot be defined." And throughout this Essay the feeling that truth and beauty and virtue are one, and that Nature is the symbol which typifies it to the soul, is the inspiring sentiment. *Noscitur a sociis* applies as well to a man's dead as to his living companions. A young friend of mine in his college days wrote an essay on Plato. When he mentioned his subject to Mr. Emerson, he got the caution, long remembered, " When you strike at a *King*, you must kill him." He himself knew well with what kings of thought to measure his own intelligence. What was grandest, loftiest, purest, in human character chiefly interested him. He rarely meddles with what is petty or ignoble. Like his " Humble Bee," the " yellow-breeched philosopher," whom he speaks of as

> " Wiser far than human seer,"

and says of him,

> " Aught unsavory or unclean
> Hath my insect never seen,"

he goes through the world where coarser minds find so much that is repulsive to dwell upon,

"Seeing only what is fair,
Sipping only what is sweet."

Why Emerson selected Michael Angelo as the subject of one of his earliest lectures is shown clearly enough by the last sentence as printed in the Essay.

"He was not a citizen of any country; he belonged to the human race; he was a brother and a friend to all who acknowledged the beauty that beams in universal nature, and who seek by labor and self-denial to approach its source in perfect goodness."

Consciously or unconsciously men describe themselves in the characters they draw. One must have the mordant in his own personality or he will not take the color of his subject. He may force himself to picture that which he dislikes or even detests; but when he loves the character he delineates, it is his own, in some measure, at least, or one of which he feels that its possibilities and tendencies belong to himself. Let us try Emerson by this test in his "Essay on Milton:" —

"It is the prerogative of this great man to stand at this hour foremost of all men in literary history, and so (shall we not say?) of all men, in the power to *inspire*. Virtue goes out of him into others." . . . "He is identified in the mind with all select and holy images, with the supreme interests of the human race." — "Better than any other he has discharged

the office of every great man, namely, to raise the
idea of Man in the minds of his contemporaries and
of posterity, — to draw after nature a life of man,
exhibiting such a composition of grace, of strength,
and of virtue as poet had not described nor hero
lived. Human nature in these ages is indebted to him
for its best portrait. Many philosophers in England,
France, and Germany, have formally dedicated their
study to this problem; and we think it impossible to
recall one in those countries who communicates the
same vibration of hope, of self-reverence, of piety, of
delight in beauty, which the name of Milton awakes."

Emerson had the same lofty aim as Milton,
" To raise the idea of man ; " he had " the power
to inspire " in a preëminent degree. If ever a
man communicatèd those *vibrations* he speaks of
as characteristic of Milton, it was Emerson. In
elevation, purity, nobility of nature, he is worthy
to stand with the great poet and patriot, who
began like him as a school-master, and ended as
the teacher in a school-house which had for its
walls the horizons of every region where English
is spoken. The similarity of their characters
might be followed by the curious into their fortunes. Both were turned away from the clerical
office by a revolt of conscience against the beliefs required of them; both lost very dear objects of affection in early manhood, and mourned
for them in tender and mellifluous threnodies.

It would be easy to trace many parallelisms in their prose and poetry, but to have dared to name any man whom we have known in our common life with the seraphic singer of the Nativity and of Paradise is a tribute which seems to savor of audacity. It is hard to conceive of Emerson as "an expert swordsman" like Milton. It is impossible to think of him as an abusive controversialist as Milton was in his controversy with Salmasius. But though Emerson never betrayed it to the offence of others, he must have been conscious, like Milton, of "a certain niceness of nature, an honest haughtiness," which was as a shield about his inner nature. Charles Emerson, the younger brother, who was of the same type, expresses the feeling in his college essay on Friendship, where it is all summed up in the line he quotes: —

"The hand of Douglas is his own."

It must be that in writing this Essay on Milton Emerson felt that he was listening in his own soul to whispers that seemed like echoes from that of the divine singer.

My friend, the Rev. James Freeman Clarke, a life-long friend of Emerson, who understood him from the first, and was himself a great part in the movement of which Emerson, more than any other man, was the leader, has kindly allowed me to make use of the following letters : —

TO REV. JAMES F. CLARKE, LOUISVILLE, KY.

PLYMOUTH, MASS., *March* 12, 1834.

MY DEAR SIR, — As the day approaches when Mr. Lewis should leave Boston, I seize a few moments in a friendly house in the first of towns, to thank you heartily for your kindness in lending me the valued manuscripts which I return. The translations excited me much, and who can estimate the value of a good thought? I trust I am to learn much more from you hereafter of your German studies, and much I hope of your own. You asked in your note concerning Carlyle. My recollections of him are most pleasant, and I feel great confidence in his character. He understands and recognizes his mission. He is perfectly simple and affectionate in his manner, and frank, as he can well afford to be, in his communications. He expressed some impatience of his total solitude, and talked of Paris as a residence. I told him I hoped not; for I should always remember him with respect, meditating in the mountains of Nithsdale. He was cheered, as he ought to be, by learning that his papers were read with interest by young men unknown to him in this continent ; and when I specified a piece which had attracted warm commendation from the New Jerusalem people here, his wife said that is always the way ; whatever he has writ that he thinks has fallen dead, he hears of two or three years afterward. — He has many, many tokens of Goethe's regard, miniatures, medals, and many letters. If you should go to Scotland one day, you would gratify him, yourself, and me, by your visit to Craigenputtock, in the parish of Dunscore, near Dumfries. He told me he had a book which he thought to publish, but was in the purpose of dividing into a series of articles for " Fraser's Magazine." I therefore subscribed for that book, which he calls the " Mud Magazine," but have seen nothing of his workmanship in the two last numbers. The mail is going, so I shall finish my letter another time.

Your obliged friend and servant,
R. WALDO EMERSON.

CONCORD, MASS., *November* 25, 1834.

MY DEAR SIR, — Miss Peabody has kindly sent me your manuscript piece on Goethe and Carlyle. I have read it with great pleasure and a feeling of gratitude, at the same time with a serious regret that it was not published. I have forgotten what reason you assigned for not printing it ; I cannot think of any sufficient one. Is it too late now ? Why not change its form a little and annex to it some account of Carlyle's later pieces, to wit : " Diderot," and " Sartor Resartus." The last is complete, and he has sent it to me in a stitched pamphlet. Whilst I see its vices (relatively to the reading public) of style, I cannot but esteem it a noble philosophical poem, reflecting the ideas, institutions, men of this very hour. And it seems to me that it has so much wit and other secondary graces as must strike a class who would not care for its primary merit, that of being a sincere exhortation to seekers of truth. If you still retain your interest in his genius (as I see not how you can avoid, having understood it and co-operated with it so truly), you will be glad to know that he values his American readers very highly; that he does not defend this offensive style of his, but calls it questionable tentative; that he is trying other modes, and is about publishing a historical piece called "The Diamond Necklace," as a part of a great work which he meditates on the subject of the French Revolution. He says it is part of his creed that history is poetry, could we tell it right. He adds, moreover, in a letter I have recently received from him, that it has been an odd dream that he might end in the western woods. Shall we not bid him come, and be Poet and Teacher of a most scattered flock wanting a shepherd? Or, as I sometimes think, would it not be a new and worse chagrin to become acquainted with the extreme deadness of our community to spiritual influences of the higher kind? Have you read Sampson Reed's "Growth of the Mind"? I rejoice to be contemporary with that man, and cannot wholly despair of the society in which he lives; there must be some oxygen yet, and La Fayette is only just dead.

Your friend,   R. WALDO EMERSON.

It occurs to me that 't is unfit to send any white paper so far as to your house, so you shall have a sentence from Carlyle's letter.

[This may be found in Carlyle's first letter, dated 12th August, 1834.]

Dr. Le Baron Russell, an intimate friend of Emerson for the greater part of his life, gives me some particulars with reference to the publication of "Sartor Resartus," which I will repeat in his own words: —

"It was just before the time of which I am speaking [that of Emerson's marriage] that the 'Sartor Resartus' appeared in 'Fraser.' Emerson lent the numbers, or the collected sheets of 'Fraser,' to Miss Jackson, and we all had the reading of them. The excitement which the book caused among young persons interested in the literature of the day at that time you probably remember. I was quite carried away by it, and so anxious to own a copy, that I determined to publish an American edition. I consulted James Munroe & Co. on the subject. Munroe advised me to obtain a subscription to a sufficient number of copies to secure the cost of the publication. This, with the aid of some friends, particularly of my classmate, William Silsbee, I readily succeeded in doing. When this was accomplished, I wrote to Emerson, who up to this time had taken no part in the enterprise, asking him to write a preface. (This is the Preface which appears in the American edition, James Munroe & Co., 1836. It was omitted in the third American from the second London edition,[1] by the same publishers, 1840.) Before the first edition appeared, and after the subscription had been secured, Munroe & Co. offered to assume the whole responsibility of the publication, and to this I assented.

[1] Revised and corrected by the author.

"This American edition of 1836 was the first appearance of the 'Sartor' in either country, as a distinct edition. Some copies of the sheets from 'Fraser,' it appears, were stitched together and sent to a few persons, but Carlyle could find no English publisher willing to take the responsibility of printing the book. This shows, I think, how much more interest was taken in Carlyle's writings in this country than in England."

On the 14th of May, 1834, Emerson wrote to Carlyle the first letter of that correspondence which has since been given to the world under the careful editorship of Mr. Charles Norton. This correspondence lasted from the date mentioned to the 2d of April, 1872, when Carlyle wrote his last letter to Emerson. The two writers reveal themselves as being in strong sympathy with each other, in spite of a radical difference of temperament and entirely opposite views of life. The hatred of unreality was uppermost with Carlyle; the love of what is real and genuine with Emerson. Those old moralists, the weeping and the laughing philosophers, find their counterparts in every thinking community. Carlyle did not weep, but he scolded; Emerson did not laugh, but in his gravest moments there was a smile waiting for the cloud to pass from his forehead. The Duet they chanted was a Miserere with a Te Deum for its Antiphon; a *De*

Profundis answered by a *Sursum Corda.* "The ground of my existence is black as death," says Carlyle. " Come and live with me a year," says Emerson, " and if you do not like New England well enough to stay, one of these years (when the 'History' has passed its ten editions, and been translated into as many languages) I will come and dwell with you."

§ 2. In September, 1835, Emerson was married to Miss Lydia Jackson, of Plymouth, Massachusetts. The wedding took place in the fine old mansion known as the Winslow House, Dr. Le Baron Russell and his sister standing up with the bridegroom and his bride. After their marriage, Mr. and Mrs. Emerson went to reside in the house in which he passed the rest of his life, and in which Mrs. Emerson and their daughter still reside. This is the "plain, square, wooden house," with horse-chestnut trees in the front yard, and evergreens around it, which has been so often described and figured. It is without pretensions, but not without an air of quiet dignity. A full and well-illustrated account of it and its arrangements and surroundings is given in " Poets' Homes," by Arthur Gilman and others, published by D. Lothrop & Company in 1879.

On the 12th of September, 1835, Emerson

delivered an "Historical Discourse, at Concord, on the Second Centennial Anniversary of the Incorporation of the Town." There is no "mysticism," no "transcendentalism" in this plain, straightforward Address. The facts are collected and related with the patience and sobriety which became the writer as one of the Dryasdusts of our very diligent, very useful, very matter-of-fact, and for the most part judiciously unimaginative Massachusetts Historical Society. It looks unlike anything else Emerson ever wrote, in being provided with abundant foot-notes and an appendix. One would almost as soon have expected to see Emerson equipped with a musket and a knapsack as to find a discourse of his clogged with annotations, and trailing a supplement after it. Oracles are brief and final in their utterances. Delphi and Cumæ are not expected to explain what they say.

It is the habit of our New England towns to celebrate their own worthies and their own deeds on occasions like this, with more or less of rhetorical gratitude and self-felicitation. The discourses delivered on these occasions are commonly worth reading, for there was never a clearing made in the forest that did not let in the light on heroes and heroines. Concord is on the whole the most interesting of all the inland towns of New England. Emerson has told its story in as painstaking, faithful a way as if he had been by nature an annalist. But with this fidelity, we find also those bold generalizations and sharp picturesque touches which reveal the poetic philosopher.

"I have read with care," he says, "the town records themselves. They exhibit a pleasing picture of a community almost exclusively agricultural, where no man has much time for words, in his search after things; of a community of great simplicity of manners, and of a manifest love of justice. I find our annals marked with a uniform good sense. — The tone of the record rises with the dignity of the event. These soiled and musty books are luminous and electric within. The old town clerks did not spell very correctly, but they contrive to make intelligible the will of a free and just community." . . . "The matters there debated (in town meetings) are such as to invite very small consideration. The ill-spelled pages of the town records contain the result. I shall be excused for confessing that I have set a value upon any symptom of meanness and private pique which I have met with in these antique books, as proof that justice was done; that if the results of our history are approved as wise and good, it was yet a free strife; if the good counsel prevailed, the sneaking counsel did not fail to be suggested; freedom and virtue, if they triumphed, triumphed in a fair field. And so be it an everlasting testimony for them, and so much ground of assurance of man's capacity for self-government."

There was nothing in this Address which the
plainest of Concord's citizens could not read un-
derstandingly and with pleasure. In fact Mr.
Emerson himself, besides being a poet and a philosopher, was also a plain Concord citizen. His
son tells me that he was a faithful attendant upon
town meetings, and, though he never spoke, was
an interested and careful listener to the debates
on town matters. That respect for "mother-
wit" and for all the wholesome human qualities
which reveals itself all through his writings was
bred from this kind of intercourse with men of
sense who had no pretensions to learning, and in
whom, for that very reason, the native qualities
came out with less disguise in their expression.
He was surrounded by men who ran to extremes
in their idiosyncrasies : Alcott in speculations,
which often led him into the fourth dimension
of mental space; Hawthorne, who brooded himself into a dream-peopled solitude; Thoreau,
the nullifier of civilization, who insisted on nib-
bling his asparagus at the wrong end, to say
nothing of idolaters and echoes. He kept his
balance among them all. It would be hard to
find a more candid and sober record of the result
of self-government in a small community than
is contained in this simple discourse, patient in
detail, large in treatment, more effective than
any unsupported generalities about the natural

rights of man, which amount to very little unless men earn the right of asserting them by attending fairly to their natural duties. So admirably is the working of a town government, as it goes on in a well-disposed community, displayed in the history of Concord's two hundred years of village life, that one of its wisest citizens had portions of the address printed for distribution, as an illustration of the American principle of self-government.

After settling in Concord, Emerson delivered courses of Lectures in Boston during several successive winters; in 1835, ten Lectures on English Literature; in 1836, twelve Lectures on the Philosophy of History; in 1837, ten Lectures on Human Culture. Some of these lectures may have appeared in print under their original titles; all of them probably contributed to the Essays and Discourses which we find in his published volumes.

On the 19th of April, 1836, a meeting was held to celebrate the completion of the monument raised in commemoration of the Concord Fight. For this occasion Emerson wrote the hymn made ever memorable by the lines : —

> Here once the embattled farmers stood,
> And fired the shot heard round the world.

The last line of this hymn quickens the heartbeats of every American, and the whole hymn is admirable in thought and expression.

Until the autumn of 1838, Emerson preached twice on Sundays to the church at East Lexington, which desired him to become its pastor. Mr. Cooke says that when a lady of the society was asked why they did not settle a friend of Emerson's whom he had urged them to invite to their pulpit, she replied: "We are a very simple people, and can understand no one but Mr. Emerson." He said of himself: "My pulpit is the Lyceum platform." Knowing that he made his Sermons contribute to his Lectures, we need not mourn over their not being reported.

In March, 1837, Emerson delivered in Boston a Lecture on War, afterwards published in Miss Peabody's "Æsthetic Papers." He recognizes war as one of the temporary necessities of a developing civilization, to disappear with the advance of mankind : —

"At a certain stage of his progress the man fights, if he be of a sound body and mind. At a certain high stage he makes no offensive demonstration, but is alert to repel injury, and of an unconquerable heart. At a still higher stage he comes into the region of holiness ; passion has passed away from him ; his warlike nature is all converted into an active medicinal principle ; he sacrifices himself, and accepts with alacrity wearisome tasks of denial and charity; but being attacked, he bears it, and turns the other

cheek, as one engaged, throughout his being, no longer
to the service of an individual, but to the common
good of all men."

In 1834 Emerson's brother Edward died, as
already mentioned, in the West India island
where he had gone for his health. In his letter
to Carlyle, of November 12th of the same year,
Emerson says: "Your letter, which I received
last week, made a bright light in a solitary and
saddened place. I had quite recently received
the news of the death of a brother in the island
of Porto Rico, whose loss to me will be a life-
long sorrow." It was of him that Emerson
wrote the lines "In Memoriam," in which he
says, —

> "There is no record left on earth
> Save on tablets of the heart,
> Of the rich, inherent worth,
> Of the grace that on him shone
> Of eloquent lips, of joyful wit ;
> He could not frame a word unfit,
> An act unworthy to be done."

Another bereavement was too soon to be recorded. On the 7th of October, 1835, he says
in a letter to Carlyle : —

"I was very glad to hear of the brother you describe,
for I have one too, and know what it is to have presence in two places. Charles Chauncy Emerson is a
lawyer now settled in this town, and, as I believe, no

better Lord Hamlet was ever. He is our Doctor on all questions of taste, manners, or action. And one of the pure pleasures I promise myself in the months to come is to make you two gentlemen know each other."

Alas for human hopes and prospects! In less than a year from the date of that letter, on the 17th of September, 1836, he writes to Carlyle : —

"Your last letter, dated in April, found me a mourner, as did your first. I have lost out of this world my brother Charles, of whom I have spoken to you, — the friend and companion of many years, the inmate of my house, a man of a beautiful genius, born to speak well, and whose conversation for these last years has treated every grave question of humanity, and has been my daily bread. I have put so much dependence on his gifts, that we made but one man together ; for I needed never to do what he could do by noble nature, much better than I. He was to have been married in this month, and at the time of his sickness and sudden death, I was adding apartments to my house for his permanent accommodation. I wish that you could have known him. At twenty-seven years the best life is only preparation. He built his foundation so large that it needed the full age of man to make evident the plan and proportions of his character. He postponed always a particular to a final and absolute success, so that his life was a silent appeal to the great and generous. But some time I shall see you and speak of him."

§ 3. In the year 1836 there was published in Boston a little book of less than a hundred very small pages, entitled "Nature." It bore no name on its title-page, but was at once attributed to its real author, Ralph Waldo Emerson.

The Emersonian adept will pardon me for burdening this beautiful Essay with a commentary which is worse than superfluous for him. For it has proved for many, — I will not say a *pons asinorum*, — but a very narrow bridge, which it made their heads swim to attempt crossing, and yet they must cross it, or one domain of Emerson's intellect will not be reached.

It differed in some respects from anything he had hitherto written. It talked a strange sort of philosophy in the language of poetry. Beginning simply enough, it took more and more the character of a rhapsody, until, as if lifted off his feet by the deepened and stronger undercurrent of his thought, the writer dropped his personality and repeated the words which " a certain poet sang " to him.

This little book met with a very unemotional reception. Its style was peculiar, — almost as unlike that of his Essays as that of Carlyle's " Sartor Resartus " was unlike the style of his " Life of Schiller." It was vague, mystic, incomprehensible, to most of those who call themselves common-sense people. Some of its expressions lent themselves easily to travesty and ridicule. But the laugh could not be very loud or very long, since it took twelve years, as Mr. Higginson tells us, to sell five hundred copies. It was a good deal like Keats's

> " doubtful tale from fairy-land
> Hard for the non-elect to understand."

The same experience had been gone through by Wordsworth.

" Whatever is too original," says De Quincey, " will be hated at the first. It must slowly mould a public for itself ; and the resistance of the early thoughtless judgments must be overcome by a counter-resistance to itself, in a better audience slowly mustering against the first. Forty and seven years it is since William Wordsworth first appeared as an author. Twenty of these years he was the scoff of the world, and his poetry a by-word of scorn. Since then, and more than once, senates have rung with acclamations to the echo of his name."

No writer is more deeply imbued with the spirit of Wordsworth than Emerson, as we cannot fail to see in turning the pages of " Nature," his first thoroughly characteristic Essay. There is the same thought in the Preface to "The Excursion " that we find in the Introduction to " Nature."

" The foregoing generations beheld God and nature face to face; we through their eyes. Why should

not we also enjoy an original relation to the universe?
Why should not we have a poetry and philosophy of
insight and not of tradition, and a religion by revelation to us, and not the history of theirs?"

> "Paradise and groves
> Elysian, Fortunate Fields — like those of old
> Sought in the Atlantic Main, why should they be
> A history only of departed things,
> Or a mere fiction of what never was?"

"Nature" is a reflective prose poem. It is
divided into eight chapters, which might almost
as well have been called cantos.

Never before had Mr. Emerson given free utterance to the passion with which the aspects of
nature inspired him. He had recently for the
first time been at once master of himself and in
free communion with all the planetary influences
above, beneath, around him. The air of the
country intoxicated him. There are sentences in
"Nature" which are as exalted as the language
of one who is just coming to himself after having been etherized. Some of these expressions
sounded to a considerable part of his early readers like the vagaries of delirium. Yet underlying
these excited outbursts there was a general tone
of serenity which reassured the anxious. The
gust passed over, the ripples smoothed themselves,
and the stars shone again in quiet reflection.

After a passionate outbreak, in which he sees

all, is nothing, loses himself in nature, in Universal Being, becomes " part or particle of God," he considers briefly, in the chapter entitled *Commodity*, the ministry of nature to the senses. A few picturesque glimpses in pleasing and poetical phrases, with a touch of archaism, and reminiscences of Hamlet and Jeremy Taylor, " the Shakspeare of divines," as he has called him, are what we find in this chapter on Commodity, or natural conveniences.

But " a nobler want of man is served by Nature, namely, the love of *Beauty*," which is his next subject. There are some touches of description here, vivid, high-colored, not so much pictures as hints and impressions for pictures.

Many of the thoughts which run through all his prose and poetry may be found here. Analogy is seen everywhere in the works of Nature. " What is common to them all, — that perfectness and harmony, is beauty." — " Nothing is quite beautiful alone : nothing but is beautiful in the whole." — " No reason can be asked or given why the soul seeks beauty." How easily these same ideas took on the robe of verse may be seen in the Poems, " Each and All," and " The Rhodora." A good deal of his philosophy comes out in these concluding sentences of the chapter : —

" Beauty in its largest and profoundest sense is

one expression for the universe ; God is the all-fair.
Truth and goodness and beauty are but different
faces of the same All. But beauty in Nature is
not ultimate. It is the herald of inward and eternal beauty, and is not alone a solid and satisfactory
good. It must therefore stand as a part and not as
yet the highest expression of the final cause of Nature."

In the "Rhodora" the flower is made to answer that

"Beauty is its own excuse for being."

In this Essay the beauty of the flower is not
enough, but it must excuse itself for being,
mainly as the symbol of something higher and
deeper than itself.

He passes next to a consideration of *Language.*
Words are signs of natural facts, particular material facts are symbols of particular spiritual
facts, and Nature is the symbol of spirit. Without going very profoundly into the subject, he
gives some hints as to the mode in which languages are formed, — whence words are derived,
how they become transformed and worn out.
But they come at first fresh from Nature.

"A man conversing in earnest, if he watch his
intellectual processes, will find that always a material image, more or less luminous, arises in his mind,
contemporaneous with every thought, which furnishes

the vestment of the thought. Hence good writing and brilliant discourse are perpetual allegories."

From this he argues that country life is a great advantage to a powerful mind, inasmuch as it furnishes a greater number of these material images. They cannot be summoned at will, but they present themselves when great exigencies call for them.

"The poet, the orator, bred in the woods, whose senses have been nourished by their fair and appeasing changes, year after year, without design and without heed, — shall not lose their lesson altogether, in the roar of cities or the broil of politics. Long hereafter, amidst agitations and terror in national councils, — in the hour of revolution, — these solemn images shall reappear in their morning lustre, as fit symbols and words of the thought which the passing events shall awaken. At the call of a noble sentiment, again the woods wave, the pines murmur, the river rolls and shines, and the cattle low upon the mountains, as he saw and heard them in his infancy. And with these forms the spells of persuasion, the keys of power, are put into his hands."

It is doing no wrong to this very eloquent and beautiful passage to say that it reminds us of certain lines in one of the best known poems of Wordsworth : —

> " These beauteous forms,
> Through a long absence, have not been to me

As is a landscape to a blind man's eye ;
But oft, in lonely rooms, and mid the din
Of towns and cities, I have owed to them
In hours of weariness sensations sweet
Felt in the blood and felt along the heart."

It is needless to quote the whole passage. The poetry of Wordsworth may have suggested the prose of Emerson, but the prose loses nothing by the comparison.

In *Discipline*, which is his next subject, he treats of the influence of Nature in educating the intellect, the moral sense, and the will. Man is enlarged and the universe lessened and brought within his grasp, because

"Time and space relations vanish as laws are known." — " The moral law lies at the centre of Nature and radiates to the circumference." — " All things with which we deal preach to us. What is a farm but a mute gospel?" — " From the child's successive possession of his several senses up to the hour when he sayeth, 'Thy will be done!' he is learning the secret that he can reduce under his will, not only particular events, but great classes, nay, the whole series of events, and so conform all facts to his character."

The unity in variety which meets us everywhere is again referred to. He alludes to the ministry of our friendships to our education. When a friend has done for our education in the way of filling our minds with sweet and solid

7

wisdom "it is a sign to us that his office is
closing, and he is commonly withdrawn from
our sight in a short time." This thought was
probably suggested by the death of his brother
Charles, which occurred a few months before
"Nature" was published. He had already
spoken in the first chapter of this little book as
if from some recent experience of his own, doubtless the same bereavement. "To a man laboring under calamity, the heat of his own fire hath
sadness in it. Then there is a kind of contempt
of the landscape felt by him who has just lost
by death a dear friend. The sky is less grand
as it shuts down over less worth in the population." This was the first effect of the loss; but
after a time he recognizes a superintending
power which orders events for us in wisdom
which we could not see at first.

The chapter on *Idealism* must be read by
all who believe themselves capable of abstract
thought, if they would not fall under the judgment of Turgot, which Emerson quotes: "He
that has never doubted the existence of matter
may be assured he has no aptitude for metaphysical inquiries." The most essential statement is this : —

"It is a sufficient account of that Appearance we
call the World, that God will teach a human mind,
and so makes it the receiver of a certain number of

congruent sensations, which we call sun and moon, man and woman, house and trade. In my utter impotence to test the authenticity of the report of my senses, to know whether the impressions they make on me correspond with outlying objects, what difference does it make, whether Orion is up there in Heaven, or some god paints the image in the firmament of the Soul?"

We need not follow the thought through the argument from illusions, like that when we look at the shore from a moving ship, and others which cheat the senses by false appearances. The poet animates Nature with his own thoughts, perceives the affinities between Nature and the soul, with Beauty as his main end. The philosopher pursues Truth, but, "not less than the poet, postpones the apparent order and relation of things to the empire of thought." Religion and ethics agree with all lower culture in degrading Nature and suggesting its dependence on Spirit. "The devotee flouts Nature." — "Plotinus was ashamed of his body." — "Michael Angelo said of external beauty, 'it is the frail and weary weed, in which God dresses the soul, which He has called into time.'" Emerson would not undervalue Nature as looked at through the senses and "the unrenewed understanding." "I have no hostility to Nature," he says, "but a child's love of it. I expand and live in the warm

day like corn and melons."—But, "seen in the
light of thought, the world always is phenom-
enal; and virtue subordinates it to the mind.
Idealism sees the world in God," — as one vast
picture, which God paints on the instant eternity,
for the contemplation of the soul.

The unimaginative reader is likely to find
himself off soundings in the next chapter, which
has for its title *Spirit*.

Idealism only denies the existence of matter;
it does not satisfy the demands of the spirit.
"It leaves God out of me." — Of these three
questions, What is matter? Whence is it?
Where to? The ideal theory answers the first
only. The reply is that matter is a phenomenon, not a substance.

"But when we come to inquire Whence is matter?
and Whereto? many truths arise to us out of the re-
cesses of consciousness. We learn that the highest
is present to the soul of man, that the dread universal
essence, which is not wisdom, or love, or beauty, or
power, but all in one, and each entirely, is that for
which all things exist, and that by which they are;
that spirit creates; that behind nature, throughout
nature, spirit is present; that spirit is one and not
compound; that spirit does not act upon us from
without, that is, in space and time, but spiritually, or
through ourselves." — "As a plant upon the earth,
so a man rests upon the bosom of God; he is nour-

ished by unfailing fountains, and draws, at his need, inexhaustible power."

Man may have access to the entire mind of the Creator, himself become a "creator in the finite."

"As we degenerate, the contrast between us and our house is more evident. We are as much strangers in nature as we are aliens from God. We do not understand the notes of birds. The fox and the deer run away from us; the bear and the tiger rend us."

All this has an Old Testament sound as of a lost Paradise. In the next chapter he dreams of Paradise regained.

This next and last chapter is entitled *Prospects*. He begins with a bold claim for the province of intuition as against induction, undervaluing the " half sight of science " as against the " untaught sallies of the spirit," the surmises and vaticinations of the mind, — the " imperfect theories, and sentences which contain glimpses of truth." In a word, he would have us leave the laboratory and its crucibles for the sibyl's cave and its tripod. We can all — or most of us, certainly — recognize something of truth, much of imagination, and more of danger in speculations of this sort. They belong to visionaries and to poets. Emerson feels distinctly enough that he is getting into the realm of

poetry. He quotes five beautiful verses from
George Herbert's " Poem on Man." Presently
he is himself taken off his feet into the air of
song, and finishes his Essay with " some traditions of man and nature which a certain poet
sang to me." — " A man is a god in ruins." —
" Man is the dwarf of himself. Once he was
permeated and dissolved by spirit. He filled
nature with his overflowing currents. Out from
him sprang the sun and moon; from man the
sun, from woman the moon."—But he no longer
fills the mere shell he had made for himself;
" he is shrunk to a drop." Still something of elemental power remains to him. " It is instinct."
Such teachings he got from his " poet." It is
a kind of New England Genesis in place of the
Old Testament one. We read in the Sermon
on the Mount : " Be ye therefore perfect as your
Father in Heaven is perfect." The discourse
which comes to us from the Trimount oracle
commands us, " Build, therefore, your own world.
As fast as you conform your life to the pure
idea in your mind, that will unfold its great proportions." The seer of Patmos foretells a heavenly Jerusalem, of which he says, " There shall
in no wise enter into it anything which defileth."
The sage of Concord foresees a new heaven on
earth. " A correspondent revolution in things
will attend the influx of the spirit. So fast will

disagreeable appearances, swine, spiders, snakes, pests, mad-houses, prisons, enemies, vanish; they are temporary and shall be no more seen."

It may be remembered that Calvin, in his Commentary on the New Testament, stopped when he came to the book of the "Revelation." He found it full of difficulties which he did not care to encounter. Yet, considered only as a poem, the vision of St. John is full of noble imagery and wonderful beauty. "Nature" is the Book of Revelation of our Saint Radulphus. It has its obscurities, its extravagances, but as a poem it is noble and inspiring. It was objected to on the score of its pantheistic character, as Wordsworth's "Lines composed near Tintern Abbey" had been long before. But here and there it found devout readers who were captivated by its spiritual elevation and great poetical beauty, among them one who wrote of it in the "Democratic Review" in terms of enthusiastic admiration.

Mr. Bowen, the Professor of Natural Theology and Moral Philosophy in Harvard University, treated this singular semi-philosophical, semi-poetical little book in a long article in the "Christian Examiner," headed "Transcendentalism," and published in the January number for 1837. The acute and learned Professor meant to deal fairly with his subject. But if one has ever seen a sagacious pointer making the acquaintance of a box-tortoise, he will have an idea of the relations between the reviewer and the reviewed as they appear in this article. The professor turns the book over and over, — inspects it from plastron to carapace, so to speak, and looks for openings everywhere, sometimes successfully, sometimes in vain. He finds good writing and sound philosophy, passages of great force and beauty of expression, marred by obscurity, under assumptions and faults of style. He was not, any more than the rest of us, acclimated to the Emersonian atmosphere, and after some not unjust or unkind comments with which many readers will heartily agree, confesses his bewilderment, saying : —

" On reviewing what we have already said of this singular work, the criticism seems to be couched in contradictory terms ; we can only allege in excuse the fact that the book is a contradiction in itself."

Carlyle says in his letter of February 13, 1837 : —

" Your little azure-colored ' Nature ' gave me true satisfaction. I read it, and then lent it about to all my acquaintances that had a sense for such things ; from whom a similar verdict always came back. You say it is the first chapter of something greater. I call it rather the Foundation and Ground-plan on

which you may build whatsoever of great and true has
been given you to build. It is the true Apocalypse,
this when the 'Open Secret' becomes revealed to a
man. I rejoice much in the glad serenity of soul
with which you look out on this wondrous Dwelling-
place of yours and mine, — with an ear for the
Ewigen Melodien, which pipe in the winds round us,
and utter themselves forth in all sounds and sights
and things ; *not* to be written down by gamut-ma-
chinery ; but which all right writing is a kind of attempt to write down."

The first edition of "Nature" had prefixed
to it the following words from Plotinus : " Nature is but an image or imitation of wisdom, the
last thing of the soul ; Nature being a thing
which doth only do, but not know." This is
omitted in after editions, and in its place we
read : —

> " A subtle chain of countless rings
> The next unto the farthest brings ;
> The eye reads omens where it goes,
> And speaks all languages the rose ;
> And striving to be man, the worm
> Mounts through all the spires of form."

The copy of "Nature" from which I take these
lines, his own, of course, like so many others
which he prefixed to his different Essays, was
printed in the year 1849, ten years before the
publication of Darwin's "Origin of Species,"
twenty years and more before the publication of

" The Descent of Man." But the " Vestiges of
Creation," published in 1844, had already pop-
ularized the resuscitated theories of Lamarck.
It seems as if Emerson had a warning from the
poetic instinct which, when it does not precede
the movement of the scientific intellect, is the
first to catch the hint of its discoveries. There
is nothing more audacious in the poet's conception of the worm looking up towards humanity,
than the naturalist's theory that the progenitor
of the human race was an acephalous mollusk.
" I will not be sworn," says Benedick, " but
love may transform me to an oyster." For
" love " read science.

Unity in variety, "*il piu nell uno*," symbolism
of Nature and its teachings, generation of phenomena, — appearances, — from spirit, to which
they correspond and which they obey ; evolution
of the best and elimination of the worst as the
law of being ; all this and much more may be
found in the poetic utterances of this slender
Essay. It fell like an aerolite, unasked for, unaccounted for, unexpected, almost unwelcome, —
a stumbling-block to be got out of the well-trod-
den highway of New England scholastic intelligence. But here and there it found a reader to
whom it was, to borrow, with slight changes, its
own quotation, —

> " The golden key
> Which opes the palace of eternity,"

inasmuch as it carried upon its face the highest certificate of truth, because it animated them to create a new world for themselves through the purification of their own souls.

Next to "Nature" in the series of his collected publications comes "The American Scholar. An Oration delivered before the Phi Beta Kappa Society at Cambridge, August 31, 1837."

The Society known by these three letters, long a mystery to the uninitiated, but which, filled out and interpreted, signify that philosophy is the guide of life, is one of long standing, the annual meetings of which have called forth the best efforts of many distinguished scholars and thinkers. Rarely has any one of the annual addresses been listened to with such profound attention and interest. Mr. Lowell says of it, that its delivery "was an event without any former parallel in our literary annals, a scene to be always treasured in the memory for its picturesqueness and its inspiration. What crowded and breathless aisles, what windows clustering with eager heads, what enthusiasm of approval, what grim silence of foregone dissent!"

Mr. Cooke says truly of this oration, that nearly all his leading ideas found expression in it. This was to be expected in an address delivered before such an audience. Every real thinker's

world of thought has its centre in a few formulæ, about which they revolve as the planets
circle round the sun which cast them off. But
those who lost themselves now and then in the
pages of "Nature" will find their way clearly
enough through those of "The American Scholar." It is a plea for generous culture; for the
development of all the faculties, many of which
tend to become atrophied by the exclusive pursuit of single objects of thought. It begins with
a note like a trumpet call.

"Thus far," he says, "our holiday has been simply
a friendly sign of the survival of the love of letters
amongst a people too busy to give to letters any more.
As such it is precious as the sign of an indestructible
instinct. Perhaps the time is already come when it
ought to be, and will be, something else ; when the
sluggard intellect of this continent will look from under its iron lids and fill the postponed expectations of
the world with something better than the exertions of
mechanical skill. Our day of dependence, our long
apprenticeship to the learning of other lands, draws
to a close. The millions that around us are rushing
into life cannot always be fed on the sere remains of
foreign harvests. Events, actions arise, that must be
sung, that will sing themselves. Who can doubt that
poetry will revive and lead in a new age, as the star
in the constellation Harp, which now flames in our
zenith, astronomers announce shall one day be the
pole-star for a thousand years ? "

Emerson finds his text in the old fable which tells that Man, as he was in the beginning, was divided into men, as the hand was divided into fingers, the better to answer the end of his being. The fable covers the doctrine that there is One Man; present to individuals only in a partial manner; and that we must take the whole of society to find the whole man. Unfortunately the unit has been too minutely subdivided, and many faculties are practically lost for want of use. "The state of society is one in which the members have suffered amputation from the trunk, and strut about so many walking monsters, — a good finger, a neck, a stomach, an elbow, but never a man. . . . Man is thus metamorphosed into a thing, into many things. . . . The priest becomes a form; the attorney a statute book; the mechanic a machine; the sailor a rope of the ship."

This complaint is by no means a new one. Scaliger says, as quoted by omnivorous old Burton: "*Nequaquam nos homines sumus sed partes hominis.*" The old illustration of this used to be found in pin-making. It took twenty different workmen to make a pin, beginning with drawing the wire and ending with sticking in the paper. Each expert, skilled in one small performance only, was reduced to a minute fraction of a fraction of humanity. If the complaint

was legitimate in Scaliger's time, it was better
founded half a century ago when Mr. Emerson
found cause for it.   It has still more serious
significance to-day, when in every profession, in
every branch of human knowledge, special ac-
quirements, special skill have greatly tended to
limit the range of men's thoughts and working
faculties.

" In this distribution of functions the scholar is the
delegated intellect. In the right state he is *Man
thinking*. In the degenerate state, when the victim
of society, he tends to become a mere thinker, or still
worse, the parrot of other men's thinking. In this
view of him, as Man thinking, the theory of his office
is continued. Him Nature solicits with all her placid,
all her monitory pictures; him the past instructs;
him the future invites."

Emerson proceeds to describe and illustrate
the influences of nature upon the mind, returning to the strain of thought with which his previous Essay has made us familiar. He next considers the influence of the past, and especially of
books as the best type of that influence. " Books
are the best of things well used; abused among
the worst."   It is hard to distil what is already
a quintessence without loss of what is just as
good as the product of our labor. A sentence
or two may serve to give an impression of the
epigrammatic wisdom of his counsel.

" Each age must write its own books, or, rather, each generation for the next succeeding. The books of an older period will not fit this."

When a book has gained a certain hold on the mind, it is liable to become an object of idolatrous regard.

" Instantly the book becomes noxious : the guide is a tyrant. The sluggish and perverted mind of the multitude, slow to open to the incursions of reason, having once so opened, having received this book, stands upon it and makes an outcry if it is disparaged. Colleges are built on it. Books are written on it by thinkers, not by Man thinking ; by men of talent, that is, who start wrong, who set out from accepted dogmas, not from their own sight of principle. Meek young men grow up in libraries, believing it their duty to accept the views which Cicero, which Locke, which Bacon have given ; forgetful that Cicero, Locke, and Bacon were only young men in libraries when they wrote these books. — One must be an inventor to read well. As the proverb says, ' He that would bring home the wealth of the Indies must carry out the wealth of the Indies.' — When the mind is braced by labor and invention, the page of whatever book we read becomes luminous with manifold allusion. Every sentence is doubly significant, and the sense of our author is as broad as the world."

It is not enough that the scholar should be a student of nature and of books. He must take a part in the affairs of the world about him.

" Action is with the scholar subordinate, but it is essential. Without it he is not yet man. Without it thought can never ripen into truth. — The true scholar grudges every opportunity of action past by, as a loss of power. It is the raw material out of which the intellect moulds her splendid products. A strange process, too, this by which experience is converted into thought as a mulberry leaf is converted into satin. The manufacture goes forward at all hours."

Emerson does not use the words " unconscious cerebration," but these last words describe the process in an unmistakable way. The beautiful paragraph in which he pictures the transformation, the transfiguration of experience, closes with a sentence so thoroughly characteristic, so Emersonially Emersonian, that I fear some readers who thought they were his disciples when they came to it went back and walked no more with him, at least through the pages of this discourse. The reader shall have the preceding sentence to prepare him for the one referred to.

" There is no fact, no event in our private history, which shall not, sooner or later, lose its adhesive, inert form, and astonish us by soaring from our body into the empyrean.

" Cradle and infancy, school and playground, the fear of boys, and dogs, and ferules, the love of little maids and berries, and many another fact that once filled the whole sky, are gone already; friend and relative, professions and party, town and country, nation and world must also soar and sing."

Having spoken of the education of the scholar by nature, by books, by action, he speaks of the scholar's duties. " They may all," he says, " be comprised in self-trust." We have to remember that the *self* he means is the highest self, that consciousness which he looks upon as open to the influx of the divine essence from which it came, and towards which all its upward tendencies lead, always aspiring, never resting ; as he sings in " The Sphinx" : —

> " The heavens that now draw him
> With sweetness untold,
> Once found, — for new heavens
> He spurneth the old."

" First one, then another, we drain all cisterns, and waxing greater by all these supplies, we crave a better and more abundant food. The man has never lived that can feed us ever. The human mind cannot be enshrined in a person who shall set a barrier on any one side of this unbounded, unboundable empire. It is one central fire, which, flaming now out of the lips of Etna, lightens the Capes of Sicily, and now out of the throat of Vesuvius, illuminates the towers and vineyards of Naples. It is one light which beams out of a thousand stars. It is one soul which animates all men."

8

And so he comes to the special application of the principles he has laid down to the American scholar of to-day. He does not spare his censure ; he is full of noble trust and manly courage. Very refreshing it is to remember in this day of specialists, when the walking fraction of humanity he speaks of would hardly include a whole finger, but rather confine itself to the single joint of the finger, such words as these : —

"The scholar is that man who must take up into himself all the ability of the time, all the contributions of the past, all the hopes of the future. He must be a university of knowledges. . . . We have listened too long to the courtly muses of Europe. The spirit of the American freeman is already suspected to be timid, imitative, tame.—The scholar is decent, indolent, complaisant.— The mind of this country, taught to aim at low objects, eats upon itself. There is no work for any but the decorous and the complaisant."

The young men of promise are discouraged and disgusted.

" What is the remedy ? They did not yet see, and thousands of young men as hopeful now crowding to the barriers for the career do not yet see, that if the single man plant himself indomitably on his instincts, and there abide, the huge world will come round to him."

Each man must be a unit, — must yield that peculiar fruit which he was created to bear.

" We will walk on our own feet ; we will work with our own hands ; we will speak our own minds. — A nation of men will for the first time exist, because each believes himself inspired by the Divine Soul which also inspires all men."

This grand Oration was our intellectual Declaration of Independence. Nothing like it had been heard in the halls of Harvard since Samuel Adams supported the affirmative of the question, " Whether it be lawful to resist the chief magistrate, if the commonwealth cannot otherwise be preserved." It was easy to find fault with an expression here and there. The dignity, not to say the formality of an Academic assembly was startled by the realism that looked for the infinite in " the meal in the firkin ; the milk in the pan." They could understand the deep thoughts suggested by " the meanest flower that blows," but these domestic illustrations had a kind of nursery homeliness about them which the grave professors and sedate clergymen were unused to expect on so stately an occasion. But the young men went out from it as if a prophet had been proclaiming to them " Thus saith the Lord." No listener ever forgot that Address, and among all the noble utterances of the speaker it may be questioned if one ever contained more truth in language more like that of immediate inspiration.

CHAPTER V.

1838–1843.   ÆT. 35–40.

§ 1. On Sunday evening, July 15, 1838, Emerson delivered an Address before the Senior
Class in Divinity College, Cambridge, which
caused a profound sensation in religious circles,
and led to a controversy, in which Emerson had
little more than the part of Patroclus when the
Greeks and Trojans fought over his body. In its
simplest and broadest statement this discourse
was a plea for the individual consciousness as
against all historical creeds, bibles, churches ;
for the soul as the supreme judge in spiritual
matters.

He begins with a beautiful picture which must

be transferred without the change of an expression : —

"In this refulgent Summer, it has been a luxury to draw the breath of life. The grass grows, the buds burst, the meadow is spotted with fire and gold in the tint of flowers. The air is full of birds, and sweet with the breath of the pine, the balm of Gilead, and the new hay. Night brings no gloom to the heart with its welcome shade. Through the transparent darkness the stars pour their almost spiritual rays. Man under them seems a young child, and his huge globe a toy. The cool night bathes the world as with a river, and prepares his eyes again for the crimson dawn."

How softly the phrases of the gentle iconoclast steal upon the ear, and how they must have hushed the questioning audience into pleased attention! The "Song of Songs, which is Solomon's," could not have wooed the listener more sweetly. "Thy lips drop as the honeycomb : honey and milk are under thy tongue, and the smell of thy garments is like the smell of Lebanon." And this was the prelude of a discourse which, when it came to be printed, fared at the hands of many a theologian, who did not think himself a bigot, as the roll which Baruch wrote with ink from the words of Jeremiah fared at the hands of Jehoiakim, the King of Judah. He listened while Jehudi read the opening passages.

But " when Jehudi had read three or four leaves he cut it with the penknife, and cast it into the fire that was on the hearth, until all the roll was consumed in the fire that was on the hearth." Such was probably the fate of many a copy of this famous discourse.

It is reverential, but it is also revolutionary. The file-leaders of Unitarianism drew back in dismay, and the ill names which had often been applied to them were now heard from their own lips as befitting this new heresy; if so mild a reproach as that of heresy belonged to this alarming manifesto. And yet, so changed is the whole aspect of the theological world since the time when that discourse was delivered that it is read as calmly to-day as a common " Election Sermon," if such are ever read at all. A few extracts, abstracts, and comments may give the reader who has not the Address before him some idea of its contents and its tendencies.

The material universe, which he has just pictured in its summer beauty, deserves our admiration. But when the mind opens and reveals the laws which govern the world of phenomena, it shrinks into a mere fable and illustration of this mind. What am I? What is? — are questions always asked, never fully answered. We would study and admire forever.

But above intellectual curiosity, there is the

sentiment of virtue. Man is born for the good, for the perfect, low as he now lies in evil and weakness. "The sentiment of virtue is a reverence and delight in the presence of certain divine laws. — These laws refuse to be adequately stated. — They elude our persevering thought; yet we read them hourly in each other's faces, in each other's actions, in our own remorse. — The intuition of the moral sentiment is an insight of the perfection of the laws of the soul. These laws execute themselves. — As we are, so we associate. The good, by affinity, seek the good; the vile, by affinity, the vile. Thus, of their own volition, souls proceed into heaven, into hell."

These facts, Emerson says, have always suggested to man that the world is the product not of manifold power, but of one will, of one mind, — that one mind is everywhere active. — "All things proceed out of the same spirit, and all things conspire with it." While a man seeks good ends, nature helps him; when he seeks other ends, his being shrinks, "he becomes less and less, a mote, a point, until absolute badness is absolute death." — "When he says 'I ought;' when love warms him; when he chooses, warned from on high, the good and great deed; then deep melodies wander through his soul from Supreme Wisdom."

"This sentiment lies at the foundation of society and successively creates all forms of worship. — This thought dwelled always deepest in the minds of men in the devout and contemplative East; not alone in Palestine, where it reached its purest expression, but in Egypt, in Persia, in India, in China. Europe has always owed to Oriental genius its divine impulses. What these holy bards said, all sane men found agreeable and true. And the unique impression of Jesus upon mankind, whose name is not so much written as ploughed into the history of this world, is proof of the subtle virtue of this infusion."

But this truth cannot be received at second hand; it is an intuition. What another announces, I must find true in myself, or I must reject it. If the word of another is taken instead of this primary faith, the church, the state, art, letters, life, all suffer degradation, — "the doctrine of inspiration is lost; the base doctrine of the majority of voices usurps the place of the doctrine of the soul."

The following extract will show the view that he takes of Christianity and its Founder, and sufficiently explain the antagonism called forth by the discourse: —

"Jesus Christ belonged to the true race of prophets. He saw with open eye the mystery of the soul. Drawn by its severe harmony, ravished with its beauty, he lived in it, and had his being there. Alone in all history he estimated the greatness of man. One man was true to what is in you and me. He saw that God incarnates himself in man, and evermore goes forth anew to take possession of his World. He said, in this jubilee of sublime emotion, 'I am Divine. Through me God acts; through me, speaks. Would you see God, see me; or see thee, when thou also thinkest as I now think.' But what a distortion did his doctrine and memory suffer in the same, in the next, and the following ages! There is no doctrine of the Reason which will bear to be taught by the Understanding. The understanding caught this high chant from the poet's lips, and said, in the next age, ' This was Jehovah come down out of heaven. I will kill you if you say he was a man.' The idioms of his language and the figures of his rhetoric have usurped the place of his truth ; and churches are not built on his principles, but on his tropes. Christianity became a Mythus, as the poetic teaching of Greece and of Egypt, before. He spoke of Miracles ; for he felt that man's life was a miracle, and all that man doth, and he knew that this miracle shines as the character ascends. But the word Miracle, as pronounced by Christian churches, gives a false impression ; it is Monster. It is not one with the blowing clover and the falling rain."

He proceeds to point out what he considers the great defects of historical Christianity. It has exaggerated the personal, the positive, the ritual. It has wronged mankind by monopolizing

all virtues for the Christian name. It is only
by his holy thoughts that Jesus serves us. "To
aim to convert a man by miracles is a profana-
tion of the soul." The preachers do a wrong to
Jesus by removing him from our human sympathies; they should not degrade his life and dia-
logues by insulation and peculiarity.

Another defect of the traditional and limited
way of using the mind of Christ is that the
Moral Nature — the Law of Laws — is not ex-
plored as the fountain of the established teaching in society. "Men have come to speak of
the revelation as somewhat long ago given and
done, as if God were dead." — "The soul is
not preached. The church seems to totter to
its fall, almost all life extinct. — The stationari-
ness of religion; the assumption that the age
of inspiration is past; that the Bible is closed;
the fear of degrading the character of Jesus by
representing him as a man; indicate with sufficient clearness the falsehood of our theology. It
is the office of a true teacher to show us that
God is, not was; that he speaketh, not spake.
The true Christianity — a faith like Christ's in
the infinitude of Man — is lost."

When Emerson came to what his earlier ancestors would have called the "practical application," some of his young hearers must have
been startled at the style of his address.

" Yourself a new - born bard of the Holy Ghost, cast behind you all conformity, and acquaint men at first hand with Deity. Look to it first and only, that fashion, custom, authority, pleasure, and money are nothing to you, — are not bandages over your eyes, that you cannot see, — but live with the privilege of the immeasurable mind."

Emerson recognizes two inestimable advantages as the gift of Christianity ; first the Sabbath, — hardly a Christian institution, — and secondly the institution of preaching. He spoke not only eloquently, but with every evidence of deep sincerity and conviction. He had sacrificed an enviable position to that inner voice of duty which he now proclaimed as the sovereign law over all written or spoken words. But he was assailing the cherished beliefs of those before him, and of Christendom generally ; not with hard or bitter words, not with sarcasm or levity, rather as one who felt himself charged with a message from the same divinity who had inspired the prophets and evangelists of old with whatever truth was in their messages. He might be wrong, but his words carried the evidence of his own serene, unshaken confidence that the spirit of all truth was with him. Some of his audience, at least, must have felt the contrast between his utterances and the formal discourses they had so long listened to, and said to them-selves, " he speaks ' as one having authority, and not as the Scribes.' "

Such teaching, however, could not be suffered to go unchallenged. Its doctrines were repudiated in the " Christian Examiner," the leading organ of the Unitarian denomination. The Rev. Henry Ware, greatly esteemed and honored, whose colleague he had been, addressed a letter to him, in which he expressed the feeling that some of the statements of Emerson's discourse would tend to overthrow the authority and influence of Christianity. To this note Emerson returned the following answer : —

" What you say about the discourse at Divinity College is just what I might expect from your truth and charity, combined with your known opinions. I am not a stick or a stone, as one said in the old time, and could not but feel pain in saying some things in that place and presence which I supposed would meet with dissent, I may say, of dear friends and benefactors of mine. Yet, as my conviction is perfect in the substantial truth of the doctrines of this discourse, and is not very new, you will see at once that it must appear very important that it be spoken; and I thought I could not pay the nobleness of my friends so mean a compliment as to suppress my opposition to their supposed views, out of fear of offence. I would rather say to them, these things look thus to me, to you otherwise. Let us say our uttermost word, and let the all-pervading truth, as it surely will, judge between us. Either of us would, I doubt not, be willingly apprised of his error. Meantime, I shall be admonished by this expression of your thought, to revise with greater care the 'address,' before it is printed (for the use of the class) : and I heartily thank you for this expression of your tried toleration and love."

Dr. Ware followed up his note with a sermon, preached on the 23d of September, in which he dwells especially on the necessity of adding the idea of personality to the abstractions of Emerson's philosophy, and sent it to him with a letter, the kindness and true Christian spirit of which were only what were inseparable from all the thoughts and feelings of that most excellent and truly apostolic man.

To this letter Emerson sent the following reply : —

CONCORD, *October* 8, 1838.

MY DEAR SIR, — I ought sooner to have acknowledged your kind letter of last week, and the sermon it accompanied. The letter was right manly and noble. The sermon, too, I have read with attention. If it assails any doctrine of mine, — perhaps I am not so quick to see it as writers generally, — certainly I did not feel any disposition to depart from my habitual contentment, that you should say your thought, whilst I say mine. I believe I must tell you what I think of my new position. It strikes me very oddly that good and wise men at Cambridge and Boston should think of raising me into an object of criticism. I have always been — from my very incapacity of methodical writing — a 'chartered libertine,' free to worship and free to rail, — lucky when I could make myself understood, but never esteemed near enough to the institutions and mind of society to deserve the notice of the masters of literature and religion. I have appreciated fully the advantages of my position, for I well know there is no scholar less willing or less able than myself to be a polemic. I could not give an account of myself, if challenged. I could not possibly give you one of the 'arguments' you cruelly hint at, on which any doctrine of mine stands; for I do not know what arguments are in reference to any expression of a thought. I delight in telling what I think; but if you ask me how I dare say so, or why it is so, I am the most helpless of mortal men. I do not even see that either of these questions admits of an answer. So that in the present droll posture of my affairs, when I see myself suddenly raised to the importance of a heretic, I am very uneasy when I advert to the supposed duties of such a personage, who is to make good his thesis against all comers. I certainly shall do no such thing. I shall read what you and other good men write, as I have always done, glad when you speak my thoughts, and skipping the page that has nothing for me. I shall go on just as before, seeing whatever I can, and telling what I see; and,

I suppose, with the same fortune that has hitherto attended me, — the joy of finding that my abler and better brothers, who work with the sympathy of society, loving and beloved, do now and then unexpectedly confirm my conceptions, and find my nonsense is only their own thought in motley, — and so I am your affectionate servant," etc.

The controversy which followed is a thing of the past ; Emerson took no part in it, and we need not return to the discussion. He knew his office and has defined it in the clearest manner in the letter just given, — " Seeing whatever I can, and telling what I see." But among his listeners and readers was a man of very different mental constitution, not more independent or fearless, but louder and more combative, whose voice soon became heard and whose strength soon began to be felt in the long battle between the traditional and immanent inspiration, — Theodore Parker. If Emerson was the moving spirit, he was the right arm in the conflict, which in one form or another has been waged up to the present day.

In the winter of 1838–39 Emerson delivered his usual winter course of Lectures. He names them in a letter to Carlyle as follows : " Ten Lectures : I. The Doctrine of the Soul ; II. Home ; III. The School ; IV. Love ; V. Genius ; VI. The Protest ; VII. Tragedy ; VIII.

Comedy; IX. Duty; X. Demonology. I designed to add two more, but my lungs played me false with unseasonable inflammation, so I discoursed no more on Human Life." Two or three of these titles only are prefixed to his published Lectures or Essays; Love, in the first volume of Essays; Demonology in " Lectures and Biographical Sketches; " and " The Comic " in " Letters and Social Aims."

I owe the privilege of making use of the two following letters to my kind and honored friend, James Freeman Clarke.

The first letter was accompanied by the Poem " The Humble-bee," which was first published by Mr. Clarke in the " Western Messenger," from the autograph copy, which begins " Fine humble-bee ! fine humble-bee ! " and has a number of other variations from the poem as printed in his collected works.

CONCORD, *December* 7, 1838.

MY DEAR SIR, — Here are the verses. They have pleased some of my friends, and so may please some of your readers, and you asked me in the spring if I had n't somewhat to contribute to your journal. I remember in your letter you mentioned the remark of some friend of yours that the verses, " Take, O take those lips away," were not Shakspeare's ; I think they are. Beaumont, nor Fletcher, nor both together were ever, I think, visited by such a starry gleam as that stanza. I know it is in "Rollo," but it is in "Measure for Measure" also; and I remember noticing that the Malones, and Stevens, and critical gentry were about evenly divided, these for Shakspeare, and those for Beaumont and Fletcher. But the internal evidence is all for one, none for the other. If he did not write it, they did not, and we shall have some fourth unknown singer. What care we *who* sung this or that. It is we at last who sing.

Your friend and servant,   R. W. EMERSON.

TO JAMES FREEMAN CLARKE.

CONCORD, *February* 27, 1839.

MY DEAR SIR, — I am very sorry to have made you wait so long for an answer to your flattering request for two such little poems. You are quite welcome to the lines "To the Rhodora;" but I think they need the superscription ["Lines on being asked 'Whence is the Flower?'"]. Of the other verses ["Good-by proud world," etc.] I send you a corrected copy, but I wonder so much at your wishing to print them that I think you must read them once again with your critical spectacles before they go further. They were written sixteen years ago, when I kept school in Boston, and lived in a corner of Roxbury called Canterbury. They have a slight misanthropy, a shade deeper than belongs to me; and as it seems nowadays I am a philosopher and am grown to have opinions, I think they must have an apologetic date, though I well know that poetry that needs a date is no poetry, and so you will wiselier suppress

9

them. I heartily wish I had any verses which with
a clear mind I could send you in lieu of these juve-
nilities. It is strange, seeing the delight we take in
verses, that we can so seldom write them, and so are
not ashamed to lay up old ones, say sixteen years, instead of improvising them as freely as the wind
blows, whenever we and our brothers are attuned to
music. I have heard of a citizen who made an annual joke. I believe I have in April or May an annual poetic *conatus* rather than *afflatus,* experiment-
ing to the length of thirty lines or so, if I may judge
from the dates of the rhythmical scraps I detect
among my MSS. I look upon this incontinence as
merely the redundancy of a susceptibility to poetry
which makes all the bards my daily treasures, and I
can well run the risk of being ridiculous once a year
for the benefit of happy reading all the other days.
In regard to the Providence Discourse, I have no
copy of it; and as far as I remember its contents, I
have since used whatever is striking in it; but I will
get the MS., if Margaret Fuller has it, and you shall
have it if it will pass muster. I shall certainly avail
myself of the good order you gave me for twelve
copies of the " Carlyle Miscellanies," so soon as they
appear. He, T. C., writes in excellent spirits of his
American friends and readers. . . . A new book, he
writes, is growing in him, though not to begin until
his spring lectures are over (which begin in May).
Your sister Sarah was kind enough to carry me the
other day to see some pencil sketches done by Stuart
Newton when in the Insane Hospital. They seemed

to me to betray the richest invention, so rich as almost to say, why draw any line since you can draw all? Genius has given you the freedom of the universe, why then come within any walls? And this seems to be the old moral which we draw from our fable, read it how or where you will, that we cannot make one good stroke until we can make every possible stroke; and when we can one, every one seems superfluous. I heartily thank you for the good wishes you send me to open the year, and I say them back again to you. Your field is a world, and all men are your spectators, and all men respect the true and great-hearted service you render. And yet it is not spectator nor spectacle that concerns either you or me. The whole world is sick of that very ail, of being seen, and of seemliness. It belongs to the brave now to trust themselves infinitely, and to sit and hearken alone. I am glad to see William Channing is one of your coadjutors. Mrs. Jameson's new book, I should think, would bring a caravan of travellers, æsthetic, artistic, and what not, up your mighty stream, or along the lakes to Mackinaw. As I read I almost vowed an exploration, but I doubt if I ever get beyond the Hudson.

Your affectionate servant,   R. W. EMERSON.

On the 24th of July, 1838, a little more than a week after the delivery of the Address before the Divinity School, Mr. Emerson delivered an Oration before the Literary Societies of Dartmouth College. If any rumor of the former

discourse had reached Dartmouth, the audience
must have been prepared for a much more startling performance than that to which they listened. The bold avowal which fluttered the
dovecotes of Cambridge would have sounded
like the crash of doom to the cautious old ten-
ants of the Hanover aviary. If there were any
drops of false or questionable doctrine in the
silver shower of eloquence under which they had
been sitting, the plumage of orthodoxy glistened
with unctuous repellents, and a shake or two on
coming out of church left the sturdy old dogmatists as dry as ever.

Those who remember the Dartmouth College
of that day cannot help smiling at the thought
of the contrast in the way of thinking between
the speaker and the larger part, or at least the
older part, of his audience. President Lord was
well known as the scriptural defender of the institution of slavery. Not long before a controversy had arisen, provoked by the setting up of
the Episcopal form of worship by one of the
Professors, the most estimable and scholarly Dr.
Daniel Oliver. Perhaps, however, the extreme
difference between the fundamental conceptions
of Mr. Emerson and the endemic orthodoxy of
that place and time was too great for any hostile
feeling to be awakened by the sweet-voiced and
peaceful-mannered speaker. There is a kind of

harmony between boldly contrasted beliefs like that between complementary colors. It is when two shades of the same color are brought side by side that comparison makes them odious to each other. Mr. Emerson could go anywhere and find willing listeners among those farthest in their belief from the views he held. Such was his simplicity of speech and manner, such his transparent sincerity, that it was next to impossible to quarrel with the gentle image-breaker.

The subject of Mr. Emerson's Address is *Literary Ethics.* It is on the same lofty plane of sentiment and in the same exalted tone of eloquence as the Phi Beta Kappa Address. The word impassioned would seem misplaced, if applied to any of Mr. Emerson's orations. But these discourses were both written and delivered in the freshness of his complete manhood. They were produced at a time when his mind had learned its powers and the work to which it was called, in the struggle which freed him from the constraint of stereotyped confessions of faith and all peremptory external authority. It is not strange, therefore, to find some of his paragraphs glowing with heat and sparkling with imaginative illustration.

"Neither years nor books," he says, "have yet availed to extirpate a prejudice rooted in me, that a scholar is the favorite of Heaven and

earth, the excellency of his country, the happiest
of men." And yet, he confesses that the scholars of this country have not fulfilled the reasonable expectation of mankind. "Men here,
as elsewhere, are indisposed to innovation and
prefer any antiquity, any usage, any livery pro-
ductive of ease or profit, to the unproductive
service of thought." For all this he offers those
correctives which in various forms underlie all
his teachings. "The resources of the scholar
are proportioned to his confidence in the attributes of the Intellect." New lessons of spiritual independence, fresh examples and illustrations, are drawn from history and biography.
There is a passage here so true to nature that it
permits a half page of quotation and a line or
two of comment : —

"An intimation of these broad rights is familiar in
the sense of injury which men feel in the assumption
of any man to limit their possible progress. We re-
sent all criticism which denies us anything that lies
in our line of advance. Say to the man of letters,
that he cannot paint a Transfiguration, or build a
steamboat, or be a grand-marshal, and he will not
seem to himself depreciated. But deny to him any
quality of literary or metaphysical power, and he is
piqued. Concede to him genius, which is a sort of
stoical *plenum* annulling the comparative, and he is
content ; but concede him talents never so rare, denying him genius, and he is aggrieved."

But it ought to be added that if the pleasure of denying the genius of their betters were denied to the mediocrities, their happiness would be forever blighted.

From the resources of the American Scholar Mr. Emerson passes to his tasks. Nature, as it seems to him, has never yet been truly studied. "Poetry has scarcely chanted its first song. The perpetual admonition of Nature to us is, 'The world is new, untried. Do not believe the past. I give you the universe a virgin to-day.'" And in the same way he would have the scholar look at history, at philosophy. The world belongs to the student, but he must put himself into harmony with the constitution of things. "He must embrace solitude as a bride." Not superstitiously, but after having found out, as a little experience will teach him, all that society can do for him with its foolish routine. I have spoken of the exalted strain into which Mr. Emerson sometimes rises in the midst of his general serenity. Here is an instance of it : —

"You will hear every day the maxims of a low prudence. You will hear that the first duty is to get land and money, place and name. 'What is this truth you seek? What is this beauty?' men will ask, with derision. If, nevertheless, God have called any of you to explore truth and beauty, be bold, be firm, be true. When you shall say, 'As others do, so will I: I renounce, I am sorry for it, my early visions : I must eat the good of the land, and let learning and romantic expectations go, until a more convenient season ; ' — then dies the man in you ; then once more perish the buds of art, and poetry, and science, as they have died already in a thousand thousand men. — Bend to the persuasion which is flowing to you from every object in nature, to be its tongue to the heart of man, and to show the besotted world how passing fair is wisdom. Why should you renounce your right to traverse the starlit deserts of truth, for the premature comforts of an acre, house, and barn ? Truth also has its roof and house and board. Make yourself necessary to the world, and mankind will give you bread ; and if not store of it, yet such as shall not take away your property in all men's possessions, in all men's affections, in art, in nature, and in hope."

The next Address Emerson delivered was " The Method of Nature," before the Society of the Adelphi, in Waterville College, Maine, August 11, 1841.

In writing to Carlyle on the 31st of July, he says : " As usual at this season of the year, I, incorrigible spouting Yankee, am writing an oration to deliver to the boys in one of our little country colleges nine days hence. . . . My whole philosophy — which is very real — teaches acquiescence and optimism. Only when I see how much work is to be done, what room for a poet

—for any spiritualist—in this great, intelligent, sensual, and avaricious America, I lament my fumbling fingers and stammering tongue." It may be remembered that Mr. Matthew Arnold quoted the expression about America, which sounded more harshly as pronounced in a public lecture than as read in a private letter.

The Oration shows the same vein of thought as the letter. Its title is "The Method of Nature." He begins with congratulations on the enjoyments and promises of this literary Anniversary.

"The scholars are the priests of that thought which establishes the foundations of the castle."—"We hear too much of the results of machinery, commerce, and the useful arts. We are a puny and a fickle folk. Avarice, hesitation, and following are our diseases. The rapid wealth which hundreds in the community acquire in trade, or by the incessant expansion of our population and arts, enchants the eyes of all the rest; this luck of one is the hope of thousands, and the bribe acts like the neighborhood of a gold mine to impoverish the farm, the school, the church, the house, and the very body and feature of man."—"While the multitude of men degrade each other, and give currency to desponding doctrines, the scholar must be a bringer of hope, and must reinforce man against himself."

I think we may detect more of the manner of

Carlyle in this Address than in any of those
which preceded it.

"Why then goest thou as some Boswell or literary
worshipper to this saint or to that? That is the only
lese-majesty. Here art thou with whom so long the
universe travailed in labor; darest thou think meanly
of thyself whom the stalwart Fate brought forth to
unite his ragged sides, to shoot the gulf, to reconcile
the irreconcilable?"

That there is an "intimate divinity" which is
the source of all true wisdom, that the duty of
man is to listen to its voice and to follow it, that
"the sanity of man needs the poise of this immanent force," that the rule is "Do what you
know, and perception is converted into character," — all this is strongly enforced and richly
illustrated in this Oration. Just how easily it
was followed by the audience, just how far they
were satisfied with its large principles wrought
into a few broad precepts, it would be easier at
this time to ask than to learn. We notice not so
much the novelty of the ideas to be found in this
discourse on "The Method of Nature," as the
pictorial beauty of their expression. The deep
reverence which underlies all Emerson's speculations is well shown in this paragraph : —

"We ought to celebrate this hour by expressions
of manly joy. Not thanks nor prayer seem quite the
highest or truest name for our communication with

the infinite, — but glad and conspiring reception, — reception that becomes giving in its turn as the receiver is only the All-Giver in part and in infancy." — "It is God in us which checks the language of petition by grander thought. In the bottom of the heart it is said: 'I am, and by me, O child! this fair body and world of thine stands and grows. I am, all things are mine; and all mine are thine.'"

We must not quarrel with his peculiar expressions. He says, in this same paragraph, " I cannot, — nor can any man, — speak precisely of things so sublime; but it seems to me the wit of man, his strength, his grace, his tendency, his art, is the grace and the presence of God. It is beyond explanation."

" We can point nowhere to anything final but tendency; but tendency appears on all hands; planet, system, constellation, total nature is growing like a field of maize in July; is becoming something else; is in rapid metamorphosis. The embryo does not more strive to be man, than yonder burr of light we call a nebula tends to be a ring, a comet, a globe, and parent of new stars." " In short, the spirit and peculiarity of that impression nature makes on us is this, that it does not exist to any one, or to any number of particular ends, but to numberless and endless benefit; that there is in it no private will, no rebel leaf or limb, but the whole is oppressed by one superincumbent tendency, obeys that redundancy or excess of life which in conscious beings we call ecstasy."

Here is another of those almost lyrical passages which seem too long for the music of
rhythm and the resonance of rhyme.

"The great Pan of old, who was clothed in a leopard skin to signify the beautiful variety of things, and
the firmament, his coat of stars, was but the representative of thee, O rich and various Man! thou pal-
ace of sight and sound, carrying in thy senses the
morning and the night and the unfathomable galaxy;
in thy brain the geometry of the City of God; in thy
heart the bower of love and the realms of right and
wrong."

His feeling about the soul, which has shown
itself in many of the extracts already given, is
summed up in the following sentence: —

"We cannot describe the natural history of the
soul, but we know that it is divine. I cannot tell if
these wonderful qualities which house to-day in this
mental home shall ever reassemble in equal activity
in a similar frame, or whether they have before had a
natural history like that of this body you see before
you; but this one thing I know, that these qualities
did not now begin to exist, cannot be sick with my
sickness, nor buried in any grave; but that they cir-
culate through the Universe: before the world was,
they were."

It is hard to see the distinction between the
omnipresent Deity recognized in our formal con-

fessions of faith and the "pantheism" which is
the object of dread to many of the faithful. But
there are many expressions in this Address
which must have sounded strangely and vaguely
to his Christian audience. "Are there not moments in the history of heaven when the human
race was not counted by individuals, but was
only the Influenced ; was God in distribution,
God rushing into manifold benefit ? " It might
be feared that the practical philanthropists would
feel that they lost by his counsels.

"The reform whose fame now fills the land with
Temperance, Anti-Slavery, Non-Resistance, No Government, Equal Labor, fair and generous as each
appears, are poor bitter things when prosecuted for
themselves as an end." — "I say to you plainly there
is no end to which your practical faculty can aim so
sacred or so large, that if pursued for itself, will not
at last become carrion and an offence to the nostril.
The imaginative faculty of the soul must be fed with
objects immense and eternal. Your end should be
one inapprehensible to the senses ; then it will be a
god, always approached, — never touched ; always
giving health."

Nothing is plainer than that it was Emerson's calling to supply impulses and not methods. He was not an organizer, but a power behind many organizers, inspiring them with lofty
motive, giving breadth to their views, always

tending to become narrow through concentration on their special objects. The Oration we have been examining was delivered in the interval between the delivery of two Addresses, one called " Man the Reformer," and another called " Lecture on the Times." In the first he preaches the dignity and virtue of manual labor ; that " a man should have a farm, or a mechanical craft for his culture." — That he cannot give up labor without suffering some loss of power. " How can the man who has learned but one art procure all the conveniences of life honestly ? Shall we say all we think ? — Perhaps with his own hands. — Let us learn the meaning of economy. — Parched corn eaten to-day that I may have roast fowl to my dinner on Sunday is a baseness ; but parched corn and a house with one apartment, that I may be free of all perturbation, that I may be serene and docile to what the mind shall speak, and quit and road-ready for the lowest mission of knowledge or good will, is frugality for gods and heroes."

This was what Emerson wrote in January, 1841. This " house with one apartment " was what Thoreau built with his own hands in 1845. In April of the former year, he went to live with Mr. Emerson, but had been on intimate terms with him previously to that time. Whether it was from him that Thoreau got the hint of the Walden cabin and the parched corn, or whether this idea was working in Thoreau's mind and was suggested to Emerson by him, is of no great consequence. Emerson, to whom he owed so much, may well have adopted some of those fancies which Thoreau entertained, and afterwards worked out in practice. He was at the philanthropic centre of a good many movements which he watched others carrying out, as a calm and kindly spectator, without losing his common sense for a moment. It would never have occurred to him to leave all the conveniences and comforts of life to go and dwell in a shanty, so as to prove to himself that he could live like a savage, or like his friends " Teague and his jade," as he called the man and brother and sister, more commonly known nowadays as Pat, or Patrick, and his old woman.

" The Americans have many virtues," he says in this Address, " but they have not Faith and Hope." Faith and Hope, Enthusiasm and Love, are the burden of this Address. But he would regulate these qualities by " a great prospective prudence," which shall mediate between the spiritual and the actual world.

In the " Lecture on the Times " he shows very clearly the effect which a nearer contact with the class of men and women who called themselves Reformers had upon him.

" The Reforms have their higher origin in an ideal justice, but they do not retain the purity of an idea. They are quickly organized in some low, inadequate form, and present no more poetic image to the mind than the evil tradition which they reprobated. They mix the fire of the moral sentiment with personal and party heats, with measureless exaggerations, and the blindness that prefers some darling measure to justice and truth. Those who are urging with most ardor what are called the greatest benefit of mankind are narrow, self-pleasing, conceited men, and affect us as the insane do. They bite us, and we run mad also. I think the work of the reformer as innocent as other work that is done around him; but when I have seen it near! — I do not like it better. It is done in the same way; it is done profanely, not piously; by management, by tactics and clamor."

All this, and much more like it, would hardly have been listened to by the ardent advocates of the various reforms, if anybody but Mr. Emerson had said it. He undervalued no sincere action except to suggest a wiser and better one. He attacked no motive which had a good aim, except in view of some larger and loftier principle. The charm of his imagination and the music of his words took away all the sting from the thoughts that penetrated to the very marrow of the entranced listeners. Sometimes it was a splendid hyperbole that illuminated a statement which by the dim light of common speech would have offended or repelled those who sat before him. He knew the force of *felix audacia* as well as any rhetorician could have taught him. He addresses the reformer with one of those daring images which defy the critics.

" As the farmer casts into the ground the finest ears of his grain, the time will come when we too shall hold nothing back, but shall eagerly convert more than we possess into means and powers, when we shall be willing to sow the sun and the moon for seeds."

He said hard things to the reformer, especially to the Abolitionist, in his " Lecture on the Times." It would have taken a long while to get rid of slavery if some of Emerson's teachings in this lecture had been accepted as the true gospel of liberty. But how much its last sentence covers with its soothing tribute !

" All the newspapers, all the tongues of to-day will of course defame what is noble; but you who hold not of to-day, not of the times, but of the Everlasting, are to stand for it; and the highest compliment man ever receives from Heaven is the sending to him its disguised and discredited angels."

The Lecture called " The Transcendentalist " will naturally be looked at with peculiar interest, inasmuch as this term has been very com-

10

monly applied to Emerson, and to many who
were considered his disciples. It has a proper
philosophical meaning, and it has also a local
and accidental application to the individuals of
a group which came together very much as any
literary club might collect about a teacher. All
this comes out clearly enough in the Lecture.
In the first place, Emerson explains that the
" *new views*," as they are called, are the oldest
of thoughts cast in a new mould.

" What is popularly called Transcendentalism
among us is Idealism : Idealism as it appears in
1842. As thinkers, mankind have ever divided into
two sects, Materialists and Idealists; the first class
founding on experience, the second on consciousness ;
the first class beginning to think from the data of the
senses, the second class perceive that the senses are
not final, and say, the senses give us representations
of things, but what are the things themselves, they
cannot tell. The materialist insists on facts, on history, on the force of circumstances and the animal
wants of man ; the idealist on the power of Thought
and of Will, on inspiration, on miracle, on individual
culture."

" The materialist takes his departure from the external world, and esteems a man as one product of
that. The idealist takes his departure from his consciousness, and reckons the world an appearance. —
His thought, that is the Universe."

The association of scholars and thinkers to

which the name of "Transcendentalists" was applied, and which made itself an organ in the periodical known as "The Dial," has been written about by many who were in the movement, and others who looked on or got their knowledge of it at second hand. Emerson was closely associated with these "same Transcendentalists," and a leading contributor to "The Dial," which was their organ. The movement borrowed its inspiration more from him than from any other source, and the periodical owed more to him than to any other writer. So far as his own relation to the circle of illuminati and the dial which they shone upon was concerned, he himself is the best witness.

In his "Historic Notes of Life and Letters in New England," he sketches in a rapid way the series of intellectual movements which led to the development of the "new views" above mentioned. "There are always two parties," he says, "the party of the Past and the party of the Future; the Establishment and the Movement."

About 1820, and in the twenty years which followed, an era of activity manifested itself in the churches, in politics, in philanthropy, in literature. In our own community the influence of Swedenborg and of the genius and character of Dr. Channing were among the more immedi-

ate early causes of the mental agitation. Emer
son attributes a great importance to the schol·
arship, the rhetoric, the eloquence, of Edward
Everett, who returned to Boston in 1820, after
five years of study in Europe.   Edward Everett
is already to a great extent a tradition, somewhat as Rufus Choate is, a voice, a fading echo,
as must be the memory of every great orator.
These wondrous personalities have their truest
and warmest life in a few old men's memories.
It is therefore with delight that one who remembers Everett in his robes of rhetorical splendor,
who recalls his full-blown, high-colored, double-
flowered periods, the rich, resonant, grave, far-
reaching music of his speech, with just enough
of nasal vibration to give the vocal sounding-
board its proper value in the harmonies of utterance, — it is with delight that such a one
reads the glowing words of Emerson whenever
he refers to Edward Everett.   It is enough if
he himself caught inspiration from those eloquent lips; but many a listener has had his
youthful enthusiasm fired by that great master
of academic oratory.

   Emerson follows out the train of influences
which added themselves to the impulse given by
Mr. Everett.   German scholarship, the growth
of science, the generalizations of Goethe, the
idealism of Schelling, the influence of Words-

worth, of Coleridge, of Carlyle, and in our immediate community, the writings of Channing, — he left it to others to say of Emerson, — all had their part in this intellectual, or if we may call it so, spiritual revival. He describes with that exquisite sense of the ridiculous which was a part of his mental ballast, the first attempt at organizing an association of cultivated, thoughtful people. They came together, the cultivated, thoughtful people, at Dr. John Collins Warren's, — Dr. Channing, the great Dr. Channing, among the rest, full of the great thoughts he wished to impart. The preliminaries went on smoothly enough with the usual small talk, —

"When a side-door opened, the whole company streamed in to an oyster supper, crowned by excellent wines [this must have been before Dr. Warren's temperance epoch], and so ended the first attempt to establish æsthetic society in Boston.

"Some time afterwards Dr. Channing opened his mind to Mr. and Mrs. Ripley, and with some care they invited a limited party of ladies and gentlemen. I had the honor to be present. — Margaret Fuller, George Ripley, Dr. Convers Francis, Theodore Parker, Dr. Hedge, Mr. Brownson, James Freeman Clarke, William H. Channing, and many others gradually drew together, and from time to time spent an afternoon at each other's houses in a serious conversation."

With them was another, " a pure Idealist, — who read Plato as an equal, and inspired his companions only in proportion as they were intellectual." He refers, of course to Mr. Alcott. Emerson goes on to say : —

" I think there prevailed at that time a general belief in Boston that there was some concert of *doctrinaires* to establish certain opinions, and inaugurate some movement in literature, philosophy, and religion, of which design the supposed conspirators were quite innocent; for there was no concert, and only here and there two or three men and women who read and wrote, each alone, with unusual vivacity. Perhaps they only agreed in having fallen upon Coleridge and Wordsworth and Goethe, then on Carlyle, with pleasure and sympathy. Otherwise their education and reading were not marked, but had the American superficialness, and their studies were solitary. I suppose all of them were surprised at this rumor of a school or sect, and certainly at the name of Transcendentalism, given, nobody knows by whom, or when it was applied."

Emerson's picture of some of these friends of his is so peculiar as to suggest certain obvious and not too flattering comments.

"In like manner, if there is anything grand and daring in human thought or virtue; any reliance on the vast, the unknown ; any presentiment, any extravagance of faith, the Spiritualist adopts it as most in nature. The Oriental mind has always tended to this largeness. Buddhism is an expression of it. The Buddhist, who thanks no man, who says, ' Do not flatter your benefactors,' but who in his conviction that every good deed can by no possibility escape its reward, will not deceive the benefactor by pretending that he has done more than he should, is a Transcendentalist.

" These exacting children advertise us of our wants. There is no compliment, no smooth speech with them ; they pay you only this one compliment, of insatiable expectation ; they aspire, they severely exact, and if they only stand fast in this watch-tower, and persist in demanding unto the end, and without end, then are they terrible friends, whereof poet and priest cannot choose but stand in awe ; and what if they eat clouds, and drink wind, they have not been without service to the race of man."

The person who adopts " any presentiment, any extravagance as most in nature," is not commonly called a Transcendentalist, but is known colloquially as a " crank." The person who does not thank, by word or look, the friend or stranger who has pulled him out of the fire or water, is fortunate if he gets off with no harder name than that of a churl.

Nothing was farther from Emerson himself than whimsical eccentricity or churlish austerity. But there was occasionally an air of bravado in some of his followers as if they had taken out a patent for some knowing machine which was to give them a monopoly of its products. They claimed more for each other than was reasonable, — so much occasionally that their pretensions became ridiculous. One was tempted to ask : " What forlorn hope have you led ? What immortal book have you written ? What great discovery have you made ? What heroic task of any kind have you performed ? " There was too much talk about earnestness and too little real work done. Aspiration too frequently got as far as the alpenstock and the brandy flask, but crossed no dangerous crevasse, and scaled no arduous summit. In short, there was a kind of " Transcendentalist " dilettanteism, which betrayed itself by a phraseology as distinctive as that of the Della Cruscans of an earlier time.

In reading the following description of the " intelligent and religious persons " who belonged to the " Transcendentalist " communion, the reader must remember that it is Emerson who draws the portrait, — a friend and not a scoffer : —

"They are not good citizens, not good members of society : unwillingly they bear their part of the public and private burdens ; they do not willingly share in the public charities, in the public religious rites, in the enterprise of education, of missions, foreign and domestic, in the abolition of the slave-trade, or in the temperance society. They do not even like to vote."

After arraigning the representatives of Transcendental or spiritual beliefs in this way, he summons them to plead for themselves, and this is what they have to say : —

" ' New, we confess, and by no means happy, is our condition : if you want the aid of our labor, we ourselves stand in greater want of the labor. We are miserable with inaction. We perish of rest and rust : but we do not like your work.'

" ' Then,' says the world, ' show me your own.'

" ' We have none.'

" ' What will you do, then ? ' cries the world.

" ' We will wait.'

" ' How long ? '

" ' Until the Universe beckons and calls us to work.'

" ' But whilst you wait you grow old and useless.'

" ' Be it so : I can sit in a corner and *perish* (as you call it), but I will not move until I have the highest command.' "

And so the dissatisfied tenant of this unhappy creation goes on with his reasons for doing nothing.

It is easy to stay away from church and from town-meetings. It is easy to keep out of the way of the contribution box and to let the subscription paper go by us to the next door. The common duties of life and the good offices so-

ciety asks of us may be left to take care of
themselves while we contemplate the infinite.
There is no safer fortress for indolence than
"the Everlasting No." The chimney-corner is
the true arena for this class of philosophers, and
the pipe and mug furnish their all-sufficient pan-
oply. Emerson undoubtedly met with some of
them among his disciples. His wise counsel did
not always find listeners in a fitting condition to
receive it. He was a sower who went forth to
sow. Some of the good seed fell among the
thorns of criticism. Some fell on the rocks of
hardened conservatism. Some fell by the way-
side and was picked up by the idlers who went
to the lecture-room to get rid of themselves.
But when it fell upon the right soil it bore a
growth of thought which ripened into a harvest
of large and noble lives.

Emerson shows up the weakness of his young
enthusiasts with that delicate wit which warns
its objects rather than wounds them. But he
makes it all up with the dreamers before he can
let them go.

"Society also has its duties in reference to this
class, and must behold them with what charity it can.
Possibly some benefit may yet accrue from them to
the state. Besides our coarse implements, there must
be some few finer instruments, — rain-gauges, ther-
mometers, and telescopes; and in society, besides far-

mers, sailors, and weavers, there must be a few persons of purer fire kept specially as gauges and meters of character; persons of a fine, detecting instinct, who note the smallest accumulations of wit and feeling in the by-stander. Perhaps too there might be room for the exciters and monitors; collectors of the heavenly spark, with power to convey the electricity to others. Or, as the storm-tossed vessel at sea speaks the frigate or "line-packet" to learn its longitude, so it may not be without its advantage that we should now and then encounter rare and gifted men, to compare the points of our spiritual compass, and verify our bearings from superior chronometers."

It must be confessed that it is not a very captivating picture which Emerson draws of some of his transcendental friends. Their faults were naturally still more obvious to those outside of their charmed circle, and some prejudice, very possibly, mingled with their critical judgments. On the other hand we have the evidence of a visitor who knew a good deal of the world as to the impression they produced upon him: —

"There has sprung up in Boston," says Dickens, in his "American Notes," "a sect of philosophers known as Transcendentalists. On inquiring what this appellation might be supposed to signify, I was given to understand that whatever was unintelligible would be certainly Transcendental. Not deriving much comfort from this elucidation, I pursued the inquiry still further, and found that the Transcendentalists are followers of my friend Mr. Carlyle, or, I should rather say, of a follower of his, Mr. Ralph Waldo Emerson. This gentleman has written a volume of Essays, in which, among much that is dreamy and fanciful (if he will pardon me for saying so), there is much more that is true and manly, honest and bold. Transcendentalism has its occasional vagaries (what school has not?), but it has good healthful qualities in spite of them; not least among the number a hearty disgust of Cant, and an aptitude to detect her in all the million varieties of her everlasting wardrobe. And therefore, if I were a Bostonian, I think I would be a Transcendentalist."

In December, 1841, Emerson delivered a Lecture entitled "The Conservative." It was a time of great excitement among the members of that circle of which he was the spiritual leader. Never did Emerson show the perfect sanity which characterized his practical judgment more beautifully than in this Lecture and in his whole course with reference to the intellectual agitation of the period. He is as fair to the conservative as to the reformer. He sees the fanaticism of the one as well as that of the other. "Conservatism tends to universal seeming and treachery; believes in a negative fate; believes that men's tempers govern them; that for me it avails not to trust in principles, they will fail me, I must bend a little; it distrusts Nature; it thinks there is a general law without a particular application, — law for all that does not include any one. Reform in its antagonism inclines to asinine resistance, to kick with hoofs; it runs to egotism and bloated self-conceit; it runs to a bodiless pretension, to unnatural refining and elevation, which ends in hypocrisy and sensual reaction. And so, whilst we do not go beyond general statements, it may be safely affirmed of these two metaphysical antagonists that each is a good half, but an impossible whole."

He has his beliefs, and, if you will, his prejudices, but he loves fair play, and though he sides with the party of the future, he will not be unjust to the present or the past.

We read in a letter from Emerson to Carlyle, dated March 12, 1835, that Dr. Channing "lay awake all night, he told my friend last week, because he had learned in the evening that some young men proposed to issue a journal, to be called ' The Transcendentalist,' as the organ of a spiritual philosophy." Again on the 30th of April of the same year, in a letter in which he lays out a plan for a visit of Carlyle to this country, Emerson says : —

"It was suggested that if Mr. C. would undertake

a journal of which we have talked much, but which we have never yet produced, he would do us great service, and we feel some confidence that it could be made to secure him a support. It is that project which I mentioned to you in a letter by Mr. Barnard, — a book to be called 'The Transcendentalist;' or, 'The Spiritual Inquirer,' or the like. . . . Those who are most interested in it designed to make gratuitous contribution to its pages, until its success could be assured."

The idea of the grim Scotchman as editor of what we came in due time to know as "The Dial!" A concert of singing mice with a savage and hungry old grimalkin as leader of the orchestra! It was much safer to be content with Carlyle's purring from his own side of the water, as thus: —

"'The Boston Transcendentalist,' whatever the fate or merit of it may prove to be, is surely an interesting symptom. There must be things not dreamt of over in that *Transoceanic* parish! I shall certainly wish well to this thing; and hail it as the sure forerunner of things better."

There were two notable products of the intellectual ferment of the Transcendental period which deserve an incidental notice here, from the close connection which Emerson had with one of them and the interest which he took in the other, in which many of his friends were more deeply concerned. These were the periodical just spoken of as a possibility realized, and the industrial community known as Brook Farm. They were to a certain extent synchronous, — the Magazine beginning in July, 1840, and expiring in April, 1844; Brook Farm being organized in 1841, and breaking up in 1847.

"The Dial" was edited at first by Margaret Fuller, afterwards by Emerson, who contributed more than forty articles in prose and verse, among them "The Conservative," "The Transcendentalist," "Chardon Street and Bible Convention," and some of his best and best known poems, "The Problem," "Woodnotes," "The Sphinx," "Fate." The other principal writers were Margaret Fuller, A. Bronson Alcott, George Ripley, James Freeman Clarke, Theodore Parker, William H. Channing, Henry Thoreau, Eliot Cabot, John S. Dwight, C. P. Cranch, William Ellery Channing, Mrs. Ellen Hooper, and her sister Mrs. Caroline Tappan. Unequal as the contributions are in merit, the periodical is of singular interest. It was conceived and carried on in a spirit of boundless hope and enthusiasm. Time and a narrowing subscription list proved too hard a trial, and its four volumes remain stranded, like some rare

and curiously patterned shell which a storm of
yesterday has left beyond the reach of the reced-
ing waves. Thoreau wrote for nearly every number. Margaret Fuller, less attractive in print
than in conversation, did her part as a contributor as well as editor. Theodore Parker came
down with his "trip-hammer" in its pages.
Mrs. Ellen Hooper published a few poems in
its columns which remain, always beautiful, in
many memories. Others, whose literary lives
have fulfilled their earlier promise, and who are
still with us, helped forward the new enterprise
with their frequent contributions. It is a pleasure to turn back to "The Dial," with all its
crudities. It should be looked through by the
side of the "Anthology." Both were April
buds, opening before the frosts were over, but
with the pledge of a better season.

We get various hints touching the new Magazine in the correspondence between Emerson
and Carlyle. Emerson tells Carlyle, a few
months before the first number appeared, that
it will give him a better knowledge of our *young
people* than any he has had. It is true that un-
fledged writers found a place to try their wings
in it, and that makes it more interesting. This
was the time above all others when out of the
mouth of babes and sucklings was to come forth
strength. The feeling that intuition was discov-

ering a new heaven and a new earth was the inspiration of these "young people" to whom Emerson refers. He has to apologize for the first number. "It is not yet much," he says; "indeed, though no copy has come to me, I know it is far short of what it should be, for they have suffered puffs and dulness to creep in for the sake of the complement of pages, but it is better than anything we had. — The Address of the Editors to the Readers is all the prose that is mine, and whether they have printed a few verses for me I do not know." They did print "The Problem." There were also some fragments of criticism from the writings of his brother Charles, and the poem called "The Last Farewell," by his brother Edward, which is to be found in Emerson's "May-day and other Pieces."

On the 30th of August, after the periodical had been published a couple of months, Emerson writes: —

"Our community begin to stand in some terror of Transcendentalism; and the *Dial*, poor little thing, whose first number contains scarce anything considerable or even visible, is just now honored by attacks from almost every newspaper and magazine; which at least betrays the irritability and the instincts of the good public."

Carlyle finds the second number of "The

Dial " better than the first, and tosses his chari-
table recognition, as if into an alms-basket, with
his usual air of superiority. He distinguishes
what is Emerson's readily, — the rest he speaks
of as the work of οἱ πολλοί for the most part.
" But it is all good and very good as a *soul ;*
wants only a body, which want means a great
deal." And again, " ' The Dial,' too, it is all
spirit like, aeri-form, aurora-borealis like. Will
no *Angel* body himself out of that ; no stalwart
Yankee *man*, with color in the cheeks of him
and a coat on his back ? "

Emerson, writing to Carlyle in March, 1842,
speaks of the " dubious approbation on the part
of you and other men," notwithstanding which
he found it with " a certain class of men and
women, though few, an object of tenderness and
religion." So, when Margaret Fuller gave it
up, at the end of the second volume, Emerson
consented to become its editor. " I cannot bid
you quit ' The Dial,' " says Carlyle, " though
it, too, alas, is Antinomian somewhat ! *Perge,
perge*, nevertheless."

In the next letter he says : —

" I love your ' Dial,' and yet it is with a kind of
shudder. You seem to me in danger of dividing
yourselves from the Fact of this present Universe, in
which alone, ugly as it is, can I find any anchorage,
and soaring away after Ideas, Beliefs, Revelations

and such like, — into perilous altitudes, as I think;
beyond the curve of perpetual frost, for one thing.
I know not how to utter what impression you give
me ; take the above as some stamping of the fore-
hoof."

A curious way of characterizing himself as a
critic, — but he was not always as well-mannered
as the Houyhnhnms.

To all Carlyle's complaints of "The Dial's"
short-comings Emerson did not pretend to give
any satisfactory answer, but his plea of guilty,
with extenuating circumstances, is very honest
and definite.

"For the *Dial* and its sins, I have no defence to
set up. We write as we can, and we know very
little about it. If the direction of these speculations
is to be deplored, it is yet a fact for literary history
that all the bright boys and girls in New England,
quite ignorant of each other, take the world so, and
come and make confession to fathers and mothers, —
the boys, that they do not wish to go into trade, the
girls, that they do not like morning calls and evening
parties. They are all religious, but hate the churches ;
they reject all the ways of living of other men, but
have none to offer in their stead. Perhaps one of
these days a great Yankee shall come, who will easily
do the unknown deed."

"All the bright boys and girls in New England," and "'The Dial' dying of inanition!"

In October, 1840, Emerson writes to Carlyle : —

" We are all a little wild here with numberless projects of social reform. Not a reading man but has a draft of a new community in his waistcoat pocket. I am gently mad myself, and am resolved to live cleanly. George Ripley is talking up a colony of agriculturists and scholars, with whom he threatens to take the field and the book. One man renounces the use of animal food ; and another of coin ; and another of domestic hired service ; and another of the state ; and on the whole we have a commendable share of reason and hope."

Mr. Ripley's project took shape in the West Roxbury Association, better known under the name of Brook Farm. Emerson was not involved in this undertaking. He looked upon it with curiosity and interest, as he would have looked at a chemical experiment, but he seems to have had only a moderate degree of faith in its practical working. " It was a noble and generous movement in the projectors to try an experiment of better living. One would say that impulse was the rule in the society, without centripetal balance ; perhaps it would not be severe to say, intellectual sans-culottism, an impatience of the formal routinary character of our educational, religious, social, and economical life in Massachusetts."

The reader will find a full detailed account
of the Brook Farm experiment in Mr. Frothingham's "Life of George Ripley," its founder,
and the first President of the Association. Emerson had only tangential relations with the experiment, and tells its story in his "Historic
Notes" very kindly and respectfully, but with
that sense of the ridiculous in the aspect of some
of its conditions which belongs to the sagacious
common-sense side of his nature. The married
women, he says, were against the community.
"It was to them like the brassy and lacquered
life in hotels. The common school was well
enough, but to the common nursery they had
grave objections. Eggs might be hatched in
ovens, but the hen on her own account much
preferred the old way. A hen without her
chickens was but half a hen." Is not the in-
audible, inward laughter of Emerson more refreshing than the explosions of our noisiest
humorists?

This is his benevolent summing up : —

"The founders of Brook Farm should have this
praise, that they made what all people try to make,
an agreeable place to live in. All comers, even the
most fastidious, found it the pleasantest of residences.
It is certain, that freedom from household routine,
variety of character and talent, variety of work, variety of means of thought and instruction, art, music,

poetry, reading, masquerade, did not permit slug-
gishness or despondency; broke up routine. There
is agreement in the testimony that it was, to most of
the associates, education; to many, the most important period of their life, the birth of valued friendships, their first acquaintance with the riches of conversation, their training in behavior. The art of let-
ter-writing, it is said, was immensely cultivated. Letters were always flying, not only from house to house,
but from room to room. It was a perpetual picnic,
a French Revolution in small, an Age of Reason in a
patty-pan."

The public edifice called the " Phalanstery "
was destroyed by fire in 1846. The Association
never recovered from this blow, and soon afterwards it was dissolved.

§ 2. Emerson's first volume of his collected
Essays was published in 1841. In the reprint
it contains the following Essays: History;
Self-Reliance; Compensation; Spiritual Laws;
Love; Friendship; Prudence; Heroism; The
Over - Soul; Circles; Intellect; Art. " The
Young American," which is now included in the
volume, was not delivered until 1844.

Once accustomed to Emerson's larger formulæ we can to a certain extent project from
our own minds his treatment of special subjects. But we cannot anticipate the daring im-

agination, the subtle wit, the curious illustrations, the felicitous language, which make the Lecture or the Essay captivating as read, and almost entrancing as listened to by the teachable disciple. The reader must be prepared for occasional extravagances. Take the Essay on History, in the first series of Essays, for instance. "Let it suffice that in the light of these two facts, namely, that the mind is One, and that nature is its correlative, history is to be read and written." When we come to the application, in the same Essay, almost on the same page, what can we make of such discourse as this ? The sentences I quote do not follow immediately, one upon the other, but their sense is continuous.

"I hold an actual knowledge very cheap. Hear the rats in the wall, see the lizard on the fence, the fungus under foot, the lichen on the log. What do I know sympathetically, morally, of either of these worlds of life ? — How many times we must say Rome and Paris, and Constantinople ! What does Rome know of rat and lizard ? What are Olympiads and Consulates to these neighboring systems of being ? Nay, what food or experience or succor have they for the Esquimau seal-hunter, for the Kamchatcan in his canoe, for the fisherman, the stevedore, the porter ? "

The connection of ideas is not obvious. One can hardly help being reminded of a certain great man's Rochester speech as commonly reported by the story-teller. "Rome in her proudest days never had a waterfall a hundred and fifty feet high! Greece in her palmiest days never had a waterfall a hundred and fifty feet high! Men of Rochester, go on! No people ever lost their liberty who had a waterfall a hundred and fifty feet high!"

We cannot help smiling, perhaps laughing, at the odd mixture of Rome and rats, of Olympiads and Esquimaux. But the underlying idea of the interdependence of all that exists in nature is far from ridiculous. Emerson says, not absurdly or extravagantly, that "every history should be written in a wisdom which divined the range of our affinities and looked at facts as symbols."

We have become familiar with his doctrine of "Self-Reliance," which is the subject of the second lecture of the series. We know that he always and everywhere recognized that the divine voice which speaks authoritatively in the soul of man is the source of all our wisdom. It is a man's true self, so that it follows that absolute, supreme self-reliance is the law of his being. But see how he guards his proclamation of self-reliance as the guide of mankind.

" Truly it demands something god-like in him who has cast off the common motives of humanity and has ventured to trust himself for a task-master. High be his heart, faithful his will, clear his sight, that he may in good earnest be doctrine, society, law, to himself, that a simple purpose may be to him as strong as iron necessity is to others ! "

" Compensation " might be preached in a synagogue, and the Rabbi would be praised for his performance. Emerson had been listening to a sermon from a preacher esteemed for his orthodoxy, in which it was assumed that judgment is not executed in this world, that the wicked are successful, and the good are miserable. This last proposition agrees with John Bunyan's view : —

> " A Christian man is never long at ease,
> When one fright's gone, another doth him seize."

Emerson shows up the " success " of the bad man and the failures and trials of the good man in their true spiritual characters, with a noble scorn of the preacher's low standard of happiness and misery, which would have made him throw his sermon into the fire.

The Essay on " Spiritual Laws " is full of pithy sayings : —

" As much virtue as there is, so much appears ; as much goodness as there is, so much reverence it commands. All the devils respect virtue. — A man passes for that he is worth. — The ancestor of every action is a thought. — To think is to act. — Let a man believe in God, and not in names and places and persons. Let the great soul incarnated in some woman's form, poor and sad and single, in some Dolly or Joan, go out to service and sweep chambers and scour floors, and its effulgent day-beams cannot be hid, but to sweep and scour will instantly appear supreme and beautiful actions, the top and radiance of human life, and all people will get mops and brooms ; until, lo ! suddenly the great soul has enshrined itself in some other form and done some other deed, and that is now the flower and head of all living nature."

This is not any the worse for being the flowering out of a poetical bud of George Herbert's. The Essay on " Love " is poetical, but the three poems, " Initial," " Dæmonic," and " Celestial Love " are more nearly equal to his subject than his prose.

There is a passage in the Lecture on " Friendship " which suggests some personal relation of Emerson's about which we cannot help being inquisitive : —

" It has seemed to me lately more possible than I knew, to carry a friendship greatly, on one side, without due correspondence on the other. Why should I cumber myself with regrets that the receiver is not capacious ? It never troubles the sun that some of his rays fall wide and vain into ungrateful space, and only a small part on the reflecting planet. Let your greatness educate the crude and cold companion. . . . Yet these things may hardly be said without a sort of treachery to the relation. The essence of friendship is entireness, a total magnanimity and trust. It must not surmise or provide for infirmity. It treats its object as a god that it may deify both."

Was he thinking of his relations with Carlyle? It is a curious subject of speculation what would have been the issue if Carlyle had come to Concord and taken up his abode under Emerson's most hospitable roof. "You shall not come nearer a man by getting into his house." How could they have got on together? Emerson was well-bred, and Carlyle was wanting in the social graces. "Come rest in this bosom" is a sweet air, heard in the distance, too apt to be followed, after a protracted season of close proximity, by that other strain, —

"No, fly me, fly me, far as pole from pole !
Rise Alps between us and whole oceans roll ! "

But Emerson may have been thinking of some very different person, perhaps some "crude and cold companion" among his disciples, who was not equal to the demands of friendly intercourse.

He discourses wisely on "Prudence," a virtue

which he does not claim for himself, and nobly on "Heroism," which was a shining part of his own moral and intellectual being.

The points which will be most likely to draw the reader's attention are the remarks on the literature of heroism; the claim for our own America, for Massachusetts and Connecticut River and Boston Bay, in spite of our love for the names of foreign and classic topography; and most of all one sentence which, coming from an optimist like Emerson, has a sound of sad sincerity painful to recognize.

"Who that sees the meanness of our politics but inly congratulates Washington that he is long already wrapped in his shroud, and forever safe; that he was laid sweet in his grave, the hope of humanity not yet subjugated in him. Who does not sometimes envy the good and brave who are no more to suffer from the tumults of the natural world, and await with curious complacency the speedy term of his own conversation with finite nature? And yet the love that will be annihilated sooner than treacherous has already made death impossible, and affirms itself no mortal, but a native of the deeps of absolute and inextinguishable being."

In the following Essay, "The Over-Soul," Emerson has attempted the impossible. He is as fully conscious of this fact as the reader of his rhapsody, — nay, he is more profoundly penetrated with it than any of his readers. In speaking of the exalted condition the soul is capable of reaching, he says, —

"Every man's words, who speaks from that life, must sound vain to those who do not dwell in the same thought on their own part. I dare not speak for it. My words do not carry its august sense; they fall short and cold. Only itself can inspire whom it will, and behold! their speech shall be lyrical and sweet, and universal as the rising of the wind. Yet I desire, even by profane words, if I may not use sacred, to indicate the heaven of this deity, and to report what hints I have collected of the transcendent simplicity and energy of the Highest Law."

"The Over-Soul" might almost be called the Over-*flow* of a spiritual imagination. We cannot help thinking of the "pious, virtuous, God-intoxicated" Spinoza. When one talks of the infinite in terms borrowed from the finite, when one attempts to deal with the absolute in the language of the relative, his words are not symbols, like those applied to the objects of experience, but the shadows of symbols, varying with the position and intensity of the light of the individual intelligence. It is a curious amusement to trace many of these thoughts and expressions to Plato, or Plotinus, or Proclus, or Porphyry, to Spinoza or Schelling, but the same tune is a different thing according to the instru-

ment on which it is played. There are songs
without words, and there are states in which, in
place of the trains of thought moving in endless
procession with ever-varying figures along the
highway of consciousness, the soul is possessed
by a single all-absorbing idea, which, in the
highest state of spiritual exaltation, becomes a
vision. Both Plotinus and Porphyry believed
they were privileged to look upon Him whom
" no man can see and live."

But Emerson states his own position so frankly
in his Essay entitled " Circles," that the reader
cannot take issue with him as against utterances
which he will not defend. There can be no doubt
that he would have confessed as much with reference to "The Over-Soul" as he has confessed
with regard to " Circles," the Essay which follows " The Over-Soul."

" I am not careful to justify myself. . . . But lest
I should mislead any when I have my own head and
obey my whims, let me remind the reader that I am
only an experimenter. Do not set the least value on
what I do, or the least discredit on what I do not, as
if I pretended to settle anything as true or false. I
unsettle all things. No facts are to me sacred ; none
are profane ; I simply experiment, an endless seeker,
with no Past at my back."

Perhaps, after reading these transcendental
essays of Emerson, we might borrow Goethe's

language about Spinoza, as expressing the feeling with which we are left.

"I am reading Spinoza with Frau von Stein. I feel myself very near to him, though his soul is much deeper and purer than mine.

"I cannot say that I ever read Spinoza straight through, that at any time the complete architecture of his intellectual system has stood clear in view before me. But when I look into him I seem to understand him, — that is, he always appears to me consistent with himself, and I can always gather from him very salutary influences for my own way of feeling and acting."

Emerson would not have pretended that he was always "consistent with himself," but these "salutary influences," restoring, enkindling, vivifying, are felt by many of his readers who would have to confess, like Dr. Walter Channing, that these thoughts, or thoughts like these, as he listened to them in a lecture, "made his head ache."

The three essays which follow "The Over-Soul," "Circles," "Intellect," "Art," would furnish us a harvest of good sayings, some of which we should recognize as parts of our own (borrowed) axiomatic wisdom.

"Beware when the great God lets loose a thinker on this planet. Then all things are at risk."

"God enters by a private door into every individual."

"God offers to every mind its choice between truth and repose. Take which you please, — you can never have both."

"Though we travel the world over to find the beautiful, we must carry it with us, or we find it not."

But we cannot reconstruct the Hanging Gardens with a few bricks from Babylon.

Emerson describes his mode of life in these years in a letter to Carlyle, dated May 10, 1838.

"I occupy, or improve, as we Yankees say, two acres only of God's earth; on which is my house, my kitchen-garden, my orchard of thirty young trees, my empty barn. My house is now a very good one for comfort, and abounding in room. Besides my house, I have, I believe, $22,000, whose income in ordinary years is six per cent. I have no other tithe or glebe except the income of my winter lectures, which was last winter $800. Well, with this income, here at home, I am a rich man. I stay at home and go abroad at my own instance. I have food, warmth, leisure, books, friends. Go away from home, I am rich no longer. I never have a dollar to spend on a fancy. As no wise man, I suppose, ever was rich in the sense of freedom to spend, because of the inundation of claims, so neither am I, who am not wise. But at home, I am rich, — rich enough for ten brothers. My wife Lidian is an incarnation of Christianity, — I call her Asia, — and keeps my philosophy from Antinomianism; my mother, whitest, mildest, most conservative of ladies, whose only exception to her universal preference for old things is her son; my boy, a piece of love and sunshine, well worth my watching from morning to night; — these, and three domestic women, who cook, and sew and run for us, make all my household. Here I sit and read and write, with very little system, and, as far as regards composition, with the most fragmentary result: paragraphs incompressible, each sentence an infinitely repellent particle."

A great sorrow visited Emerson and his household at this period of his life. On the 30th of October, 1841, he wrote to Carlyle: " My little boy is five years old to-day, and almost old enough to send you his love."

Three months later, on the 28th of February, 1842, he writes once more : —

" My dear friend, you should have had this letter and these messages by the last steamer ; but when it sailed, my son, a perfect little boy of five years and three months, had ended his earthly life. You can never sympathize with me ; you can never know how much of me such a young child can take away. A few weeks ago I accounted myself a very rich man, and now the poorest of all. What would it avail to tell you anecdotes of a sweet and wonderful boy, such as we solace and sadden ourselves with at home every morning and evening ? From a perfect health and as happy a life and as happy influences as ever child

12

enjoyed, he was hurried out of my arms in three short days by scarlatina. We have two babes yet, one girl of three years, and one girl of three months and a week, but a promise like that Boy's I shall never see. How often I have pleased myself that one day I should send to you this Morning Star of mine, and stay at home so gladly behind such a representative. I dare not fathom the Invisible and Untold to inquire what relations to my Departed ones I yet sustain."

This was the boy whose memory lives in the tenderest and most pathetic of Emerson's poems, the " Threnody," — a lament not unworthy of comparison with Lycidas for dignity, but full of the simple pathos of Cowper's well-remembered lines on the receipt of his mother's picture, in the place of Milton's sonorous academic phrases.

CHAPTER VI.

1843–1848. ÆT. 40–45.

EMERSON was American in aspect, temperament, way of thinking, and feeling; American, with an atmosphere of Oriental idealism ; American, so far as he belonged to any limited part of the universe. He believed in American institutions, he trusted the future of the American race. In the address first mentioned in the contents of this chapter, delivered February 7, 1844, he claims for this country all that the most ardent patriot could ask. Not a few of his fellow-countrymen will feel the significance of the following contrast.

"The English have many virtues, many advan-

---

[1] These two addresses are to be found in the first and eleventh volumes, respectively, of the last collective edition of Emerson's works, namely, "Nature, Addresses, and Lectures," and "Miscellanies."

tages, and the proudest history in the world; but they need all and more than all the resources of the past to indemnify a heroic gentleman in that country for the mortifications prepared for him by the system of society, and which seem to impose the alternative to resist or to avoid it. . . . It is for Englishmen to consider, not for us; we only say, Let us live in America, too thankful for our want of feudal institutions. . . . If only the men are employed in conspiring with the designs of the Spirit who led us hither, and is leading us still, we shall quickly enough advance out of all hearing of others' censures, out of all regrets of our own, into a new and more excellent social state than history has recorded."

Thirty years have passed since the lecture from which these passages are taken was delivered. The "Young American" of that day is the more than middle-aged American of the present. The intellectual independence of our country is far more solidly established than when this lecture was written. But the social alliance between certain classes of Americans and English is more and more closely cemented from year to year, as the wealth of the new world burrows its way among the privileged classes of the old world. It is a poor ambition for the possessor of suddenly acquired wealth to have it appropriated as a feeder of the impaired fortunes of a deteriorated household, with a family record of which its representatives are unworthy.

The plain and wholesome language of Emerson is on the whole more needed now than it was when spoken. His words have often been extolled for their stimulating quality; following the same analogy, they are, as in this address, in a high degree tonic, bracing, strengthening to the American, who requires to be reminded of his privileges that he may know and find himself equal to his duties.

On the first day of August, 1844, Emerson delivered in Concord an address on the Anniversary of the Emancipation of the Negroes in the British West India Islands. This discourse would not have satisfied the Abolitionists. It was too general in its propositions, full of humane and generous sentiments, but not looking to their extreme and immediate method of action.

Emerson's second series of Essays was published in 1844. There are many sayings in the Essay called "The Poet," which are meant for the initiated, rather than for him who runs, to read : —

" All that we call sacred history attests that the birth of a poet is the principal event in chronology."

Does this sound wild and extravagant? What were the political ups and downs of the Hebrews,

— what were the squabbles of the tribes with each other, or with their neighbors, compared to the birth of that poet to whom we owe the Psalms, — the sweet singer whose voice is still the dearest of all that ever sang to the heart of mankind?

The poet finds his materials everywhere, as Emerson tells him in this eloquent apostrophe: —

"Thou true land-bird! sea-bird! air-bird! Wherever snow falls, or water flows, or birds fly, wherever day and night meet in twilight, wherever the blue heaven is hung by clouds, or sown with stars, wherever are forms with transparent boundaries, wherever are outlets into celestial space, wherever is danger and awe and love, there is Beauty, plenteous as rain, shed for thee, and though thou should'st walk the world over, thou shalt not be able to find a condition inopportune or ignoble."

"Experience" is, as he says himself, but a fragment. It bears marks of having been written in a less tranquil state of mind than the other essays. His most important confession is this: —

"All writing comes by the grace of God, and all doing and having. I would gladly be moral and keep due metes and bounds, which I dearly love, and allow the most to the will of man; but I have set my heart on honesty in this chapter, and I can see nothing at last, in success or failure, than more or less of vital force supplied from the Eternal."

The Essay on "Character" requires no difficult study, but is well worth the trouble of reading. A few sentences from it show the prevailing tone and doctrine.

"Character is Nature in the highest form. It is of no use to ape it, or to contend with it. Somewhat is possible of resistance and of persistence and of creation to this power, which will foil all emulation."

" There is a class of men, individuals of which appear at long intervals, so eminently endowed with insight and virtue, that they have been unanimously saluted as *divine*, and who seem to be an accumulation of that power we consider.

" The history of those gods and saints which the world has written, and then worshipped, are documents of character. The ages have exulted in the manners of a youth who owed nothing to fortune, and who was hanged at the Tyburn of his nation, who, by the pure quality of his nature, shed an epic splendor around the facts of his death which has transfigured every particular into an universal symbol for the eyes of mankind. This great defeat is hitherto our highest fact."

In his Essay on "Manners," Emerson gives us his ideas of a gentleman : —

" The gentleman is a man of truth, lord of his own actions and expressing that lordship in his behavior, not in any manner dependent and servile either on persons or opinions or possessions. Beyond this fact

of truth and real force, the word denotes good-nature
or benevolence : manhood first, and then gentleness.
— Power first, or no leading class. — God knows that
all sorts of gentlemen knock at the door : but whenever used in strictness, and with any emphasis, the
name will be found to point at original energy. —
The famous gentlemen of Europe have been of this
strong type : Saladin, Sapor, the Cid, Julius Cæsar,
Scipio, Alexander, Pericles, and the lordliest personages. They sat very carelessly in their chairs, and
were too excellent themselves to value any condition
at a high rate. — I could better eat with one who
did not respect the truth or the laws than with a
sloven and unpresentable person. — The person who
screams, or uses the superlative degree, or converses
with heat, puts whole drawing-rooms to flight. — I
esteem it a chief felicity of this country that it excels
in woman."

So writes Emerson, and proceeds to speak of
woman in language which seems almost to pant
for rhythm and rhyme.

This essay is plain enough for the least " transcendental " reader. Franklin would have approved it, and was himself a happy illustration
of many of the qualities which go to the Emersonian ideal of good manners, a typical American, equal to his position, always as much so in
the palaces and salons of Paris as in the Conti-
nental Congress, or the society of Philadelphia.

"Gifts " is a dainty little Essay with some nice

distinctions and some hints which may help to give form to a generous impulse : —

" The only gift is a portion of thyself. Thou must bleed for me. Therefore the poet brings his poem ; the shepherd, his lamb ; the farmer, corn ; the miner, a gem ; the sailor, coral and shells ; the painter, his picture ; the girl, a handkerchief of her own sewing."

" Flowers and fruits are always fit presents; flowers, because they are a proud assertion that a ray of beauty outvalues all the utilities of the world. — Fruits are acceptable gifts, because they are the flower of commodities, and admit of fantastic values being attached to them."

" It is a great happiness to get off without injury and heart-burning from one who has had the ill-luck to be served by you. It is a very onerous business, this of being served, and the debtor naturally wishes to give you a slap."

Emerson hates the superlative, but he does unquestionably love the tingling effect of a witty over-statement.

We have recognized most of the thoughts in the Essay entitled " Nature," in the previous Essay by the same name, and others which we have passed in review. But there are poetical passages which will give new pleasure.

Here is a variation of the formula with which we are familiar : —

" Nature is the incarnation of a thought, and turns to a thought again, as ice becomes water and gas. The world is mind precipitated, and the volatile essence is forever escaping again into the state of free thought."

And here is a quaint sentence with which we may take leave of this Essay : —

" They say that by electro-magnetism, your salad shall be grown from the seed, whilst your fowl is roasting for dinner : it is a symbol of our modern aims and endeavors, — of our condensation and acceleration of objects ; but nothing is gained : nature cannot be cheated : man's life is but seventy salads long, grow they swift or grow they slow."

This is pretty and pleasant, but as to the literal value of the prediction, M. Jules Verne would be the best authority to consult. Poets are fond of that branch of science which, if the imaginative Frenchman gave it a name, he would probably call *Onditologie.*

It is not to be supposed that the most sanguine optimist could be satisfied with the condition of the American political world at the present time, or when the Essay on " Politics " was written, some years before the great war which changed the aspects of the country in so many respects, still leaving the same party names, and many of the characters of the old parties unchanged. This is Emerson's view of them as they then were : —

" Of the two great parties, which, at this hour, almost share the nation between them, I should say that one has the best cause, and the other contains the best men. The philosopher, the poet, or the religious man, will, of course, wish to cast his vote with the democrat, for free trade, for wide suffrage, for the abolition of legal cruelties in the penal code, and for facilitating in every manner the access of the young and the poor to the sources of wealth and power. But he can rarely accept the persons whom the so-called popular party propose to him as representatives of these liberties. They have not at heart the ends which give to the name of democracy what hope and virtue are in it. The spirit of our American radicalism is destructive and aimless; it is not loving; it has no ulterior and divine ends; but is destructive only out of hatred and selfishness. On the other side, the conservative party, composed of the most moderate, able, and cultivated part of the population, is timid, and merely defensive of property. It indicates no right, it aspires to no real good, it brands no crime, it proposes no generous policy, it does not build nor write, nor cherish the arts, nor foster religion, nor establish schools, nor encourage science, nor emancipate the slave, nor befriend the poor, or the Indian, or the immigrant. From neither party, when in power, has the world any benefit to expect in science, art, or humanity, at all commensurate with the resources of the nation."

The metaphysician who looks for a closely

reasoned argument on the famous old question which so divided the schoolmen of old will find a very moderate satisfaction in the Essay entitled "Nominalism and Realism." But there are many discursive remarks in it worth gathering and considering. We have the complaint of the Cambridge "Phi Beta Kappa Oration," reiterated, that there is no complete man, but only a collection of fragmentary men.

As a Platonist and a poet there could not be any doubt on which side were all his prejudices; but he takes his ground cautiously.

"In the famous dispute with the Nominalists, the Realists had a good deal of reason. General ideas are essences. They are our gods: they round and ennoble the most practical and sordid way of living.

"Though the uninspired man certainly finds persons a conveniency in household matters, the divine man does not respect them: he sees them as a rack of clouds, or a fleet of ripples which the wind drives over the surface of the water. But this is flat rebellion. Nature will not be Buddhist: she resents generalizing, and insults the philosopher in every moment with a million of fresh particulars."

New England Reformers. — Would any one venture to guess how Emerson would treat this subject? With his unsparing, though amiable radicalism, his excellent common sense, his delicate appreciation of the ridiculous, too deep for laughter, as Wordsworth's thoughts were too deep for tears, in the midst of a band of enthusiasts and not very remote from a throng of fanatics, what are we to look for from our philosopher who unites many characteristics of Berkeley and of Franklin?

We must remember when this lecture was written, for it was delivered on a Sunday in the year 1844. The Brook Farm experiment was an index of the state of mind among one section of the Reformers of whom he was writing. To remodel society and the world into a "happy family" was the aim of these enthusiasts. Some attacked one part of the old system, some another; some would build a new temple, some would rebuild the old church, some would worship in the fields and woods, if at all; one was for a phalanstery, where all should live in common, and another was meditating the plan and place of the wigwam where he was to dwell apart in the proud independence of the woodchuck and the musquash. Emerson had the largest and kindliest sympathy with their ideals and aims, but he was too clear-eyed not to see through the whims and extravagances of the unpractical experimenters who would construct a working world with the lay figures they had put together, instead of flesh and blood men and women and children with all their congenital and acquired perversities.   He describes these Reformers **in** his own good-naturedly half-satirical way : —

" They defied each other like a congress of kings, each of whom had a realm to rule, and a way of his own that made concert unprofitable. What a fertility of projects for the salvation of the world !   One apostle thought all men should go to farming ; and another that no man should buy or sell ; that the use of money was the cardinal evil ; another that the mischief was in our diet, that we eat and drink damnation.   These made unleavened bread, and were foes to the death to fermentation.   It was in vain urged by the housewife that God made yeast as well as dough, and loves fermentation just as dearly as he does vegetation ; that fermentation develops the saccharine element in the grain, and makes it more palatable and more digestible.   No, they wish the pure wheat, and will die but it shall not ferment.   Stop, dear nature, these innocent advances of thine ; let us scotch these ever-rolling wheels !   Others attacked the system of agriculture, the use of animal manures in farming ; and the tyranny of man over brute nature ; these abuses polluted his food.   The ox must be taken from the plough, and the horse from the cart, the hundred acres of the farm must be spaded, and the man must walk wherever boats and locomotives will not carry him.   Even the insect world was to be defended, — that had been too long neglected, and a society for the protection of ground-worms, slugs, and mosquitoes was to be incorporated without delay. With these appeared the adepts of homœopathy, of hydropathy, of mesmerism, of phrenology, and their wonderful theories of the Christian miracles ! "

We have already seen the issue of the famous Brook Farm experiment, which was a practical outcome of the reforming agitation.

Emerson has had the name of being a leader in many movements in which he had very limited confidence, this among others to which the idealizing impulse derived from him lent its force, but for the organization of which he was in no sense responsible.

He says in the lecture we are considering : —

" These new associations are composed of men and women of superior talents and sentiments; yet it may easily be questioned whether such a community will draw, except in its beginnings, the able and the good; whether these who have energy will not prefer their choice of superiority and power in the world to the humble certainties of the association ; whether such a retreat does not promise to become an asylum to those who have tried and failed rather than a field to the strong ; and whether the members will not necessarily be fractions of men, because each finds that he cannot enter into it without some compromise."

His sympathies were not allowed to mislead him ; he knew human nature too well to believe in a Noah's ark full of idealists.

All this time he was lecturing for his support, giving courses of lectures in Boston and other cities, and before the country lyceums in and out of New England.

His letters to Carlyle show how painstaking, how methodical, how punctual he was in the business which interested his distant friend. He was not fond of figures, and it must have cost him a great effort to play the part of an accountant.

He speaks also of receiving a good deal of company in the summer, and that some of this company exacted much time and attention, — more than he could spare, — is made evident by his gentle complaints, especially in his poems, which sometimes let out a truth he would hardly have uttered in prose.

In 1846 Emerson's first volume of poems was published. Many of the poems had been long before the public — some of the best, as we have seen, having been printed in " The Dial." It is only their being brought together for the first time which belongs especially to this period, and we can leave them for the present, to be looked over by and by in connection with a second volume of poems published in 1867, under the title, " May-Day and other Pieces."

In October, 1847, he left Concord on a second visit to England, which will be spoken of in the following chapter.

CHAPTER VII.

1848–1853. ÆT. 45–50.

A NEW periodical publication was begun in Boston in 1847, under the name of the "Massachusetts Quarterly Review." Emerson wrote the "Editor's Address," but took no further active part in it, Theodore Parker being the real editor. The last line of this address is characteristic: "We rely on the truth for aid against ourselves."

On the 5th of October, 1847, Emerson sailed for Europe on his second visit, reaching Liverpool on the 22d of that month. Many of his admirers were desirous that he should visit England and deliver some courses of lectures. Mr. Alexander Ireland, who had paid him friendly attentions during his earlier visit, and whose im-

pressions of him in the pulpit have been given
on a previous page, urged his coming.   Mr.
Conway quotes passages from a letter of Emerson's which show that he had some hesitation
in accepting the invitation, not unmingled with
a wish to be heard by the English audiences
favorably disposed towards him.

" I feel no call," he said, " to make a visit of
literary propagandism in England.   All my impulses to work of that kind would rather employ
me at home."   He does not like the idea of
"coaxing" or advertising to get him an audience.
He would like to read lectures before institutions
or friendly persons who sympathize with his
studies.   He has had a good many decisive tokens
of interest from British men and women, but he
doubts whether he is much and favorably known
in any one city, except perhaps in London.   It
proved, however, that there was a very wide-
spread desire to hear him, and applications for
lectures flowed in from all parts of the kingdom.

From Liverpool he proceeded immediately to
Manchester, where Mr. Ireland received him at
the Victoria station.   After spending a few hours
with him, he went to Chelsea to visit Carlyle,
and at the end of a week returned to Manchester to begin the series of lecturing engagements
which had been arranged for him.   Mr. Ireland's

account of Emerson's visits and the interviews between him and many distinguished persons is full of interest, but the interest largely relates to the persons visited by Emerson. He lectured at Edinburgh, where his liberal way of thinking and talking made a great sensation in orthodox circles. But he did not fail to find enthusiastic listeners. A young student, Mr. George Cupples, wrote an article on these lectures from which, as quoted by Mr. Ireland, I borrow a single sentence, — one only, but what could a critic say more?

Speaking of his personal character, as revealed through his writings, he says: "In this respect, I take leave to think that Emerson is the most mark-worthy, the loftiest, and most heroic mere man that ever appeared." Emerson has a lecture on the superlative, to which he himself was never addicted. But what would youth be without its extravagances, — its preterpluperfect in the shape of adjectives, its unmeasured and unstinted admiration?

I need not enumerate the celebrated literary personages and other notabilities whom Emerson met in England and Scotland. He thought "the two finest mannered literary men he met in England were Leigh Hunt and De Quincey." His diary might tell us more of the impressions made upon him by the distinguished people he

met, but it is impossible to believe that he ever
passed such inhuman judgments on the least
desirable of his new acquaintances as his friend
Carlyle has left as a bitter legacy behind him.
Carlyle's merciless discourse about Coleridge
and Charles Lamb, and Swinburne's carnivorous
lines, which take a barbarous vengeance on him
for his offence, are on the level of political rhetoric rather than of scholarly criticism or characterization.   Emerson never forgot that he was
dealing with human beings.   He could not have
long endured the asperities of Carlyle, and that
" loud shout of laughter," which Mr. Ireland
speaks of as one of his customary explosions,
would have been discordant to Emerson's ears,
which were offended by such noisy manifestations.

During this visit Emerson made an excursion
to Paris, which furnished him materials for a
lecture on France delivered in Boston, in 1856,
but never printed.

From the lectures delivered in England he selected a certain number for publication.   These
make up the volume entitled " Representative
Men," which was published in 1850.   I will
give very briefly an account of its contents. The
title was a happy one, and has passed into literature and conversation as an accepted and convenient phrase.   It would teach us a good deal

merely to consider the names he has selected as typical, and the ground of their selection. We get his classification of men considered as leaders in thought and in action. He shows his own affinities and repulsions, and, as everywhere, writes his own biography, no matter about whom or what he is talking. There is hardly any book of his better worth study by those who wish to understand, not Plato, not Plutarch, not Napoleon, but Emerson himself. All his great men interest us for their own sake; but we know a good deal about most of them, and Emerson holds the mirror up to them at just such an angle that we see his own face as well as that of his hero, unintentionally, unconsciously, no doubt, but by a necessity which he would be the first to recognize.

Emerson swears by no master. He admires, but always with a reservation. Plato comes nearest to being his idol, Shakespeare next. But he says of all great men: "The power which they communicate is not theirs. When we are exalted by ideas, we do not owe this to Plato, but to the idea, to which also Plato was debtor."

Emerson loves power as much as Carlyle does; he likes "rough and smooth," "scourges of God," and "darlings of the human race." He likes Julius Cæsar, Charles the Fifth, of Spain, Charles the Twelfth, of Sweden, Richard Plantagenet, and Bonaparte.

"I applaud," he says, "a sufficient man, an officer equal to his office; captains, ministers, senators. I like a master standing firm on legs of iron, well born, rich, handsome, eloquent, loaded with advantages, drawing all men by fascination into tributaries and supporters of his power. Sword and staff, or talents sword-like or staff-like, carry on the work of the world. But I find him greater when he can abolish himself and all heroes by letting in this element of reason, irrespective of persons, this subtilizer and irresistible upward force, into our thoughts, destroying individualism; the power is so great that the potentate is nothing. —

"The genius of humanity is the right point of view of history. The qualities abide; the men who exhibit them have now more, now less, and pass away; the qualities remain on another brow. — All that respects the individual is temporary and prospective, like the individual himself, who is ascending out of his limits into a catholic existence."

No man can be an idol for one who looks in this way at all men. But Plato takes the first place in Emerson's gallery of six great personages whose portraits he has sketched. And of him he says: —

"Among secular books Plato only is entitled to Omar's fanatical compliment to the Koran, when he said, 'Burn the libraries; for their value is in this book.' Out of Plato come all things that are still written and debated among men of thought." —

"In proportion to the culture of men they become his scholars." — "How many great men Nature is incessantly sending up out of night to be *his men!* — His contemporaries tax him with plagiarism. — But the inventor only knows how to borrow. When we are praising Plato, it seems we are praising quotations from Solon and Sophron and Philolaus. Be it so. Every book is a quotation; and every house is a quotation out of all forests and mines and stone quarries; and every man is a quotation from all his ancestors."

The reader will, I hope, remember this last general statement when he learns from what wide fields of authorship Emerson filled his storehouses.

A few sentences from Emerson will show us the probable source of some of the deepest thought of Plato and his disciples.

The conception of the fundamental Unity, he says, finds its highest expression in the religious writings of the East, especially in the Indian Scriptures. "'The whole world is but a manifestation of Vishnu, who is identical with all things, and is to be regarded by the wise as not differing from but as the same as themselves. I neither am going nor coming; nor is my dwelling in any one place; nor art thou, thou; nor are others, others; nor am I, I.' As if he had said, 'All is for the soul, and the soul is Vishnu; and animals and stars are transient paintings; and light is whitewash ; and durations are deceptive ; and form is imprisonment ; and heaven itself a decoy.' " All of which we see reproduced in Emerson's poem "Brahma." — "The country of unity, of immovable institutions, the seat of a philosophy delighting in abstractions, of men faithful in doctrine and in practice to the idea of a deaf, unimplorable, immense fate, is Asia ; and it realizes this faith in the social institution of caste. On the other side, the genius of Europe is active and creative : it resists caste by culture ; its philosophy was a discipline ; it is a land of arts, inventions, trade, freedom." — " Plato came to join, and by contact to enhance, the energy of each."

But Emerson says, — and some will smile at hearing him say it of another, — " The acutest German, the lovingest disciple, could never tell what Platonism was ; indeed, admirable texts can be quoted on both sides of every great question from him."

The transcendent intellectual and moral supe-riorities of this " Euclid of holiness," as Emerson calls him, with his " soliform eye and his boni-form soul," — the two quaint adjectives being from the mint of Cudworth, — are fully dilated upon in the addition to the original article called " Plato : New Readings."

Few readers will be satisfied with the Essay entitled "Swedenborg; or, the Mystic." The believers in his special communion as a revealer of divine truth will find him reduced to the level of other seers. The believers of the different creeds of Christianity will take offence at the statement that "Swedenborg and Behmen both failed by attaching themselves to the Christian symbol, instead of to the moral sentiment, which carries innumerable christianities, humanities, divinities in its bosom." The men of science will smile at the exorbitant claims put forward in behalf of Swedenborg as a scientific discoverer. "Philosophers" will not be pleased to be reminded that Swedenborg called them "cockatrices," "asps," or "flying serpents;" "literary men" will not agree that they are "conjurers and charlatans," and will not listen with patience to the praises of a man who so called them. As for the poets, they can take their choice of Emerson's poetical or prose estimate of the great Mystic, but they cannot very well accept both. In "The Test," the Muse says: —

"I hung my verses in the wind,
    Time and tide their faults may find;
    All were winnowed through and through,
    Five lines lasted good and true . . .
    Sunshine cannot bleach the snow,
    Nor time unmake what poets know.

> Have you eyes to find the five
> Which five hundred did survive ? "

In the verses which follow we learn that the five immortal poets referred to are Homer, Dante, Shakespeare, *Swedenborg*, and Goethe.

And now, in the Essay we have just been looking at, I find that " his books have no melody, no emotion, no humor, no relief to the dead prosaic level. We wander forlorn in a lack-lustre landscape. No bird ever sang in these gardens of the dead. The entire want of poetry in so transcendent a mind betokens the disease, and like a hoarse voice in a beautiful person, is a kind of warning." Yet Emerson says of him that " He lived to purpose: he gave a verdict. He elected goodness as the clue to which the soul must cling in this labyrinth of nature."

Emerson seems to have admired Swedenborg at a distance, but seen nearer, he liked Jacob Behmen a great deal better.

" Montaigne ; or, the Skeptic," is easier reading than the last-mentioned Essay. Emerson accounts for the personal regard which he has for Montaigne by the story of his first acquaintance with him. But no other reason was needed than that Montaigne was just what Emerson describes him as being.

" There have been men with deeper insight ; but,

one would say, never a man with such abundance of thought : he is never dull, never insincere, and has the genius to make the reader care for all that he cares for.

"The sincerity and marrow of the man reaches to his sentences. I know not anywhere the book that seems less written. It is the language of conversation transferred to a book. Cut these words and they would bleed ; they are vascular and alive. —

"Montaigne talks with shrewdness, knows the world and books and himself, and uses the positive degree ; never shrieks, or protests, or prays : no weakness, no convulsion, no superlative : does not wish to jump out of his skin, or play any antics, or annihilate space or time, but is stout and solid ; tastes every moment of the day ; likes pain because it makes him feel himself and realize things ; as we pinch ourselves to know that we are awake. He keeps the plain ; he rarely mounts or sinks ; likes to feel solid ground and the stones underneath. His writing has no enthusiasms, no aspiration ; contented, self-respecting, and keeping the middle of the road. There is but one exception, — in his love for Socrates. In speaking of him, for once his cheek flushes and his style rises to passion."

The writer who draws this portrait must have many of the same characteristics. Much as Emerson loved his dreams and his dreamers, he must have found a great relief in getting into "the middle of the road" with Montaigne, after wandering in difficult by-paths which too often

led him round to the point from which he
started.

As to his exposition of the true relations of
skepticism to affirmative and negative belief, the
philosophical reader must be referred to the
Essay itself.

In writing of " Shakespeare ; or, the Poet,"
Emerson naturally gives expression to his leading ideas about the office of the poet and of
poetry.

" Great men are more distinguished by range
and extent than by originality." A poet has
" a heart in unison with his time and country."
— " There is nothing whimsical and fantastic
in his production, but sweet and sad earnest,
freighted with the weightiest convictions, and
pointed with the most determined aim which
any man or class knows of in his times."

When Shakespeare was in his youth the drama
was the popular means of amusement. It was
" ballad, epic, newspaper, caucus, lecture, Punch,
and library, at the same time. The best proof
of its vitality is the crowd of writers which suddenly broke into this field." Shakespeare found
a great mass of old plays existing in manuscript
and reproduced from time to time on the stage.
He borrowed in all directions : " A great poet
who appears in illiterate times absorbs into his

sphere all the light which is anywhere radiating." Homer, Chaucer, Saadi, felt that all wit was their wit. "Chaucer is a huge borrower." Emerson gives a list of authors from whom he drew. This list is in many particulars erroneous, as I have learned from a letter of Professor Lounsbury's which I have had the privilege of reading, but this is a detail which need not delay us.

The reason why Emerson has so much to say on this subject of borrowing, especially when treating of Plato and of Shakespeare, is obvious enough. He was arguing in his own cause, — not defending himself, as if there were some charge of plagiarism to be met, but making the proud claim of eminent domain in behalf of the masters who knew how to use their acquisitions.

"Shakespeare is the only biographer of Shakespeare ; and even he can tell nothing except to the Shakespeare in us." — "Shakespeare is as much out of the category of eminent authors as he is out of the crowd. A good reader can in a sort nestle into Plato's brain and think from thence ; but not into Shakespeare's. We are still out of doors."

After all the homage which Emerson pays to the intellect of Shakespeare, he weighs him with the rest of mankind, and finds that he shares "the halfness and imperfection of humanity."

"He converted the elements which waited on his

command into entertainment. He was master of the revels to mankind."

And so, after this solemn verdict on Shakespeare, after looking at the forlorn conclusions of our old and modern oracles, priest and prophet, Israelite, German, and Swede, he says: "It must be conceded that these are half views of half men. The world still wants its poet-priest, who shall not trifle with Shakespeare the player, nor shall grope in graves with Swedenborg the mourner; but who shall see, speak, and act with equal inspiration."

It is not to be expected that Emerson should have much that is new to say about "Napoleon; or, the Man of the World."

The stepping-stones of this Essay are easy to find: —

"The instinct of brave, active, able men, throughout the middle class everywhere, has pointed out Napoleon as the incarnate democrat. —

"Napoleon is thoroughly modern, and at the highest point of his fortunes, has the very spirit of the newspapers." As Plato borrowed, as Shakespeare borrowed, as Mirabeau "plagiarized every good thought, every good word that was spoken in France," so Napoleon is not merely "representative, but a monopolizer and usurper of other minds."

He was "a man of stone and iron,"—equipped

for his work by nature as Sallust describes Catiline as being. "He had a directness of action never before combined with such comprehension. Here was a man who in each moment and emergency knew what to do next. He saw only the object; the obstacle must give way."

"When a natural king becomes a titular king everybody is pleased and satisfied." —

"I call Napoleon the agent or attorney of the middle class of modern society. — He was the agitator, the destroyer of prescription, the internal improver, the liberal, the radical, the inventor of means, the opener of doors and markets, the subverter of monopoly and abuse."

But he was without generous sentiments, "a boundless liar," and finishing in high colors the outline of his moral deformities, Emerson gives us a climax in two sentences which render further condemnation superfluous : —

"In short, when you have penetrated through all the circles of power and splendor, you were not dealing with a gentleman, at last, but with an impostor and rogue; and he fully deserves the epithet of Jupiter Scapin, or a sort of Scamp Jupiter.

"So this exorbitant egotist narrowed, impoverished, and absorbed the power and existence of those who served him; and the universal cry of France and of Europe in 1814 was, Enough of him; '*Assez de Bonaparte.*'"

It was to this feeling that the French poet Barbier, whose death we have but lately seen announced, gave expression in the terrible satire in which he pictured France as a fiery courser bestridden by her spurred rider, who drove her in a mad career over heaps of rocks and ruins.

But after all, Carlyle's "*carrière ouverte aux talens*," is the expression for Napoleon's great message to mankind.

"Goethe ; or, the Writer," is the last of the Representative Men who are the subjects of this book of Essays. Emerson says he had read the fifty-five volumes of Goethe, but no other German writers, at least in the original. It must have been in fulfilment of some pious vow that he did this. After all that Carlyle had written about Goethe, he could hardly help studying him. But this Essay looks to me as if he had found the reading of Goethe hard work. It flows rather languidly, toys with side issues as a stream loiters round a nook in its margin, and finds an excuse for play in every pebble. Still, he has praise enough for his author. "He has clothed our modern existence with poetry." — "He has said the best things about nature that ever were said. — He flung into literature in his Mephistopheles the first organic figure that has been added for some ages, and which will remain

as long as the Prometheus. — He is the type of
culture, the amateur of all arts and sciences and
events; artistic, but not artist; spiritual, but not
spiritualist. — I join Napoleon with him, as being both representatives of the impatience and
reaction of nature against the morgue of conventions, — two stern realists, who, with their scholars, have severally set the axe at the root of the
tree of cant and seeming, for this time and for
all time."

This must serve as an *ex pede* guide to reconstruct the Essay which finishes the volume.

In 1852 there was published a Memoir of Margaret Fuller Ossoli, in which Emerson, James
Freeman Clarke, and William Henry Channing
each took a part. Emerson's account of her
conversation and extracts from her letters and
diaries, with his running commentaries and his
interpretation of her mind and character, are a
most faithful and vivid portraiture of a woman
who is likely to live longer by what is written
of her than by anything she ever wrote herself.

14

CHAPTER VIII.

1853–1858. Æt. 50–55.

Lectures in various Places. — Anti - Slavery Addresses. — Woman. A Lecture read before the Woman's Rights Convention. — Samuel Hoar. Speech at Concord. — Publication of "English Traits." — The "Atlantic Monthly." — The "Saturday Club."

AFTER Emerson's return from Europe he delivered lectures to different audiences, — one on Poetry, afterwards published in "Letters and Social Aims," a course of lectures in Freeman Place Chapel, Boston, some of which have been published, one on the Anglo-Saxon Race, and many others. In January, 1855, he gave one of the lectures in a course of Anti-Slavery Addresses delivered in Tremont Temple, Boston. In the same year he delivered an address before the Anti-Slavery party of New York. His plan for the extirpation of slavery was to buy the slaves from the planters, not conceding their right to ownership, but because "it is the only practical course, and is innocent." It would cost two thousand millions, he says, according to the present estimate, but "was there ever any contribution that was so enthusiastically paid as this would be?"

His optimism flowers out in all its innocent luxuriance in the paragraph from which this is quoted. Of course with notions like these he could not be hand in hand with the Abolitionists. He was classed with the Free Soilers, but he seems to have formed a party by himself in his project for buying up the negroes. He looked at the matter somewhat otherwise in 1863, when the settlement was taking place in a different currency, — in steel and not in gold: —

> "Pay ransom to the owner,
>   And fill the bag to the brim.
>   Who is the owner? The slave is owner,
>   And ever was. Pay him."

His sympathies were all and always with freedom. He spoke with indignation of the outrage on Sumner; he took part in the meeting at Concord expressive of sympathy with John Brown. But he was never in the front rank of the aggressive Anti-Slavery men. In his singular "Ode inscribed to W. H. Channing" there is a hint of a possible solution of the slavery problem which implies a doubt as to the permanence of the cause of all the trouble.

> "The over-god
>   Who marries Right to Might,

> Who peoples, unpeoples, —
> He who exterminates
> Races by stronger races,
> Black by white faces, —
> Knows to bring honey
> Out of the lion."

Some doubts of this kind helped Emerson to justify himself when he refused to leave his "honeyed thought" for the busy world where

> "Things are of the snake."

The time came when he could no longer sit quietly in his study, and, to borrow Mr. Cooke's words, "As the agitation proceeded, and brave men took part in it, and it rose to a spirit of moral grandeur, he gave a heartier assent to the outward methods adopted."

No woman could doubt the reverence of Emerson for womanhood. In a lecture read to the "Woman's Rights Convention" in 1855, he takes bold, and what would then have been considered somewhat advanced, ground in the controversy then and since dividing the community. This is the way in which he expresses himself:

"I do not think it yet appears that women wish this equal share in public affairs. But it is they and not we that are to determine it. Let the laws be purged of every barbarous remainder, every barbarous impediment to women. Let the public dona-

tions for education be equally shared by them, let
them enter a school as freely as a church, let them
have and hold and give their property as men do
theirs ; — and in a few years it will easily appear
whether they wish a voice in making the laws that
are to govern them. If you do refuse them a vote,
you will also refuse to tax them, — according to our
Teutonic principle, No representation, no tax. — The
new movement is only a tide shared by the spirits of
man and woman ; and you may proceed in the faith
that whatever the woman's heart is prompted to desire, the man's mind is simultaneously prompted to
accomplish."

Emerson was fortunate enough to have had
for many years as a neighbor, that true New
England Roman, Samuel Hoar. He spoke of
him in Concord before his fellow-citizens, shortly
after his death, in 1856. He afterwards prepared a sketch of Mr. Hoar for "Putnam's Magazine," from which I take one prose sentence and
the verse with which the sketch concluded : —

" He was a model of those formal but reverend
manners which make what is called a gentleman of
the old school, so called under an impression that the
style is passing away, but which, I suppose, is an op-
tical illusion, as there are always a few more of the
class remaining, and always a few young men to
whom these manners are native."

The single verse I quote is compendious enough

and descriptive enough for an Elizabethan monumental inscription.

> " With beams December planets dart
>   His cold eye truth and conduct scanned ;
> July was in his sunny heart,
>   October in his liberal hand."

Emerson's " English Traits," forming one volume of his works, was published in 1856. It is a thoroughly fresh and original book. It is not a tourist's guide, not a detailed description of sights which tired the traveller in staring at them, and tire the reader who attacks the wearying pages in which they are recorded. Shrewd observation there is indeed, but its strength is in broad generalization and epigrammatic characterizations. They are not to be received as in any sense final ; they are not like the verifiable facts of science ; they are more or less sagacious, more or less well founded opinions formed by a fair-minded, sharp-witted, kind-hearted, open-souled philosopher, whose presence made every one well-disposed towards him, and consequently left him well-disposed to all the world.

A glance at the table of contents will give an idea of the objects which Emerson proposed to himself in his tour, and which take up the principal portion of his record. Only one *place* is given as the heading of a chapter, — *Stonehenge.* The other eighteen chapters have general titles, *Land, Race, Ability, Manners,* and others of similar character.

He uses plain English in introducing us to the Pilgrim fathers of the British Aristocracy : —

"Twenty thousand thieves landed at Hastings. These founders of the House of Lords were greedy and ferocious dragoons, sons of greedy and ferocious pirates. They were all alike, they took everything they could carry ; they burned, harried, violated, tortured, and killed, until everything English was brought to the verge of ruin. Such, however, is the illusion of antiquity and wealth, that decent and dignified men now existing boast their descent from these filthy thieves, who showed a far juster conviction of their own merits by assuming for their types the swine, goat, jackal, leopard, wolf, and snake, which they severally resembled."

The race preserves some of its better characteristics.

"They have a vigorous health and last well into middle and old age. The old men are as red as roses, and still handsome. A clear skin, a peach-bloom complexion, and good teeth are found all over the island."

English " Manners " are characterized, according to Emerson, by pluck, vigor, independence. "Every one of these islanders is an island himself, safe, tranquil, incommunicable." They are positive, methodical, cleanly, and formal, loving routine and conventional ways; loving truth and religion, to be sure, but inexorable on points of form.

"They keep their old customs, costumes, and pomps, their wig and mace, sceptre and crown. A severe decorum rules the court and the cottage. Pretension and vaporing are once for all distasteful. They hate nonsense, sentimentalism, and high-flown expressions; they use a studied plainness."

"In an aristocratical country like England, not the Trial by Jury, but the dinner is the capital institution."

"They confide in each other, — English believes in English." — "They require the same adherence, thorough conviction, and reality in public men."

"As compared with the American, I think them cheerful and contented. Young people in this country are much more prone to melancholy."

Emerson's observation is in accordance with that of Cotton Mather nearly two hundred years ago.

"*New England*, a country where splenetic Maladies are prevailing and pernicious, perhaps above any other, hath afforded numberless instances, of even pious people, who have contracted those *Melancholy Indispositions*, which have unhinged them from all service or comfort; yea, not a few persons have been hurried thereby to lay *Violent Hands* upon themselves at the last. These are among the *unsearchable Judgments* of God."

If there is a little exaggeration about the following portrait of the Englishman, it has truth enough to excuse its high coloring, and the likeness will be smilingly recognized by every stout Briton.

"They drink brandy like water, cannot expend their quantities of waste strength on riding, hunting, swimming, and fencing, and run into absurd follies with the gravity of the Eumenides. They stoutly carry into every nook and corner of the earth their turbulent sense; leaving no lie uncontradicted; no pretension unexamined. They chew hasheesh; cut themselves with poisoned creases, swing their hammock in the boughs of the Bohon Upas, taste every poison, buy every secret; at Naples, they put St. Januarius's blood in an alembic; they saw a hole into the head of the 'winking virgin' to know why she winks; measure with an English foot-rule every cell of the inquisition, every Turkish Caaba, every Holy of Holies; translate and send to Bentley the arcanum, bribed and bullied away from shuddering Bramins; and measure their own strength by the terror they cause."

This last audacious picture might be hung up as a prose pendant to Marvell's poetical description of Holland and the Dutch.

"A saving stupidity marks and protects their perception as the curtain of the eagle's eye. Our swifter Americans, when they first deal with English, pro-

nounce them stupid; but, later, do them justice as
people who wear well, or hide their strength. — High
and low, they are of an unctuous texture. — Their
daily feasts argue a savage vigor of body. — Half
their strength they put not forth. The stability of
England is the security of the modern world."

Perhaps nothing in any of his vigorous paragraphs is more striking than the suggestion that
" if hereafter the war of races often predicted,
and making itself a war of opinions also (a
question of despotism and liberty coming from
Eastern Europe), should menace the English
civilization, these sea-kings may take once again
to their floating castles and find a new home and
a second millennium of power in their colonies."

In reading some of Emerson's pages it seems
as if another Arcadia, or the new Atlantis, had
emerged as the fortunate island of Great Britain,
or that he had reached a heaven on earth where
neith.. moth nor rust doth corrupt, and where
thieves do not break through nor steal, — or if
they do, never think of denying that they have
done it. But this was a generation ago, when
the noun "shoddy," and the verb "to scamp,"
had not grown such familiar terms to English
ears as they are to-day. Emerson saw the
country on its best side. Each traveller makes
his own England. A Quaker sees chiefly broad
brims, and the island looks to him like a field of
mushrooms.

The transplanted Church of England is rich and prosperous and fashionable enough not to be disturbed by Emerson's flashes of light that have not come through its stained windows.

"The religion of England is part of good-breeding. When you see on the continent the well-dressed Englishman come into his ambassador's chapel, and put his face for silent prayer into his smooth-brushed hat, one cannot help feeling how much national pride prays with him, and the religion of a gentleman.

"The church at this moment is much to be pitied. She has nothing left but possession. If a bishop meets an intelligent gentleman, and reads fatal interrogation in his eyes, he has no resource but to take wine with him."

Sydney Smith had a great reverence for a bishop, — so great that he told a young lady that he used to roll a crumb of bread in his hand, from nervousness, when he sat next one at a dinner-table, — and if next an archbishop, used to roll crumbs with both hands, — but Sydney Smith would have enjoyed the tingling felicity of this last stinging touch of wit, left as lightly and gracefully as a *banderillero* leaves his little gayly ribboned dart in the shoulders of the bull with whose unwieldy bulk he is playing.

Emerson handles the formalism and the half belief of the Established Church very freely, but he closes his chapter on Religion with soft-spoken words.

" Yet if religion be the doing of all good, and for its sake the suffering of all evil, *souffrir de tout le monde, et ne faire souffrir personne,* that divine secret has existed in England from the days of Alfred to those of Romilly, of Clarkson, and of Florence Nightingale, and in thousands who have no fame."

" English Traits " closes with Emerson's speech at Manchester, at the annual banquet of the " Free Trade Athenæum." This was merely an occasional after - dinner reply to a toast which called him up, but it had sentences in it which, if we can imagine Milton to have been called up in the same way, he might well have spoken and done himself credit in their utterance.

The total impression left by the book is that Emerson was fascinated by the charm of English society, filled with admiration of the people, tempted to contrast his New Englanders in many respects unfavorably with Old Englanders, mainly in their material and vital stamina; but with all this not blinded for a moment to the thoroughly insular limitations of the phlegmatic islander. He alternates between a turn of genuine admiration and a smile as at a people that has not outgrown its playthings. This is in truth the natural and genuine feeling of a self-governing citizen of a commonwealth where thrones and wigs and mitres seem like so many

pieces of stage property. An American need
not be a philosopher to hold these things cheap.
He cannot help it. Madame Tussaud's exhibition, the Lord-Mayor's gilt coach, and a corona-
tion, if one happens to be in season, are all
sights to be seen by an American traveller, but
the reverence which is born with the British
subject went up with the smoke of the gun that
fired the long echoing shot at the little bridge
over the sleepy river which works its way along
through the wide-awake town of Concord.

In November, 1857, a new magazine was established in Boston, bearing the name of "The
Atlantic Monthly." Professor James Russell
Lowell was editor-in-chief, and Messrs. Phillips
and Sampson, who were the originators of the
enterprise, were the publishers. Many of the old
contributors to "The Dial" wrote for the new
magazine, among them Emerson. He contributed twenty-eight articles in all, more than half
of them verse, to different numbers, from the first
to the thirty-seventh volume. Among them are
several of his best known poems, such as "The
Romany Girl," "Days," "Brahma," "Waldein-
samkeit," "The Titmouse," "Boston Hymn,"
"Saadi," and "Terminus."

At about the same time there grew up in Boston a literary association, which became at last
well known as the "Saturday Club," the mem-

bers dining together on the last Saturday of
every month.

The Magazine and the Club have existed and
flourished to the present day. They have often
been erroneously thought to have some organic
connection, and the "Atlantic Club" has been
spoken of as if there was or had been such an
institution, but it never existed.

Emerson was a member of the Saturday Club
from the first; in reality before it existed as an
empirical fact, and when it was only a Platonic
idea. The Club seems to have shaped itself
around him as a nucleus of crystallization, two or
three friends of his having first formed the habit
of meeting him at dinner at "Parker's," the
"Will's Coffee-House" of Boston. This little
group gathered others to itself and grew into
a club as Rome grew into a city, almost without knowing how. During its first decade the
Saturday Club brought together, as members
or as visitors, many distinguished persons. At
one end of the table sat Longfellow, florid,
quiet, benignant, soft-voiced, a most agreeable
rather than a brilliant talker, but a man upon
whom it was always pleasant to look, — whose
silence was better than many another man's conversation. At the other end of the table sat
Agassiz, robust, sanguine, animated, full of talk,
boy-like in his laughter. The stranger who

should have asked who were the men ranged
along the sides of the table would have heard in
answer the names of Hawthorne, Motley, Dana,
Lowell, Whipple, Peirce, the distinguished math-
ematician, Judge Hoar, eminent at the bar and
in the cabinet, Dwight, the leading musical critic
of Boston for a whole generation, Sumner, the
academic champion of freedom, Andrew, "the
great War Governor" of Massachusetts, Dr.
Howe, the philanthropist, William Hunt, the
painter, with others not unworthy of such company. And with these, generally near the Longfellow end of the table, sat Emerson, talking in
low tones and carefully measured utterances to
his neighbor, or listening, and recording on his
mental phonograph any stray word worth remembering. Emerson was a very regular attendant at the meetings of the Saturday Club,
and continued to dine at its table, until within
a year or two of his death.

Unfortunately the Club had no Boswell, and
its golden hours passed unrecorded.

CHAPTER IX.

1858–1863.   Æt. 55–60.

THE Essay on Persian Poetry, published in the
" Atlantic Monthly " in 1858, should be studied
by all readers who are curious in tracing the influence of Oriental poetry on Emerson's verse.
In many of the shorter poems and fragments
published since " May-Day," as well as in the
" Quatrains " and others of the later poems in
that volume, it is sometimes hard to tell what is
from the Persian from what is original.

On the 25th of January, 1859, Emerson attended the Burns Festival, held at the Parker
House in Boston, on the Centennial Anniversary
of the poet's birth.   He spoke after the dinner
to the great audience with such beauty and
eloquence that all who listened to him have remembered it as one of the most delightful addresses they ever heard.   Among his hearers was

Mr. Lowell, who says of it that "every word seemed to have just dropped down to him from the clouds." Judge Hoar, who was another of his hearers, says, that though he has heard many of the chief orators of his time, he never witnessed such an effect of speech upon men. I was myself present on that occasion, and underwent the same fascination that these gentlemen and the varied audience before the speaker experienced. His words had a passion in them not usual in the calm, pure flow most natural to his uttered thoughts; white-hot iron we are familiar with, but white-hot silver is what we do not often look upon, and his inspiring address glowed like silver fresh from the cupel.

I am allowed the privilege of printing the following letter addressed to a lady of high intellectual gifts, who was one of the earliest, most devoted, and most faithful of his intimate friends : —

CONCORD, *May* 13, 1859.

Please, dear C., not to embark for home until I have despatched these lines, which I will hasten to finish. Louis Napoleon will not bayonet you the while, — keep him at the door. So long I have promised to write! so long I have thanked your long suffering! I have let pass the unreturning opportunity your visit to Germany gave to acquaint you with Gisela von Arnim (Bettina's daughter), and Joachim

15

the violinist, and Hermann Grimm the scholar, her friends. Neither has E., — wandering in Europe with hope of meeting you, — yet met. This contumacy of mine I shall regret as long as I live. How palsy creeps over us, with gossamer first, and ropes afterwards! and the witch has the prisoner when once she has put her eye on him, as securely as after the bolts are drawn. — Yet I and all my little company watch every token from you, and coax Mrs. H. to read us letters. I learned with satisfaction that you did not like Germany. Where then did Goethe find his lovers? Do all the women have bad noses and bad mouths? And will you stop in England, and bring home the author of " Counterparts " with you? Or did —— write the novels and send them to London, as I fancied when I read them? How strange that you and I alone to this day should have his secret! I think our people will never allow genius, without it is alloyed by talent. But —— is paralyzed by his whims, that I have ceased to hope from him. I could wish your experience of your friends were more animating than mine, and that there were any horoscope you could not cast from the first day. The faults of youth are never shed, no, nor the merits, and creeping time convinces ever the more of our impotence, and of the irresistibility of our bias. Still this is only science, and must remain science. Our *praxis* is never altered for that. We must forever hold our companions responsible, or they are not companions but stall-fed.

I think, as we grow older, we decrease as indi-

viduals, and as if in an immense audience who hear
stirring music, none essays to offer a new stave, but
we only join emphatically in the chorus. We volun-
teer no opinion, we despair of guiding people, but are
confirmed in our perception that Nature is all right,
and that we have a good understanding with it. We
must shine to a few brothers, as palms or pines or
roses among common weeds, not from greater absolute
value, but from a more convenient nature. But 't is
almost chemistry at last, though a meta-chemistry.
I remember you were such an impatient blasphemer,
however musically, against the adamantine identities,
in your youth, that you should take your turn of resignation now, and be a preacher of peace. But there
is a little raising of the eyebrow, now and then, in
the most passive acceptance, — if of an intellectual
turn. Here comes out around me at this moment the
new June, — the leaves say June, though the calendar
says May, — and we must needs hail our young relatives again, though with something of the gravity of
adult sons and daughters receiving a late-born brother
or sister. Nature herself seems a little ashamed of a
law so monstrous, billions of summers, and now the
old game again without a new bract or sepal. But
you will think me incorrigible with my generalities,
and you so near, and will be here again this summer ; perhaps with A. W. and the other travellers.
My children scan curiously your E.'s drawings, as
they have seen them.

The happiest winds fill the sails of you and yours !

R. W. EMERSON.

In the year 1860, Theodore Parker died, and Emerson spoke of his life and labors at the meeting held at the Music Hall to do honor to his memory. Emerson delivered discourses on Sundays and week-days in the Music Hall to Mr. Parker's society after his death. In 1862, he lost his friend Thoreau, at whose funeral he delivered an address which was published in the "Atlantic Monthly" for August of the same year. Thoreau had many rare and admirable qualities, and Thoreau pictured by Emerson is a more living personage than White of Selborne would have been on the canvas of Sir Joshua Reynolds.

The Address on the Emancipation Proclamation was delivered in Boston in September, 1862. The feeling that inspired it may be judged by the following extract : —

"Happy are the young, who find the pestilence cleansed out of the earth, leaving open to them an honest career. Happy the old, who see Nature purified before they depart. Do not let the dying die ; hold them back to this world, until you have charged their ear and heart with this message to other spiritual societies, announcing the melioration of our planet : —

"'Incertainties now crown themselves assured,
   And Peace proclaims olives of endless age.'"

The "Conduct of Life" was published in 1860. The chapter on "Fate" might leave the reader with a feeling that what he is to do, as well as what he is to be and to suffer, is so largely predetermined for him, that his will, though formally asserted, has but a questionable fraction in adjusting him to his conditions as a portion of the universe. But let him hold fast to this reassuring statement : —

"If we must accept Fate, we are not less compelled to affirm liberty, the significance of the individual, the grandeur of duty, the power of character. — We are sure, that, though we know not how, necessity does comport with liberty, the individual with the world, my polarity with the spirit of the times."

But the value of the Essay is not so much in any light it throws on the mystery of volition, as on the striking and brilliant way in which the limitations of the individual and the inexplicable rule of law are illustrated.

"Nature is no sentimentalist, — does not cosset or pamper us. We must see that the world is rough and surly, and will not mind drowning a man or a woman ; but swallows your ship like a grain of dust. — The way of Providence is a little rude. The habit of snake and spider, the snap of the tiger and other leapers and bloody jumpers, the crackle of the bones of his prey in the coil of the anaconda, — these are in the system, and our habits are like theirs. You have just dined, and however scrupulously the slaughter-house is concealed in the graceful distance of miles, there is complicity, — expensive races, — race living at the expense of race. — Let us not deny it up and down. Providence has a wild, rough, incalculable road to its end, and it is of no use to try to whitewash its huge, mixed instrumentalities, or to dress up that terrific benefactor in a clean shirt and white neckcloth of a student in divinity."

Emerson cautions his reader against the danger of the doctrines which he believed in so fully : —

"They who talk much of destiny, their birth-star, etc., are in a lower dangerous plane, and invite the evils they fear."

But certainly no physiologist, no cattle-breeder, no Calvinistic predestinarian could put his view more vigorously than Emerson, who dearly loves a picturesque statement, has given it in these words, which have a dash of science, a flash of imagination, and a hint of the delicate wit that is one of his characteristics : —

"People are born with the moral or with the material bias ; — uterine brothers with this diverging destination : and I suppose, with high magnifiers, Mr. Fraunhofer or Dr. Carpenter might come to distinguish in the embryo at the fourth day, this is a whig and that a free-soiler."

Let us see what Emerson has to say of "Power : " —

"All successful men have agreed in one thing —

they were *causationists*. They believed that things went not by luck, but by law ; that there was not a weak or a cracked link in the chain that joins the first and the last of things.

" The key to the age may be this, or that, or the other, as the young orators describe ; — the key to all ages is, — Imbecility ; imbecility in the vast majority of men at all times, and, even in heroes, in all but certain eminent moments ; victims of gravity, custom, and fear. This gives force to the strong, — that the multitude have no habit of self-reliance or original action. —

" We say that success is constitutional ; depends on a *plus* condition of mind and body, on power of work, on courage ; that is of main efficacy in carrying on the world, and though rarely found in the right state for an article of commerce, but oftener in the supernatural or excess, which makes it dangerous and destructive, yet it cannot be spared, and must be had in that form, and absorbents provided to take off its edge."

The " two economies which are the best *succedanea* " for deficiency of temperament are concentration and drill. This he illustrates by example, and he also lays down some good, plain, practical rules which " Poor Richard " would have cheerfully approved. He might have accepted also the Essay on " Wealth " as having a good sense so like his own that he could hardly tell the difference between them.

" Wealth begins in a tight roof that keeps the rain and wind out ; in a good pump that yields you plenty of sweet water ; in two suits of clothes, so as to change your dress when you are wet ; in dry sticks to burn ; in a good double-wick lamp, and three meals ; in a horse or locomotive to cross the land ; in a boat to cross the sea ; in tools to work with ; in books to read ; and so, in giving, on all sides, by tools and auxiliaries, the greatest possible extension to our powers, as if it added feet, and hands, and eyes, and blood, length to the day, and knowledge and good will. Wealth begins with these articles of necessity. —

" To be rich is to have a ticket of admission to the masterworks and chief men of each race. —

" The pulpit and the press have many commonplaces denouncing the thirst for wealth ; but if men should take these moralists at their word, and leave off aiming to be rich, the moralists would rush to re-kindle at all hazards this love of power in the people, lest civilization should be undone."

Who can give better counsels on " Culture " than Emerson ? But we must borrow only a few sentences from his essay on that subject. All kinds of secrets come out as we read these Essays of Emerson's. We know something of his friends and disciples who gathered round him and sat at his feet. It is not hard to believe that he was drawing one of those composite portraits Mr. Galton has given us specimens of when he wrote as follows : —

" The pest of society is egotism. This goitre of egotism is so frequent among notable persons that we must infer some strong necessity in nature which it subserves ; such as we see in the sexual attraction. The preservation of the species was a point of such necessity that Nature has secured it at all hazards by immensely overloading the passion, at the risk of perpetual crime and disorder. So egotism has its root in the cardinal necessity by which each individual persists to be what he is.

" The antidotes against this organic egotism are, the range and variety of attraction, as gained by acquaintance with the world, with men of merit, with classes of society, with travel, with eminent persons, and with the high resources of philosophy, art, and religion : books, travel, society, solitude."

" We can ill spare the commanding social benefits of cities ; they must be used ; yet cautiously and haughtily, — and will yield their best values to him who can best do without them. Keep the town for occasions, but the habits should be formed to retirement. Solitude, the safeguard of mediocrity, is to genius the stern friend, the cold, obscure shelter, where moult the wings which will bear it farther than suns and stars."

We must remember, too, that " the calamities are our friends. Try the rough water as well as the smooth. Rough water can teach lessons worth knowing. Don't be so tender at making an enemy now and then. He who aims high, must dread an easy home and popular manners."

Emerson cannot have had many enemies, if any, in his calm and noble career. He can have cherished no enmity, on personal grounds at least. But he refused his hand to one who had spoken ill of a friend whom he respected. It was " the hand of Douglas " again, — the same feeling that Charles Emerson expressed in the youthful essay mentioned in the introduction to this volume.

Here are a few good sayings about " Behavior."

" There is always a best way of doing everything, if it be to boil an egg.   Manners are the happy ways of doing things; each once a stroke of genius or of love, — now repeated and hardened into usage."

Thus it is that Mr. Emerson speaks of " Manners" in his Essay under the above title.

" The basis of good manners is self-reliance. — Manners require time, as nothing is more vulgar than haste. —

" Men take each other's measure, when they meet for the first time, — and every time they meet. —

" It is not what talents or genius a man has, but how he is to his talents, that constitutes friendship and character.   The man that stands by himself, the universe stands by him also."

In his Essay on "Worship," Emerson ventures the following prediction : —

"The religion which is to guide and fulfil the present and coming ages, whatever else it be, must be intellectual. The scientific mind must have a faith which is science. — There will be a new church founded on moral science, at first cold and naked, a babe in a manger again, the algebra and mathematics of ethical law, the church of men to come, without shawms or psaltery or sackbut; but it will have heaven and earth for its beams and rafters; science for symbol and illustration; it will fast enough gather beauty, music, picture, poetry."

It is a bold prophecy, but who can doubt that all improbable and unverifiable traditional knowledge of all kinds will make way for the established facts of science and history when these last reach it in their onward movement? It may be remarked that he now speaks of science more respectfully than of old. I suppose this Essay was of later date than "Beauty," or "Illusions." But accidental circumstances made such confusion in the strata of Emerson's published thought that one is often at a loss to know whether a sentence came from the older or the newer layer.

We come to "Considerations by the Way." The common-sense side of Emerson's mind has so much in common with the plain practical in-

telligence of Franklin that it is a pleasure to find
the philosopher of the nineteenth century quoting
the philosopher of the eighteenth.

"Franklin said, 'Mankind are very superficial and
dastardly: they begin upon a thing, but, meeting with
a difficulty, they fly from it discouraged: but they
have the means if they would employ them.'"

"Shall we judge a country by the majority, or
by the minority? By the minority, surely." Here
we have the doctrine of the "saving remnant,"
which we have since recognized in Mr. Matthew
Arnold's well-remembered lecture. Our republican philosopher is clearly enough outspoken on
this matter of the *vox populi*. "Leave this hypo-
critical prating about the masses. Masses are
rude, lame, unmade, pernicious in their demands,
and need not to be flattered, but to be schooled.
I wish not to concede anything to them, but to
tame, drill, divide, and break them up, and draw
individuals out of them."

Père Bouhours asked a question about the
Germans which found its answer in due time.
After reading what Emerson says about "the
masses," one is tempted to ask whether a philosopher can ever have "a constituency" and be
elected to Congress? Certainly the essay just
quoted from would not make a very promising
campaign document.

Perhaps there was no great necessity for Emerson's returning to the subject of "Beauty," to which he had devoted a chapter of "Nature," and of which he had so often discoursed incidentally. But he says so many things worth reading in the Essay thus entitled in the "Conduct of Life" that we need not trouble ourselves about repetitions. The Essay is satirical and poetical rather than philosophical. Satirical when he speaks of science with something of that old feeling betrayed by his brother Charles when he was writing in 1828; poetical in the flight of imagination with which he enlivens, entertains, stimulates, inspires, — or as some may prefer to say, — amuses his listeners and readers.

The reader must decide which of these effects is produced by the following passage : —

"The feat of the imagination is in showing the convertibility of everything into every other thing. Facts which had never before left their stark common sense suddenly figure as Eleusinian mysteries. My boots and chair and candlestick are fairies in disguise, meteors, and constellations. All the facts in Nature are nouns of the intellect, and make the grammar of the eternal language. Every word has a double, treble, or centuple use and meaning. What! has my stove and pepper-pot a false bottom? I cry you mercy, good shoe-box! I did not know you were a jewel-case. Chaff and dust begin to sparkle, and are clothed about with immortality. And there is a joy in perceiving the representative or symbolic character of a fact, which no base fact or event can ever give. There are no days so memorable as those which vibrated to some stroke of the imagination."

One is reminded of various things in reading this sentence. An ounce of alcohol, or a few whiffs from an opium-pipe, may easily make a day memorable by bringing on this imaginative delirium, which is apt, if often repeated, to run into visions of rodents and reptiles. A coarser satirist than Emerson indulged his fancy in "Meditations on a Broomstick," which My Lady Berkeley heard seriously and to edification. Meditations on a "Shoe-box" are less promising, but no doubt something could be made of it. A poet must select, and if he stoops too low he cannot lift the object he would fain idealize.

The habitual readers of Emerson do not mind an occasional over-statement, extravagance, paradox, eccentricity; they find them amusing and not misleading. But the accountants, for whom two and two always make four, come upon one of these passages and shut the book up as wanting in sanity. Without a certain sensibility to the humorous, no one should venture upon Emerson. If he had seen the lecturer's smile as he delivered one of his playful statements of a runaway truth, fact unhorsed by imagination, some-

times by wit, or humor, he would have found a
meaning in his words which the featureless
printed page could never show him.

The Essay on " Illusions " has little which we
have not met with, or shall not find repeating
itself in the Poems.

During this period Emerson contributed many
articles in prose and verse to the " Atlantic
Monthly," and several to " The Dial," a second
periodical of that name published in Cincinnati.
Some of these have been, or will be, elsewhere
referred to.

CHAPTER X.

1863–1868. Æt. 60–65.

THE "Boston Hymn" was read by Emerson in the Music Hall, on the first day of January, 1863. It is a rough piece of verse, but noble from beginning to end. One verse of it, beginning "Pay ransom to the owner," has been already quoted; these are the three that precede it : —

> "I cause from every creature
> His proper good to flow:
> As much as he is and doeth
> So much shall he bestow.
>
> "But laying hands on another
> To coin his labor and sweat,
> He goes in pawn to his victim
> For eternal years in debt.

> " To-day unbind the captive,
>   So only are ye unbound :
> Lift up a people from the dust,
>   Trump of their rescue, sound ! "

" Voluntaries," published in the same year in the " Atlantic Monthly," is more dithyrambic in its measure and of a more Pindaric elevation than the plain song of the " Boston Hymn."

> " But best befriended of the God
>   He who, in evil times,
>   Warned by an inward voice,
> Heeds not the darkness and the dread,
>   Biding by his rule and choice,
> Feeling only the fiery thread
> Leading over heroic ground,
> Walled with mortal terror round,
> To the aim which him allures,
> And the sweet heaven his deed secures.
> Peril around, all else appalling,
> Cannon in front and leaden rain
> Him duly through the clarion calling
> To the van called not in vain."

It is in this poem that we find the lines which, a moment after they were written, seemed as if they had been carved on marble for a thousand years : —

> " So nigh is grandeur to our dust,
>   So near is God to man,
> When Duty whispers low, *Thou must,*
>   The youth replies, *I can.*"

16

"Saadi" was published in the "Atlantic Monthly" in 1864, "My Garden" in 1866, "Terminus" in 1867. In the same year these last poems with many others were collected in a small volume, entitled "May-Day, and Other Pieces." The general headings of these poems are as follows: May-Day. — The Adirondacs. — Occasional and Miscellaneous Pieces. — Nature and Life. — Elements. — Quatrains. — Translations. — Some of these poems, which were written at long intervals, have been referred to in previous pages. "The Adirondacs" is a pleasant narrative, but not to be compared for its poetical character with "May-Day," one passage from which, beginning,

"I saw the bud-crowned Spring go forth,"

is surpassingly imaginative and beautiful. In this volume will be found "Brahma," "Days," and others which are well known to all readers of poetry.

Emerson's delineations of character are remarkable for high-relief and sharp-cut lines. In his Remarks at the Funeral Services for Abraham Lincoln, held in Concord, April 19, 1865, he drew the portrait of the homespun-robed chief of the Republic with equal breadth and delicacy: —

"Here was place for no holiday magistrate, no fair weather sailor; the new pilot was hurried to the helm in a tornado. In four years, — four years of battle-days, — his endurance, his fertility of resources, his magnanimity, were sorely tried and never found wanting. There, by his courage, his justice, his even temper, his fertile counsel, his humanity, he stood a heroic figure in the centre of a heroic epoch. He is the true history of the American people in his time. Step by step he walked before them; slow with their slowness, quickening his march by theirs, the true representative of this continent; an entirely public man; father of his country; the pulse of twenty millions throbbing in his heart, the thought of their minds articulated by his tongue."

In his " Remarks at the Organization of the Free Religious Association," Emerson stated his leading thought about religion in a very succinct and sufficiently " transcendental " way : intelligibly for those who wish to understand him; mystically to those who do not accept or wish to accept the doctrine shadowed forth in his poem, " The Sphinx."

— " As soon as every man is apprised of the Divine Presence within his own mind, — is apprised that the perfect law of duty corresponds with the laws of chemistry, of vegetation, of astronomy, as face to face in a glass; that the basis of duty, the order of society, the power of character, the wealth

of culture, the perfection of taste, all draw their
essence from this moral sentiment; then we have a
religion that exalts, that commands all the social and
all the private action."

Nothing could be more wholesome in a
meeting of creed-killers than the suggestive remark, —

— "What I expected to find here was, some practical suggestions by which we were to reanimate and
reorganize for ourselves the true Church, the pure
worship. Pure doctrine always bears fruit in pure
benefits. It is only by good works, it is only on the
basis of active duty, that worship finds expression. —
The interests that grow out of a meeting like this,
should bind us with new strength to the old eternal
duties."

In a later address before the same association,
Emerson says : —

"I object, of course, to the claim of miraculous
dispensation, — certainly not to the *doctrine* of Christianity. — If you are childish and exhibit your saint
as a worker of wonders, a thaumaturgist, I am repelled. That claim takes his teachings out of nature,
and permits official and arbitrary senses to be grafted
on the teachings."

The " Progress of Culture " was delivered as
a Phi Beta Kappa oration just thirty years after
his first address before the same society. It is
very instructive to compare the two orations

written at the interval of a whole generation:
one in 1837, at the age of thirty-four; the other
in 1867, at the age of sixty-four. Both are
hopeful, but the second is more sanguine than
the first. He recounts what he considers the
recent gains of the reforming movement: —

"Observe the marked ethical quality of the inno-
vations urged or adopted. The new claim of woman
to a political status is itself an honorable testimony to
the civilization which has given her a civil status new
in history. Now that by the increased humanity of
law she controls her property, she inevitably takes the
next step to her share in power."

He enumerates many other gains, from the
war or from the growth of intelligence, — " All,
one may say, in a high degree revolutionary,
teaching nations the taking of governments into
their own hands, and superseding kings."

He repeats some of his fundamental formulæ.

"The foundation of culture, as of character, is at
last the moral sentiment.

"Great men are they who see that spiritual is
stronger than any material force, that thoughts rule
the world.

"Periodicity, reaction, are laws of mind as well as
of matter."

And most encouraging it is to read in 1884
what was written in 1867, — especially in the
view of future possibilities.

"Bad kings and governors help us, if only they are bad enough." *Non tali auxilio,* we exclaim, with a shudder of remembrance, and are very glad to read these concluding words: "I read the promise of better times and of greater men."

In the year 1866, Emerson reached the age which used to be spoken of as the "grand climacteric." In that year Harvard University conferred upon him the degree of Doctor of Laws, the highest honor in its gift.

In that same year, having left home on one of his last lecturing trips, he met his son, Dr. Edward Waldo Emerson, at the Brevoort House, in New York. Then, and in that place, he read to his son the poem afterwards published in the "Atlantic Monthly," and in his second volume, under the title "Terminus." This was the first time that Dr. Emerson recognized the fact that his father felt himself growing old. The thought, which must have been long shaping itself in the father's mind, had been so far from betraying itself that it was a shock to the son to hear it plainly avowed. The poem is one of his noblest; he could not fold his robes about him with more of serene dignity than in these solemn lines. The reader may remember that one passage from it has been quoted for a particular purpose, but here is the whole poem : —

TERMINUS.

It is time to be old,
To take in sail :—
The god of bounds,
Who sets to seas a shore,
Came to me in his fatal rounds,
And said : " No more !
No farther shoot
Thy broad ambitious branches, and thy root.
Fancy departs : no more invent ;
Contract thy firmament
To compass of a tent.
There 's not enough for this and that,
Make thy option which of two ;
Economize the failing river,
Not the less revere the Giver,
Leave the many and hold the few,
Timely wise accept the terms,
Soften the fall with wary foot ;
A little while
Still plan and smile,
And, — fault of novel germs, —
Mature the unfallen fruit.
Curse, if thou wilt, thy sires,
Bad husbands of their fires,
Who when they gave thee breath,
Failed to bequeath
The needful sinew stark as once,
The baresark marrow to thy bones,
But left a legacy of ebbing veins,
Inconstant heat and nerveless reins, —
Amid the Muses, left thee deaf and dumb,
Amid the gladiators, halt and numb.

" As the bird trims her to the gale
 I trim myself to the storm of time,
 I man the rudder, reef the sail,
 Obey the voice at eve obeyed at prime :
'Lowly faithful, banish fear,
 Right onward drive unharmed ;
 The port, well worth the cruise, is near,
 And every wave is charmed.' "

CHAPTER XI.

1868–1873. Æt. 65–70.

DURING three successive years, 1868, 1869,
1870, Emerson delivered a series of Lectures at
Harvard University on the "Natural History of
the Intellect." These Lectures, as I am told by
Dr. Emerson, cost him a great deal of labor, but
I am not aware that they have been collected or
reported. They will be referred to in the course
of this chapter, in an extract from Prof. Thayer's "Western Journey with Mr. Emerson."
He is there reported as saying that he cared
very little for metaphysics. It is very certain
that he makes hardly any use of the ordinary
terms employed by metaphysicians. If he does
not hold the words "subject and object" with
their adjectives, in the same contempt that Mr.

Ruskin shows for them, he very rarely employs either of these expressions. Once he ventures on the *not me*, but in the main he uses plain English handles for the few metaphysical tools he has occasion to employ.

" Society and Solitude " was published in 1870. The first Essay in the volume bears the same name as the volume itself.

In this first Essay Emerson is very fair to the antagonistic claims of solitary and social life. He recognizes the organic necessity of solitude. We are driven " as with whips into the desert." But there is danger in this seclusion. " Now and then a man exquisitely made can live alone and must; but coop up most men and you undo them. — Here again, as so often, Nature delights to put us between extreme antagonisms, and our safety is in the skill with which we keep the diagonal line. — The conditions are met, if we keep our independence yet do not lose our sympathy."

The Essay on " Civilization " is pleasing, putting familiar facts in a very agreeable way. The framed or stone-house in place of the cave or the camp, the building of roads, the change from war, hunting, and pasturage to agriculture, the division of labor, the skilful combinations of civil government, the diffusion of knowledge through the press, are well worn subjects which he treats agreeably, if not with special brilliancy : —

"Right position of woman in the State is another index. — Place the sexes in right relations of mutual respect, and a severe morality gives that essential charm to a woman which educates all that is delicate, poetic, and self-sacrificing ; breeds courtesy and learning, conversation and wit, in her rough mate, so that I have thought a sufficient measure of civilization is the influence of good women."

My attention was drawn to one paragraph for a reason which my reader will readily understand, and I trust look upon good-naturedly : —

"The ship, in its latest complete equipment, is an abridgment and compend of a nation's arts : the ship steered by compass and chart, longitude reckoned by lunar observation and by chronometer, driven by steam ; and in wildest sea-mountains, at vast distances from home, —

"'The pulses of her iron heart
    Go beating through the storm.'"

I cannot be wrong, it seems to me, in supposing those two lines to be an incorrect version of these two from a poem of my own called "The Steamboat : "

"The beating of her restless heart
    Still sounding through the storm."

It is never safe to quote poetry from memory,

at least while the writer lives, for he is ready to
" cavil on the ninth part of a hair " where his
verses are concerned.   But extreme accuracy was
not one of Emerson's special gifts, and vanity
whispers to the misrepresented versifier that

> 't is better to be quoted wrong
> Than to be quoted not at all.

This Essay of Emerson's is irradiated by a
single precept that is worthy to stand by the side
of that which Juvenal says came from heaven.
How could the man in whose thought such a
meteoric expression suddenly announced itself
fail to recognize it as divine ?   It is not strange
that he repeats it on the page next the one
where we first see it.   Not having any golden
letters to print it in, I will underscore it for
italics, and doubly underscore it in the second
extract for small capitals : —

" Now that is the wisdom of a man, in every instance of his labor, to *hitch his wagon to a star*, and
see his chore done by the gods themselves." —

" ' It was a great instruction,' said a saint in Crom-
well's war, ' that the best courages are but beams of
the Almighty.'   HITCH YOUR WAGON TO A STAR.
Let us not fag in paltry works which serve our pot
and bag alone.   Let us not lie and steal.   No god
will help.   We shall find all their teams going the
other way, — Charles's Wain, Great Bear, Orion,
Leo, Hercules : every god will leave us.   Work rather

for those interests which the divinities honor and promote, — justice, love, freedom, knowledge, utility." —

Charles's Wain and the Great Bear, he should have been reminded, are the same constellation; the *Dipper* is what our people often call it, and the country folk all know "the pīnters," which guide their eyes to the North Star.

I find in the Essay on "Art" many of the thoughts with which we are familiar in Emerson's poem, "The Problem." It will be enough to cite these passages: —

" We feel in seeing a noble building which rhymes well, as we do in hearing a perfect song, that it is spiritually organic; that it had a necessity in nature for being; was one of the possible forms in the Divine mind, and is now only discovered and executed by the artist, not arbitrarily composed by him. And so every genuine work of art has as much reason for being as the earth and the sun. —

— " The Iliad of Homer, the songs of David, the odes of Pindar, the tragedies of Æschylus, the Doric temples, the Gothic cathedrals, the plays of Shakspeare, all and each were made not for sport, but in grave earnest, in tears and smiles of suffering and loving men. —

— " The Gothic cathedrals were built when the builder and the priest and the people were overpowered by their faith. Love and fear laid every stone. —

"Our arts are happy hits. We are like the musician on the lake, whose melody is sweeter than he knows."

The discourse on "Eloquence" is more systematic, more professorial, than many of the others. A few brief extracts will give the key to its general purport : —

"Eloquence must be grounded on the plainest narrative. Afterwards, it may warm itself until it exhales symbols of every kind and color, speaks only through the most poetic forms ; but, first and last, it must still be at bottom a biblical statement of fact. —

"He who will train himself to mastery in this science of persuasion must lay the emphasis of education, not on popular arts, but on character and insight. —

— "The highest platform of eloquence is the moral sentiment. —

— "Its great masters . . . were grave men, who preferred their integrity to their talent, and esteemed that object for which they toiled, whether the prosperity of their country, or the laws, or a reformation, or liberty of speech, or of the press, or letters, or morals, as above the whole world and themselves also."

"Domestic Life" begins with a picture of childhood so charming that it sweetens all the good counsel which follows like honey round the rim of the goblet which holds some tonic draught : —

" Welcome to the parents the puny struggler, strong in his weakness, his little arms more irresistible than the soldier's, his lips touched with persuasion which Chatham and Pericles in manhood had not. His unaffected lamentations when he lifts up his voice on high, or, more beautiful, the sobbing child, — the face all liquid grief, as he tries to swallow his vexation, — soften all hearts to pity, and to mirthful and clamorous compassion. The small despot asks so little that all reason and all nature are on his side. His ignorance is more charming than all knowledge, and his little sins more bewitching than any virtue. His flesh is angels' flesh, all alive. — All day, between his three or four sleeps, he coos like a pigeon-house, sputters and spurs and puts on his faces of importance ; and when he fasts, the little Pharisee fails not to sound his trumpet before him."

Emerson has favored his audiences and readers with what he knew about "Farming." Dr. Emerson tells me that this discourse was read as an address before the " Middlesex Agricultural Society," and printed in the " Transactions " of that association. He soon found out that the hoe and the spade were not the tools he was meant to work with, but he had some general ideas about farming which he expressed very happily : —

" The farmer's office is precise and important, but you must not try to paint him in rose-color ; you cannot make pretty compliments to fate and gravitation, whose minister he is. — This hard work will always be done by one kind of man; not by scheming speculators, nor by soldiers, nor professors, nor readers of Tennyson; but by men of endurance, deep-chested, long-winded, tough, slow and sure, and timely."

Emerson's chemistry and physiology are not profound, but they are correct enough to make a fine richly colored poetical picture in his imaginative presentation. He tells the commonest facts so as to make them almost a surprise: —

"By drainage we went down to a subsoil we did not know, and have found there is a Concord under old Concord, which we are now getting the best crops from; a Middlesex under Middlesex; and, in fine, that Massachusetts has a basement story more valuable and that promises to pay a better rent than all the superstructure."

In "Works and Days" there is much good reading, but I will call attention to one or two points only, as having a slight special interest of their own. The first is the boldness of Emerson's assertions and predictions in matters belonging to science and art. Thus, he speaks of "the transfusion of the blood, — which, in Paris, it was claimed, enables a man to change his blood as often as his linen!" And once more,

" We are to have the balloon yet, and the next war
will be fought in the air."

Possibly ; but it is perhaps as safe to predict
that it will be fought on wheels ; the soldiers on
bicycles, the officers on tricycles.

The other point I have marked is that we find
in this Essay a prose version of the fine poem
printed in " May-Day " under the title " Days."
I shall refer to this more particularly hereafter.

It is wronging the Essay on " Books " to make
extracts from it. It is all an extract, taken from
years of thought in the lonely study and the public libraries. If I commit the wrong I have
spoken of, it is under protest against myself.
Every word of this Essay deserves careful reading. But here are a few sentences I have
selected for the reader's consideration : —

" There are books ; and it is practicable to read
them because they are so few. —

" I visit occasionally the Cambridge Library, and
I can seldom go there without renewing the conviction that the best of it all is already within the four
walls of my study at home. —

" The three practical rules which I have to offer
are, 1. Never read any book that is not a year old.
2. Never read any but famed books. 3. Never
read any but what you like, or, in Shakspeare's
phrase, —

17

" 'No profit goes where is no pleasure ta'en ;
    In brief, Sir, study what you most affect.' "

Emerson has a good deal to say about conversation in his Essay on " Clubs," but nothing very
notable on the special subject of the Essay.
Perhaps his diary would have something of interest with reference to the " Saturday Club," of
which he was a member, which, in fact, formed
itself around him as a nucleus, and which he attended very regularly. But he was not given to
personalities, and among the men of genius and
of talent whom he met there no one was quieter,
but none saw and heard and remembered more.
He was hardly what Dr. Johnson would have
called a " clubable " man, yet he enjoyed the
meetings in his still way, or he would never have
come from Concord so regularly to attend them.
He gives two good reasons for the existence of a
club like that of which I have been speaking : —

" I need only hint the value of the club for bringing masters in their several arts to compare and
expand their views, to come to an understanding on
these points, and so that their united opinion shall
have its just influence on public questions of education and politics."

" A principal purpose also is the hospitality of the
club, as a means of receiving a worthy foreigner with
mutual advantage."

I do not think " public questions of education

and politics" were very prominent at the social meetings of the "Saturday Club," but "worthy foreigners," and now and then one not so worthy, added variety to the meetings of the company, which included a wide range of talents and callings.

All that Emerson has to say about "Courage" is worth listening to, for he was a truly brave man in that sphere of action where there are more cowards than are found in the battle-field. He spoke his convictions fearlessly; he carried the spear of Ithuriel, but he wore no breastplate save that which protects him

> "Whose armor is his honest thought,
>   And simple truth his utmost skill."

He mentions three qualities as attracting the wonder and reverence of mankind: 1. Disinterestedness; 2. Practical Power; 3. Courage. "I need not show how much it is esteemed, for the people give it the first rank. They forgive everything to it. And any man who puts his life in peril in a cause which is esteemed becomes the darling of all men." — There are good and inspiriting lessons for young and old in this Essay or Lecture, which closes with the spirited ballad of "George Nidiver," written "by a lady to whom all the particulars of the fact are exactly known."

Men will read any essay or listen to any lecture which has for its subject, like the one now before me, "Success." Emerson complains of the same things in America which Carlyle groaned over in England : —

"We countenance each other in this life of show, puffing advertisement, and manufacture of public opinion ; and excellence is lost sight of in the hunger for sudden performance and praise. —

"Now, though I am by no means sure that the reader will assent to all my propositions, yet I think we shall agree in my first rule for success, — that we shall drop the brag and the advertisement and take Michael Angelo's course, ' to confide in one's self and be something of worth and value.' "

Reading about "Success" is after all very much like reading in old books of alchemy. "How not to do it," is the lesson of all the books and treatises. Geber and Albertus Magnus, Roger Bacon and Raymond Lully, and the whole crew of "pauperes alcumistæ," all give the most elaborate directions showing their student how to fail in transmuting Saturn into Luna and Sol and making a billionaire of himself. "Success" in its vulgar sense, — the gaining of money and position, — is not to be reached by following the rules of an instructor. Our "self-made men," who govern the country by their wealth and influence, have found their place by

adapting themselves to the particular circumstances in which they were placed, and not by
studying the broad maxims of " Poor Richard,"
or any other moralist or economist. — For such
as these is meant the cheap cynical saying quoted
by Emerson, "*Rien ne réussit mieux que le
succès.*"

But this is not the aim and end of Emerson's
teaching: —

"I fear the popular notion of success stands in
direct opposition in all points to the real and wholesome success. One adores public opinion, the other
private opinion; one fame, the other desert; one
feats, the other humility; one lucre, the other love;
one monopoly, and the other hospitality of mind."

And so, though there is no alchemy in this
Lecture, it is profitable reading, assigning its
true value to the sterling gold of character, the
gaining of which is true success, as against the
brazen idol of the market-place.

The Essay on " Old Age " has a special value
from its containing two personal reminiscences:
one of the venerable Josiah Quincy, a brief
mention; the other the detailed record of a visit
in the year 1825, Emerson being then twenty-
two years old, to ex-President John Adams, soon
after the election of his son to the Presidency.
It is enough to allude to these, which every
reader will naturally turn to first of all.

But many thoughts worth gathering are dropped along these pages. He recounts the benefits of age ; the perilous capes and shoals it has weathered ; the fact that a success more or less signifies little, so that the old man may go below his own mark with impunity ; the feeling that he has found expression, — that his condition, in particular and in general, allows the utterance of his mind ; the pleasure of completing his secular affairs, leaving all in the best posture for the future : —

"When life has been well spent, age is a loss of what it can well spare, muscular strength, organic instincts, gross bulk, and works that belong to these. But the central wisdom which was old in infancy is young in fourscore years, and dropping off obstructions, leaves in happy subjects the mind purified and wise. I have heard that whoever loves is in no condition old. I have heard that whenever the name of man is spoken, the doctrine of immortality is announced ; it cleaves to his constitution. The mode of it baffles our wit, and no whisper comes to us from the other side. But the inference from the working of intellect, hiving knowledge, hiving skill, — at the end of life just ready to be born, — affirms the inspirations of affection and of the moral sentiment."

Other literary labors of Emerson during this period were the Introduction to "Plutarch's Morals" in 1870, and a Preface to William El-

lery Channing's Poem, "The Wanderer," in
1871. He made a speech at Howard University,
Washington, in 1872.

In the year 1871 Emerson made a visit to
California with a very pleasant company, concerning which Mr. John M. Forbes, one of whose
sons married Emerson's daughter Edith, writes
to me as follows. Professor James B. Thayer, to
whom he refers, has more recently written and
published an account of this trip, from which
some extracts will follow Mr. Forbes's letter: —

BOSTON, *February* 6, 1884.

MY DEAR DR., — What little I can give will be
of a very rambling character.

One of the first memories of Emerson which comes
up is my meeting him on the steamboat at returning
from Detroit East. I persuaded him to stop over at
Niagara, which he had never seen. We took a carriage and drove around the circuit. It was in early
summer, perhaps in 1848 or 1849. When we came
to Table Rock on the British side, our driver took us
down on the outer part of the rock in the carriage.
We passed on by rail, and the next day's papers
brought us the telegraphic news that Table Rock had
fallen over; perhaps we were among the last persons
on it!

About 1871 I made up a party for California, including Mr. Emerson, his daughter Edith, and a
number of gay young people. We drove with B——,
the famous Vermont coachman, up to the Geysers,

and then made the journey to the Yosemite Valley by wagon and on horseback. I wish I could give you more than a mere outline picture of the sage at this time. With the thermometer at 100° he would sometimes drive with the buffalo robes drawn up over his knees, apparently indifferent to the weather, gazing on the new and grand scenes of mountain and valley through which we journeyed. I especially remember once, when riding down the steep side of a mountain, his reins hanging loose, the bit entirely out of the horse's mouth, without his being aware that this was an unusual method of riding Pegasus, so fixed was his gaze into space, and so unconscious was he, at the moment, of his surroundings.

In San Francisco he visited with us the dens of the opium smokers, in damp cellars, with rows of shelves around, on which were deposited the stupefied Mongolians; perhaps the lowest haunts of humanity to be found in the world. The contrast between them and the serene eye and undisturbed brow of the sage was a sight for all beholders.

When we reached Salt Lake City on our way home he made a point of calling on Brigham Young, then at the summit of his power. The Prophet, or whatever he was called, was a burly, bull-necked man of hard sense, really leading a great industrial army. He did not seem to appreciate who his visitor was, at any rate gave no sign of so doing, and the chief interest of the scene was the wide contrast between these leaders of spiritual and of material forces.

I regret not having kept any notes of what was

said on this and other occasions, but if by chance you could get hold of Professor J. B. Thayer, who was one of our party, he could no doubt give you some notes that would be valuable.

Perhaps the latest picture that remains in my mind of our friend is his wandering along the beaches and under the trees at Naushon, no doubt carrying home large stealings from my domain there, which lost none of their value from being transferred to his pages. Next to his private readings which he gave us there, the most notable recollection is that of his intense amusement at some comical songs which our young people used to sing, developing a sense of humor which a superficial observer would hardly have discovered, but which you and I know he possessed in a marked degree.

Yours always,
J. M. FORBES.

Professor James B. Thayer's little book, " A Western Journey with Mr. Emerson," is a very entertaining account of the same trip concerning which Mr. Forbes wrote the letter just given. Professor Thayer kindly read many of his notes to me before his account was published, and allows me to make such use of the book as I see fit. Such liberty must not be abused, and I will content myself with a few passages in which Emerson has a part. No extract will interest the reader more than the following : —

" ' How *can* Mr. Emerson,' said one of the younger

members of the party to me that day, 'be so agreeable, all the time, without getting tired!' It was the *naive* expression of what we all had felt. There was never a more agreeable travelling companion; he was always accessible, cheerful, sympathetic, considerate, tolerant; and there was always that same respectful interest in those with whom he talked, even the humblest, which raised them in their own estimation. One thing particularly impressed me, — the sense that he seemed to have of a certain great amplitude of time and leisure. It was the behavior of one who really *believed* in an immortal life, and had adjusted his conduct accordingly; so that, beautiful and grand as the natural objects were, among which our journey lay, they were matched by the sweet elevation of character, and the spiritual charm of our gracious friend. Years afterwards, on that memorable day of his funeral at Concord, I found that a sentence from his own Essay on Immortality haunted my mind, and kept repeating itself all the day long; it seemed to point to the sources of his power: 'Meantime the true disciples saw through the letter the doctrine of eternity, which dissolved the poor corpse, and Nature also, and gave grandeur to the passing hour.'"

This extract will be appropriately followed by another alluding to the same subject.

"The next evening, Sunday, the twenty-third, Mr. Emerson read his address on 'Immortality,' at Dr. Stebbins's church. It was the first time that he had spoken on the Western coast; never did he speak better. It was, in the main, the same noble Essay that has since been printed.

"At breakfast the next morning we had the news-paper, the 'Alta California.' It gave a meagre out-line of the address, but praised it warmly, and closed with the following observations: 'All left the church feeling that an elegant tribute had been paid to the creative genius of the Great First Cause, and that a masterly use of the English language had contributed to that end.'"

The story used to be told that after the Reverend Horace Holley had delivered a prayer on some public occasion, Major Ben. Russell, of ruddy face and ruffled shirt memory, Editor of "The Columbian Centinel," spoke of it in his paper the next day as "the most eloquent prayer ever addressed to a Boston audience."

The "Alta California's" "elegant tribute" is not quite up to this rhetorical altitude.

"'The minister,' said he, 'is in no danger of losing his position; he represents the moral sense and the humanities.' He spoke of his own reasons for leaving the pulpit, and added that 'some one had lately come to him whose conscience troubled him about retaining the name of Christian; he had replied that he him-self had no difficulty about it. When he was called a Platonist, or a Christian, or a Republican, he wel-comed it. It did not bind him to what he did not like. What is the use of going about and setting up a flag of negation?'"

"I made bold to ask him what he had in mind in naming his recent course of lectures at Cambridge, 'The Natural History of the Intellect.' This opened a very interesting conversation; but, alas! I could recall but little of it, — little more than the mere hintings of what he said. He cared very little for metaphysics. But he thought that as a man grows he observes certain facts about his own mind, — about memory, for example These he had set down from time to time. As for making any methodical history, he did not undertake it."

Emerson met Brigham Young at Salt Lake City, as has been mentioned, but neither seems to have made much impression upon the other. Emerson spoke of the Mormons. Some one had said, "They impress the common people, through their imagination, by Bible-names and imagery." "Yes," he said, "it is an after-clap of Puritanism. But one would think that after this Father Abraham could go no further."

The charm of Boswell's Life of Johnson is that it not merely records his admirable conversation, but also gives us many of those lesser peculiarities which are as necessary to a true biography as lights and shades to a portrait on canvas. We are much obliged to Professor Thayer therefore for the two following pleasant recollections which he has been good-natured enough to preserve for us, and with which we will take leave of his agreeable little volume : —

"At breakfast we had, among other things, pie. This article at breakfast was one of Mr. Emerson's weaknesses. A pie stood before him now. He offered to help somebody from it, who declined ; and then one or two others, who also declined ; and then Mr. —— ; he too declined. 'But Mr. —— !' Mr. Emerson remonstrated, with humorous emphasis, thrusting the knife under a piece of the pie, and putting the entire weight of his character into his manner, — 'but Mr. ——, *what is pie for?*'"

A near friend of mine, a lady, was once in the cars with Emerson, and when they stopped for the refreshment of the passengers he was very desirous of procuring something at the station for her solace. Presently he advanced upon her with a cup of tea in one hand and a wedge of pie in the other, — such a wedge ! She could hardly have been more dismayed if one of Cæsar's *cunei*, or wedges of soldiers, had made a charge against her.

Yet let me say here that pie, often foolishly abused, is a good creature, at the right time and in angles of thirty or forty degrees. In semicircles and quadrants it may sometimes prove too much for delicate stomachs. But here was Emerson, a hopelessly confirmed pie-eater, never, so far as I remember, complaining of dyspepsia ;

and there, on the other side, was Carlyle, feeding largely on wholesome oatmeal, groaning with indigestion all his days, and living with half his self-consciousness habitually centred beneath his diaphragm.

Like his friend Carlyle and like Tennyson, Emerson had a liking for a whiff of tobacco-smoke : —

" When alone," he said, " he rarely cared to finish a whole cigar. But in company it was singular to see how different it was. To one who found it difficult to meet people, as he did, the effect of a cigar was agreeable ; one who is smoking may be as silent as he likes, and yet be good company. And so Hawthorne used to say that he found it. On this journey Mr. Emerson generally smoked a single cigar after our mid-day dinner, or after tea, and occasionally after both. This was multiplying, several times over, anything that was usual with him at home."

Professor Thayer adds in a note : —

" Like Milton, Mr. Emerson 'was extraordinary temperate in his Diet,' and he used even less tobacco. Milton's quiet day seems to have closed regularly with a pipe ; he 'supped,' we are told, 'upon . . . some light thing ; and after a pipe of tobacco and a glass of water went to bed.'"

As Emerson's name has been connected with that of Milton in its nobler aspects, it can do no harm to contemplate him, like Milton, indulging in this semi-philosophical luxury.

One morning in July, 1872, Mr. and Mrs. Emerson woke to find their room filled with smoke and fire coming through the floor of a closet in the room over them. The alarm was given, and the neighbors gathered and did their best to put out the flames, but the upper part of the house was destroyed, and with it were burned many papers of value to Emerson, including his father's sermons. Emerson got wet and chilled, and it seems too probable that the shock hastened that gradual loss of memory which came over his declining years.

His kind neighbors did all they could to save his property and relieve his temporary needs. A study was made ready for him in the old Court House, and the "Old Manse," which had sheltered his grandfather, and others nearest to him, received him once more as its tenant.

On the 15th of October he spoke at a dinner given in New York in honor of James Anthony Froude, the historian, and in the course of this same month he set out on his third visit to Europe, accompanied by his daughter Ellen. We have little to record of this visit, which was suggested as a relief and recreation while his home was being refitted for him. He went to Egypt, but so far as I have learned the Sphinx had no message for him, and in the state of mind in which he found himself upon the mysterious and dream-compelling Nile it may be suspected that the landscape with its palms and pyramids was an unreal vision, — that, as to his Humble-bee,

"All was picture as he passed."

But while he was voyaging his friends had not forgotten him. The sympathy with him in his misfortune was general and profound. It did not confine itself to expressions of feeling, but a spontaneous movement organized itself almost without effort. If any such had been needed, the attached friend whose name is appended to the Address to the Subscribers to the Fund for rebuilding Mr. Emerson's house would have been as energetic in this new cause as he had been in the matter of procuring the reprint of "Sartor Resartus." I have his kind permission to publish the whole correspondence relating to the friendly project so happily carried out.

To the Subscribers to the Fund for the Rebuilding of Mr. Emerson's House, after the Fire of July 24, 1872 :

The death of Mr. Emerson has removed any objection which may have before existed to the printing of the following correspondence. I have now caused this to be done, that each subscriber may have the satisfaction of possessing a copy of the touching and affectionate letters in which he expressed his delight in this, to him, most unexpected demonstration of personal regard and attachment, in the offer to restore for him his ruined home.

No enterprise of the kind was ever more fortunate and successful in its purpose and in its results. The prompt and cordial response to the proposed subscription was most gratifying. No contribution was solicited from any one. The simple suggestion to a few friends of Mr. Emerson that an opportunity was now offered to be of service to him was all that was needed. From the first day on which it was made, the day after the fire, letters began to come in, with cheques for large and small amounts, so that in less than three weeks I was enabled to send to Judge Hoar the sum named in his letter as received by him on the 13th of August, and presented by him to Mr. Emerson the next morning, at the Old Manse, with fitting words.

Other subscriptions were afterwards received, increasing the amount on my book to eleven thousand six hundred and twenty dollars. A part of this was handed directly to the builder at Concord. The balance was sent to Mr. Emerson October 7, and acknowledged by him in his letter of October 8, 1872.

All the friends of Mr. Emerson who knew of the plan which was proposed to rebuild his house, seemed to feel that it was a privilege to be allowed to express in this way the love and veneration with which he was regarded, and the deep debt of gratitude which they owed to him, and there is no doubt that a much

18

larger amount would have been readily and gladly offered, if it had been required, for the object in view.

Those who have had the happiness to join in this friendly " conspiracy " may well take pleasure in the thought that what they have done has had the effect to lighten the load of care and anxiety which the calamity of the fire brought with it to Mr. Emerson, and thus perhaps to prolong for some precious years the serene and noble life that was so dear to all of us.

My thanks are due to the friends who have made me the bearer of this message of good-will.

LE BARON RUSSELL.
BOSTON, *May* 8, 1882.

BOSTON, *August* 13, 1872.
DEAR MR. EMERSON:

It seems to have been the spontaneous desire of your friends, on hearing of the burning of your house, to be allowed the pleasure of rebuilding it.

A few of them have united for this object, and now request your acceptance of the amount which I have to-day deposited to your order at the Concord Bank, through the kindness of our friend, Judge Hoar. They trust that you will receive it as an expression of sincere regard and affection from friends, who will, one and all, esteem it a great privilege to be permitted to assist in the restoration of your home.

And if, in their eagerness to participate in so grateful a work, they may have exceeded the estimate of your architect as to what is required for that purpose, they beg that you will devote the remainder to such other objects as may be most convenient to you.

> Very sincerely yours,
> LE BARON RUSSELL.

CONCORD, *August* 14, 1872.

DR. LE B. RUSSELL:

Dear Sir,—I received your letters, with the check for ten thousand dollars inclosed, from Mr. Barrett last evening. This morning I deposited it to Mr. Emerson's credit in the Concord National Bank, and took a bank book for him, with his little balance entered at the top, and this following, and carried it to him with your letter. I told him, by way of prelude, that some of his friends had made him treasurer of an association who wished him to go to England and examine Warwick Castle and other noted houses that had been recently injured by fire, in order to get the best ideas possible for restoration, and then to apply them to a house which the association was formed to restore in this neighborhood.

When he understood the thing and had read your letter, he seemed very deeply moved. He said that he had been allowed so far in life to stand on his own feet, and that he hardly knew what to say,— that the kindness of his friends was very great. I said what I thought was best in reply, and told him that this was the spontaneous act of friends, who wished the privilege of expressing in this way their respect and affection, and was done only by those who thought it a privilege to do so. I mentioned Hillard as you desired, and also Mrs. Tappan, who, it seems, had written to him and offered any assistance he might need, to the extent of five thousand dollars, personally.

I think it is all right, but he said he must see the list of contributors, and would then say what he had to say about it. He told me that Mr. F. C. Lowell, who was his classmate and old friend, Mr. Bangs, Mrs. Gurney, and a few other friends, had already sent him five thousand dollars, which he seemed to think was as much as he could bear. This makes the whole a very gratifying result, and perhaps explains the absence of some names on your book.

I am glad that Mr. Emerson, who is feeble and ill, can learn what a debt of obligation his friends feel to him, and thank you heartily for what you have done about it.   Very truly yours,

E. R. HOAR.

CONCORD, *August* 16, 1872.

MY DEAR LE BARON:

I have wondered and melted over your letter and its accompaniments till it is high time that I should reply to it, if I can. My misfortunes, as I have lived along so far in this world, have been so few that I have never needed to ask direct aid of the host of good men and women who have cheered my life, though many a gift has come to me. And this late calamity, however rude and devastating, soon began to look more wonderful in its salvages than in its ruins, so that I can hardly feel any right to this munificent endowment with which you, and my other friends through you, have astonished me. But I cannot read your letter or think of its message without delight, that my companions and friends bear me so noble a good-will, nor without some new aspirations in the old heart toward a better deserving. Judge Hoar has, up to this time, withheld from me the names of my benefactors, but you may be sure that I shall not rest till I have learned them, every one, to repeat to myself at night and at morning.

Your affectionate friend and debtor,

R. W. EMERSON.

DR. LE BARON RUSSELL

CONCORD, *October* 8, 1872.

MY DEAR DOCTOR LE BARON :

I received last night your two notes, and the cheque, enclosed in one of them, for one thousand and twenty dollars.

Are my friends bent on killing me with kindness ? No, you will say, but to make me live longer. I thought myself sufficiently loaded with benefits already, and you add more and more. It appears that you all will rebuild my house and rejuvenate me by sending me in my old days abroad on a young man's excursion.

I am a lover of men, but this recent wonderful experience of their tenderness surprises and occupies my thoughts day by day. Now that I have all or almost all the names of the men and women who have conspired in this kindness to me (some of whom I have never personally known), I please myself with the thought of meeting each and asking, Why have we not met before? Why have you not told me that we thought alike? Life is not so long, nor sympathy of thought so common, that we can spare the society of those with whom we best agree. Well, 't is probably my own fault by sticking ever to my solitude. Perhaps it is not too late to learn of these friends a better lesson.

Thank them for me whenever you meet them, and say to them that I am not wood or stone, if I have not yet trusted myself so far as to go to each one of them directly.

My wife insists that I shall also send her acknowledgments to them and you.

Yours and theirs affectionately,

R. W. EMERSON.

Dr. LE BARON RUSSELL.

The following are the names of the subscribers to the fund for rebuilding Mr. Emerson's house: —

Mrs. Anne S. Hooper.
Miss Alice S. Hooper.
Mrs. Caroline Tappan.
Miss Ellen S. Tappan.
Miss Mary A. Tappan.
Mr. T. G. Appleton.
Mrs. Henry Edwards.
Miss Susan E. Dorr.
Misses Wigglesworth.
Mr. Edward Wigglesworth.
Mr. J. Elliot Cabot.
Mrs. Sarah S. Russell.

Friends in New York and Philadelphia, through Mr. Williams.
Mr. William Whiting.
Mr. Frederick Beck.
Mr. H. P. Kidder.
Mrs. Abel Adams.
Mrs. George Faulkner.
Hon. E. R. Hoar.
Mr. James B. Thayer.
Mr. John M. Forbes.
Mr. James H. Beal.

Mrs. Anna C. Lodge.
Mr. H. H. Hunnewell.
Mr. James A. Dupee.
Mrs. M. F. Sayles.
J. R. Osgood & Co.
Mr. Francis Geo. Shaw.
Mr. William P. Mason.
Mr. Sam'l G. Ward.
Mr. Geo. C. Ward.
Mr. John E. Williams.

Mr. T. Jefferson Coolidge.
Mrs. S. Cabot.
Mrs. Anna C. Lowell.
Miss Helen L. Appleton.
Mr. Richard Soule.
Dr. R. W. Hooper.
Mr. William Gray.
Mr. J. I. Bowditch.
Mrs. Lucia J. Briggs.
Dr. Le Baron Russell.

In May, 1873, Emerson returned to Concord. His friends and fellow-citizens received him with every token of affection and reverence. A set of signals was arranged to announce his arrival. Carriages were in readiness for him and his family, a band greeted him with music, and passing under a triumphal arch, he was driven to his renewed old home amidst the welcomes and the blessings of his loving and admiring friends and neighbors.

CHAPTER XII.

1873-1878. ÆT. 70-75.

Publication of "Parnassus." — Emerson Nominated as Candi-
date for the Office of Lord Rector of Glasgow University. —
Publication of "Letters and Social Aims." Contents :
Poetry and Imagination. — Social Aims. — Eloquence. —
Resources. — The Comic. — Quotation and Originality. —
Progress of Culture. — Persian Poetry. — Inspiration. —
Greatness. — Immortality. — Address at the Unveiling of
the Statue of "The Minute-Man" at Concord.—Publication
of Collected Poems.

In December, 1874, Emerson published "Par-
nassus," a Collection of Poems by British and
American authors. Many readers may like to see
his subdivisions and arrangement of the pieces
he has brought together. They are as follows :
"Nature." — "Human Life." — "Intellectual."
— "Contemplation." — "Moral and Religious."
— "Heroic." — "Personal." — "Pictures." —
"Narrative Poems and Ballads." — "Songs." —
"Dirges and Pathetic Poems." — "Comic and
Humorous." — "Poetry of Terror." — "Oracles
and Counsels."

I have borrowed so sparingly from the rich
mine of Mr. George Willis Cooke's "Ralph

Waldo Emerson, His Life, Writings, and Philosophy," that I am pleased to pay him the respectful tribute of taking a leaf from his excellent work.

"This collection," he says,

"was the result of his habit, pursued for many years, of copying into his commonplace book any poem which specially pleased him. Many of these favorites had been read to illustrate his lectures on the English poets. The book has no worthless selections, almost everything it contains bearing the stamp of genius and worth. Yet Emerson's personality is seen in its many intellectual and serious poems, and in the small number of its purely religious selections. With two or three exceptions he copies none of those devotional poems which have attracted devout souls. — His poetical sympathies are shown in the fact that one third of the selections are from the seventeenth century. Shakespeare is drawn on more largely than any other, no less than eighty-eight selections being made from him. The names of George Herbert, Herrick, Ben Jonson, and Milton frequently appear. Wordsworth appears forty-three times, and stands next to Shakespeare; while Burns, Byron, Scott, Tennyson, and Chaucer make up the list of favorites. Many little known pieces are included, and some whose merit is other than poetical. — This selection of poems is eminently that of a poet of keen intellectual tastes. It is not popular in character, omitting many public favorites, and introducing very much which can never be acceptable to the general reader. The Preface is full of interest for its comments on many of the poems and poets appearing in these selections."   .

I will only add to Mr. Cooke's criticism these two remarks : First, that I have found it impossible to know under which of his divisions to look for many of the poems I was in search of ; and as, in the earlier copies at least, there was no paged index where each author's pieces were collected together, one had to hunt up his fragments with no little loss of time and patience, under various heads, " imitating the careful search that Isis made for the mangled body of Osiris." The other remark is that each one of Emerson's American fellow-poets from whom he has quoted would gladly have spared almost any of the extracts from the poems of his brother-bards, if the editor would only have favored us with some specimens of his own poetry, with a single line of which he has not seen fit to indulge us.

In 1874 Emerson received the nomination by the independent party among the students of Glasgow University for the office of Lord Rector. He received five hundred votes against seven hundred for Disraeli, who was elected. He says in a letter to Dr. J. Hutchinson Sterling : —

" I count that vote as quite the fairest laurel that has ever fallen on me ; and I cannot but feel deeply grateful to my young friends in the University, and to yourself, who have been my counsellor and my too partial advocate."

Mr. Cabot informs us in his Prefatory Note to "Letters and Social Aims," that the proof sheets of this volume, now forming the eighth of the collected works, showed even before the burning of his house and the illness which followed from the shock, that his loss of memory and of mental grasp was such as to make it unlikely that he would in any case have been able to accomplish what he had undertaken. Sentences, even whole pages, were repeated, and there was a want of order beyond what even he would have tolerated : —

"There is nothing here that he did not write, and he gave his full approval to whatever was done in the way of selection and arrangement; but I cannot say that he applied his mind very closely to the matter."

This volume contains eleven Essays, the subjects of which, as just enumerated, are very various. The longest and most elaborate paper is that entitled "Poetry and Imagination." I have room for little more than the enumeration of the different headings of this long Essay. By these it will be seen how wide a ground it covers. They are "Introductory;" "Poetry;" "Imag-

ination ; " " Veracity ; " " Creation ; " " Melody,
Rhythm, Form ; " " Bards and Trouveurs ; "
" Morals ; " " Transcendency." Many thoughts
with which we are familiar are reproduced,
expanded, and illustrated in this Essay. Unity
in multiplicity, the symbolism of nature, and
others of his leading ideas appear in new phrases,
not unwelcome, for they look fresh in every re-
statement. It would be easy to select a score
of pointed sayings, striking images, large generalizations. Some of these we find repeated in
his verse. Thus : —

"Michael Angelo is largely filled with the Creator
that made and makes men. How much of the original
craft remains in him, and he a mortal man ! "

And so in the well remembered lines of " The
Problem " : —

"Himself from God he could not free."

" He knows that he did not make his thought, —
no, his thought made him, and made the sun and
stars."

"Art might obey but not surpass.
    The passive Master lent his hand
    To the vast soul that o'er him planned."

Hope is at the bottom of every Essay of
Emerson's as it was at the bottom of Pandora's
box : —

" I never doubt the riches of nature, the gifts of

the future, the immense wealth of the mind. O yes, poets we shall have, mythology, symbols, religion of our own.

— " Sooner or later that which is now life shall be poetry, and every fair and manly trait shall add a richer strain to the song."

Under the title " Social Aims " he gives some wise counsel concerning manners and conversation. One of these precepts will serve as a specimen — if we have met with it before it is none the worse for wear : —

" Shun the negative side. Never worry people with your contritions, nor with dismal views of politics or society. Never name sickness ; even if you could trust yourself on that perilous topic, beware of unmuzzling a valetudinarian, who will give you enough of it."

We have had one Essay on " Eloquence " already. One extract from this new discourse on the same subject must serve our turn : —

" These are ascending stairs, — a good voice, winning manners, plain speech, chastened, however, by the schools into correctness ; but we must come to the main matter, of power of statement, — know your fact ; hug your fact. For the essential thing is heat, and heat comes of sincerity. Speak what you know and believe ; and are personally in it ; and are answerable for every word. Eloquence is *the power to*

*translate a truth into language perfectly intelligible
to the person to whom you speak."*

The italics are Emerson's.

If our learned and excellent John Cotton used
to sweeten his mouth before going to bed with
a bit of Calvin, we may as wisely sweeten and
strengthen our sense of existence with a morsel or
two from Emerson's Essay on " Resources " : —

" A Schopenhauer, with logic and learning and wit,
teaching pessimism, — teaching that this is the worst
of all possible worlds, and inferring that sleep is better than waking, and death than sleep, — all the talent in the world cannot save him from being odious.
But if instead of these negatives you give me affirma-
tives; if you tell me that there is always life for the
living ; that what man has done man can do ; that
this world belongs to the energetic ; that there is always a way to everything desirable ; that every man
is provided, in the new bias of his faculty, with a key
to nature, and that man only rightly knows himself
as far as he has experimented on things, — I am in-
vigorated, put into genial and working temper ; the
horizon opens, and we are full of good-will and gratitude to the Cause of Causes."

The Essay or Lecture on " The Comic " may
have formed a part of a series he had contem-
plated on the intellectual processes. Two or three
sayings in it will show his view sufficiently : —

" The essence of all jokes, of all comedy, seems to

be an honest or well-intended halfness; a non-performance of what is pretended to be performed, at the same time that one is giving loud pledges of performance.

"If the essence of the Comic be the contrast in the intellect between the idea and the false performance, there is good reason why we should be affected by the exposure. We have no deeper interest than our integrity, and that we should be made aware by joke and by stroke of any lie we entertain. Besides, a perception of the comic seems to be a balance-wheel in our metaphysical structure. It appears to be an essential element in a fine character. — A rogue alive to the ludicrous is still convertible. If that sense is lost, his fellow-men can do little for him."

These and other sayings of like purport are illustrated by well-preserved stories and anecdotes not for the most part of very recent date.

"Quotation and Originality" furnishes the key to Emerson's workshop. He believed in quotation, and borrowed from everybody and every book. Not in any stealthy or shame-faced way, but proudly, royally, as a king borrows from one of his attendants the coin that bears his own image and superscription.

"All minds quote. Old and new make the warp and woof of every moment. There is no thread that is not a twist of these two strands. — We quote not only books and proverbs, but arts, sciences, religion, customs, and laws; nay, we quote temples and houses, tables and chairs by imitation. —

" The borrowing is often honest enough and comes of magnanimity and stoutness.   A great man quotes bravely, and will not draw on his invention when his memory serves him with a word as good.

" Next to the originator of a good sentence is the first quoter of it." —

— " The Progress of Culture," his second Phi Beta Kappa oration, has already been mentioned.

— The lesson of self-reliance, which he is never tired of inculcating, is repeated and enforced in the Essay on " Greatness."

" There are certain points of identity in which these masters agree.   Self-respect is the early form in which greatness appears. — Stick to your own ; don't inculpate yourself in the local, social, or national crime, but follow the path your genius traces like the galaxy of heaven for you to walk in.

" Every mind has a new compass, a new direction of its own, differencing its genius and aim from every other mind. — We call this specialty the *bias* of each individual.   And none of us will ever accomplish anything excellent or commanding except when he listens to this whisper which is heard by him alone."

If to follow this native bias is the first rule, the second is concentration. — To the bias of the individual mind must be added the most catholic receptivity for the genius of others.

"Shall I tell you the secret of the true scholar? It is this : Every man I meet is my master in some point, and in that I learn of him." —

" The man whom we have not seen, in whom no regard of self degraded the adorer of the laws, — who by governing himself governed others ; sportive in manner, but inexorable in act; who sees longevity in his cause; whose aim is always distinct to him ; who is suffered to be himself in society; who carries fate in his eye ; — he it is whom we seek, encouraged in every good hour that here or hereafter he shall be found."

What has Emerson to tell us of " Inspiration ? "

"I believe that nothing great or lasting can be done except by inspiration, by leaning on the secret augury. —

" How many sources of inspiration can we count ? As many as our affinities. But to a practical purpose we may reckon a few of these."

I will enumerate them briefly as he gives them, but not attempting to reproduce his comments on each : —

1. Health. 2. The experience of writing letters. 3. The renewed sensibility which comes after seasons of decay or eclipse of the faculties.

4. The power of the will. 5. Atmospheric causes, especially the influence of morning. 6. Solitary converse with nature. 7. Solitude of itself, like that of a country inn in summer, and of a city hotel in winter. 8. Conversation. 9. New poetry; by which, he says, he means chiefly old poetry that is new to the reader.

"Every book is good to read which sets the reader in a working mood."

What can promise more than an Essay by Emerson on "Immortality"? It is to be feared that many readers will transfer this note of interrogation to the Essay itself. What is the definite belief of Emerson as expressed in this discourse, — what does it mean? We must tack together such sentences as we can find that will stand for an answer : —

"I think all sound minds rest on a certain preliminary conviction, namely, that if it be best that conscious personal life, shall continue, it will continue; if not best, then it will not; and we, if we saw the whole, should of course see that it was better so."

This is laying the table for a Barmecide feast of nonentity, with the possibility of a real banquet to be provided for us. But he continues : —

"Schiller said, 'What is so universal as death must be benefit.'"

He tells us what Michael Angelo said, how

Plutarch felt, how Montesquieu thought about
the question, and then glances off from it to the
terror of the child at the thought of life without
end, to the story of the two skeptical statesmen
whose unsatisfied inquiry through a long course
of years he holds to be a better affirmative evidence than their failure to find a confirmation
was negative. He argues from our delight in
permanence, from the delicate contrivances and
adjustments of created things, that the contriver
cannot be forever hidden, and says at last
plainly : —

"Everything is prospective, and man is to live
hereafter. That the world is for his education is the
only sane solution of the enigma."

But turn over a few pages and we may
read : —

"I confess that everything connected with our
personality fails. Nature never spares the individual ;
we are always balked of a complete success ; no prosperity is promised to our self-esteem. We have our
indemnity only in the moral and intellectual reality
to which we aspire. That is immortal, and we only
through that. The soul stipulates for no private good.
That which is private I see not to be good. 'If truth
live, I live ; if justice live, I live,' said one of the old
saints, 'and these by any man's suffering are enlarged
and enthroned.'"

Once more we get a dissolving view of Emer-

son's creed, if such a word applies to a statement like the following : —

— " I mean that I am a better believer, and all
serious souls are better believers in the immortality
than we can give grounds for. The real evidence is
too subtle, or is higher than we can write down in
propositions, and therefore Wordsworth's 'Ode' is the
best modern essay on the subject."

Wordsworth's " Ode " is a noble and beautiful dream ; is it anything more ? The reader
who would finish this Essay, which I suspect to
belong to an early period of Emerson's development, must be prepared to plunge into mysticism
and lose himself at last in an Oriental apologue.
The eschatology which rests upon an English
poem and an Indian fable belongs to the realm
of reverie and of imagination rather than the
domain of reason.

On the 19th of April, 1875, the hundredth
anniversary of the " Fight at the Bridge," Emerson delivered a short Address at the unveiling
of the statue of " The Minute-Man," erected at
the place of the conflict, to commemorate the
event. This is the last Address he ever wrote,
though he delivered one or more after this date.
From the manuscript which lies before me I
extract a single passage : —

" In the year 1775 we had many enemies and

many friends in England, but our one benefactor was King George the Third. The time had arrived for the political severance of America, that it might play its part in the history of this globe, and the inscrutable divine Providence gave an insane king to England. In the resistance of the Colonies, he alone was immovable on the question of force. England was so dear to us that the Colonies could only be absolutely disunited by violence from England, and only one man could compel the resort to violence. Parliament wavered, Lord North wavered, all the ministers wavered, but the king had the insanity of one idea; he was immovable, he insisted on the impossible, so the army was sent, America was instantly united, and the Nation born."

There is certainly no mark of mental failure in this paragraph, written at a period when he had long ceased almost entirely from his literary labors.

Emerson's collected "Poems" constitute the ninth volume of the recent collected edition of his works. They will be considered in a following chapter.

CHAPTER XIII.

1878–1882. Æt. 75–79.

Last Literary Labors. — Addresses and Essays. — " Lectures
and Biographical Sketches." — " Miscellanies."

THE decline of Emerson's working faculties
went on gently and gradually, but he was not
condemned to entire inactivity. His faithful
daughter, Ellen, followed him with assiduous,
quiet, ever watchful care, aiding his failing memory, bringing order into the chaos of his manuscript, an echo before the voice whose words it
was to shape for him when his mind faltered
and needed a momentary impulse.

With her helpful presence and support he
ventured from time to time to read a paper be-
fore a select audience. Thus, March 30, 1878,
he delivered a Lecture in the Old South Church,
— " Fortune of the Republic." On the 5th of
May, 1879, he read a Lecture in the Chapel of
Divinity College, Harvard University, — " The
Preacher." In 1881 he read a paper on Carlyle
before the Massachusetts Historical Society. —
He also published a paper in the " North Amer-

ican Review," in 1878, — " The Sovereignty of
Ethics," and one on " Superlatives," in "The
Century" for February, 1882.

But in these years he was writing little or
nothing. All these papers were taken from
among his manuscripts of different dates. The
same thing is true of the volumes published
since his death ; they were only compilations
from his stores of unpublished matter, and their
arrangement was the work of Mr. Emerson's
friend and literary executor, Mr. Cabot. These
volumes cannot be considered as belonging to
any single period of his literary life.

Mr. Cabot prefixes to the tenth volume of
Emerson's collected works, which bears the title,
" Lectures and Biographical Sketches," the fol-
lowing : —

"NOTE.

" Of the pieces included in this volume the following, namely, those from ' The Dial,' ' Character,'
' Plutarch,' and the biographical sketches of Dr.
Ripley, of Mr. Hoar, and of Henry Thoreau, were
printed by Mr. Emerson before I took any part in
the arrangement of his papers. The rest, except the
sketch of Miss Mary Emerson, I got ready for his
use in readings to his friends, or to a limited public.
He had given up the regular practice of lecturing,
but would sometimes, upon special request, read a
paper that had been prepared for him from his manuscripts, in the manner described in the Preface to

' Letters and Social Aims,' — some former lecture serving as a nucleus for the new. Some of these papers he afterwards allowed to be printed ; others, namely, 'Aristocracy,' ' Education,' 'The Man of Letters,' 'The Scholar,' 'Historic Notes of Life and Letters in New England,' 'Mary Moody Emerson,' are now published for the first time."

Some of these papers I have already had occasion to refer to. From several of the others I will make one or two extracts, — a difficult task, so closely are the thoughts packed together. From " Demonology " : —

" I say to the table-rappers

'I will believe
Thou wilt not utter what thou dost not know,'
And so far will I trust thee, gentle Kate ! "

" Meantime far be from me the impatience which cannot brook the supernatural, the vast ; far be from me the lust of explaining away all which appeals to the imagination, and the great presentiments which haunt us. Willingly I too say Hail ! to the unknown, awful powers which transcend the ken of the understanding."

I will not quote anything from the Essay called " Aristocracy." But let him who wishes to know what the word means to an American whose life has come from New England soil, whose ancestors have breathed New England air for many generations, read it, and he will find a new interpretation of a very old and often greatly wronged appellation.

"Perpetual Forces" is one of those prose poems, — of his earlier epoch, I have no doubt, — in which he plays with the facts of science with singular grace and freedom.

What man could speak more fitly, with more authority of "Character," than Emerson? When he says, "If all things are taken away, I have still all things in my relation to the Eternal," we feel that such an utterance is as natural to his pure spirit as breathing to the frame in which it was imprisoned.

We have had a glimpse of Emerson as a school-master, but behind and far above the teaching drill-master's desk is the chair from which he speaks to us of "Education." Compare the short and easy method of the wise man of old, — "He that spareth his rod hateth his son," with this other, "Be the companion of his thought, the friend of his friendship, the lover of his virtue, — but no kinsman of his sin."

"The Superlative" will prove light and pleasant reading after these graver essays. Μηδὲν ἄγαν, — *ne quid nimis*, — nothing in excess, was his precept as to adjectives.

Two sentences from "The Sovereignty of Ethics" will go far towards reconciling elderly readers who have not forgotten the Westminster Assembly's Catechism with this sweet-souled dealer in spiritual dynamite : —

" Luther would cut his hand off sooner than write theses against the pope if he suspected that he was bringing on with all his might the pale negations of Boston Unitarianism. —

" If I miss the inspiration of the saints of Calvinism, or of Platonism, or of Buddhism, our times are not up to theirs, or, more truly, have not yet their own legitimate force."

So, too, this from " The Preacher " : —

" All civil mankind have agreed in leaving one day for contemplation against six for practice. I hope that day will keep its honor and its use. — The Sabbath changes its forms from age to age, but the substantial benefit endures."

The special interest of the Address called " The Man of Letters " is, that it was delivered during the war. He was no advocate for peace where great principles were at the bottom of the conflict : —

" War, seeking for the roots of strength, comes upon the moral aspects at once. — War ennobles the age. — Battle, with the sword, has cut many a Gordian knot in twain which all the wit of East and West, of Northern and Border statesmen could not untie."

" The Scholar " was delivered before two
Societies at the University of Virginia so late as
the year 1876. If I must select any of its wise
words, I will choose the questions which he has
himself italicized to show his sense of their importance : —

"For all men, all women, Time, your country, your
condition, the invisible world are the interrogators :
*Who are you? What do you? Can you obtain
what you wish? Is there method in your consciousness? Can you see tendency in your life? Can
you help any soul?*

" Can he answer these questions ? Can he dispose
of them ? Happy if you can answer them mutely in
the order and disposition of your life ! Happy for
more than yourself, a benefactor of men, if you can
answer them in works of wisdom, art, or poetry ;
bestowing on the general mind of men organic cre-
ations, to be the guidance and delight of all who know
them."

The Essay on " Plutarch " has a peculiar value
from the fact that Emerson owes more to him
than to any other author except Plato, who is
one of the only two writers quoted oftener than
Plutarch. *Mutato nomine*, the portrait which
Emerson draws of the Greek moralist might
stand for his own : —

" Whatever is eminent in fact or in fiction, in
opinion, in character, in institutions, in science —

natural, moral, or metaphysical, or in memorable sayings drew his attention and came to his pen with more or less fulness of record.

"A poet in verse or prose must have a sensuous eye, but an intellectual co-perception. Plutarch's memory is full and his horizon wide. Nothing touches man but he feels to be his.

" Plutarch had a religion which Montaigne wanted, and which defends him from wantonness ; and though Plutarch is as plain spoken, his moral sentiment is always pure. —

" I do not know where to find a book — to borrow a phrase of Ben Jonson's — 'so rammed with life,' and this in chapters chiefly ethical, which are so prone to be heavy and sentimental. — His vivacity and abundance never leave him to loiter or pound on an incident. —

"In his immense quotation and allusion we quickly cease to discriminate between what he quotes and what he invents. — 'T is all Plutarch, by right of eminent domain, and all property vests in this emperor.

"It is in consequence of this poetic trait in his mind, that I confess that, in reading him, I embrace the particulars, and carry a faint memory of the argument or general design of the chapter ; but he is not less welcome, and he leaves the reader with a relish and a necessity for completing his studies.

" He is a pronounced idealist, who does not hesitate to say, like another Berkeley, 'Matter is itself privation.' —

"Of philosophy he is more interested in the results

than in the method. He has a just instinct of the presence of a master, and prefers to sit as a scholar with Plato than as a disputant.

" His natural history is that of a lover and poet, and not of a physicist.

" But though curious in the questions of the schools on the nature and genesis of things, his extreme interest in every trait of character, and his broad humanity, lead him constantly to Morals, to the study of the Beautiful and Good. Hence his love of heroes, his rule of life, and his clear convictions of the high destiny of the soul. La Harpe said that ' Plutarch is the genius the most naturally moral that ever existed.'

" Plutarch thought ' truth to be the greatest good that man can receive, and the goodliest blessing that God can give.'

" All his judgments are noble. He thought with Epicurus that it is more delightful to do than to receive a kindness.

" Plutarch was well-born, well-conditioned — eminently social, he was a king in his own house, surrounded himself with select friends, and knew the high value of good conversation. —

" He had that universal sympathy with genius which makes all its victories his own ; though he never used verse, he had many qualities of the poet in the power of his imagination, the speed of his mental associations, and his sharp, objective eyes. But what specially marks him, he is a chief example of the illumination of the intellect by the force of morals."

How much of all this would have been recognized as just and true if it had been set down in
an obituary notice of Emerson!

I have already made use of several of the other
papers contained in this volume, and will merely
enumerate all that follow the " Plutarch." Some
of the titles will be sure to attract the reader.
They are "Historic Notes of Life and Letters in
New England;" "The Chardon Street Convention;" "Ezra Ripley, D. D.;" "Mary Moody
Emerson;" "Samuel Hoar;" "Thoreau;"
"Carlyle." —

Mr. Cabot prefaces the eleventh and last
volume of Emerson's writings with the following "Note": —

"The first five pieces in this volume, and the
'Editorial Address' from the 'Massachusetts Quarterly Review,' were published by Mr. Emerson long
ago. The speeches at the John Brown, the Walter
Scott, and the Free Religious Association meetings
were published at the time, no doubt with his consent,
but without any active co-operation on his part. The
'Fortune of the Republic' appeared separately in
1879; the rest have never been published. In none
was any change from the original form made by me,
except in the 'Fortune of the Republic,' which was
made up of several lectures for the occasion upon
which it was read."

The volume of "Miscellanies" contains no less than twenty - three pieces of very various lengths and relating to many different subjects. The five referred to as having been previously published are, "The Lord's Supper," the "Historical Discourse in Concord," the "Address at the Dedication of the Soldiers' Monument in Concord," the "Address on Emancipation in the British West Indies," and the Lecture or Essay on "War," — all of which have been already spoken of.

Next in order comes a Lecture on the "Fugitive Slave Law." Emerson says, "I do not often speak on public questions. — My own habitual view is to the well-being of scholars." But he leaves his studies to attack the institution of slavery, from which he says he himself has never suffered any inconvenience, and the "Law," which the abolitionists would always call the "Fugitive Slave *Bill.*" Emerson had a great admiration for Mr. Webster, but he did not spare him as he recalled his speech of the seventh of March, just four years before the delivery of this Lecture. He warns against false leadership : —

"To make good the cause of Freedom, you must draw off from all foolish trust in others. — He only who is able to stand alone is qualified for society. And that I understand to be the end for which a soul exists in this world, — to be himself the counterbalance of all falsehood and all wrong. — The Anglo-Saxon race is proud and strong and selfish. — England maintains trade, not liberty."

Cowper had said long before this : —

> " doing good,
> Disinterested good, is not our trade."

And America found that England had not learned that trade when, fifteen years after this discourse was delivered, the conflict between the free and slave states threatened the ruin of the great Republic, and England forgot her Anti-slavery in the prospect of the downfall of "a great empire which threatens to overshadow the whole earth."

It must be remembered that Emerson had never been identified with the abolitionists. But an individual act of wrong sometimes gives a sharp point to a blunt dagger which has been kept in its sheath too long : —

" The events of the last few years and months and days have taught us the lessons of centuries. I do not see how a barbarous community and a civilized community can constitute one State. I think we must get rid of slavery or we must get rid of freedom."

These were his words on the 26th of May, 1856, in his speech on "The Assault upon Mr. Sumner."

A few months later, in his "Speech on the Affairs of Kansas," delivered almost five years before the first gun was fired at Fort Sumter, he spoke the following fatally prophetic and commanding words: —

"The hour is coming when the strongest will not be strong enough. A harder task will the new revolution of the nineteenth century be than was the revolution of the eighteenth century. I think the American Revolution bought its glory cheap. If the problem was new, it was simple. If there were few people, they were united, and the enemy three thousand miles off. But now, vast property, gigantic interests, family connections, webs of party, cover the land with a net-work that immensely multiplies the dangers of war.

"Fellow-citizens, in these times full of the fate of the Republic, I think the towns should hold town meetings, and resolve themselves into Committees of Safety, go into permanent sessions, adjourning from week to week, from month to month. I wish we could send the sergeant-at-arms to stop every American who is about to leave the country. Send home every one who is abroad, lest they should find no country to return to. Come home and stay at home while there is a country to save. When it is lost it will be time enough then for any who are luckless enough to remain alive to gather up their clothes and depart to some land where freedom exists."

Two short speeches follow, one delivered at a

20

meeting for the relief of the family of John Brown, on the 18th of November, 1859, the other after his execution : —

"Our blind statesmen," he says, "go up and down, with committees of vigilance and safety, hunting for the origin of this new heresy. They will need a very vigilant committee indeed to find its birthplace, and a very strong force to root it out. For the arch-Abolitionist, older than Brown, and older than the Shenandoah Mountains, is Love, whose other name is Justice, which was before Alfred, before Lycurgus, before Slavery, and will be after it."

From his "Discourse on Theodore Parker" I take the following vigorous sentence : —

"His commanding merit as a reformer is this, that he insisted beyond all men in pulpits, — I cannot think of one rival, — that the essence of Christianity is its practical morals; it is there for use, or it is nothing; and if you combine it with sharp trading, or with ordinary city ambitions to gloze over municipal corruptions, or private intemperance, or successful fraud, or immoral politics, or unjust wars, or the cheating of Indians, or the robbery of frontier nations, or leaving your principles at home to follow on the high seas or in Europe a supple complaisance to tyrants, — it is hypocrisy, and the truth is not in you; and no love of religious music, or of dreams of Swedenborg, or praise of John Wesley, or of Jeremy Taylor, can save you from the Satan which you are."

The Lecture on " American Civilization," made up from two Addresses, one of which was delivered at Washington on the 31st of January, 1862, is, as might be expected, full of anti-slavery. That on the " Emancipation Proclamation," delivered in Boston in September, 1862, is as full of " silent joy " at the advent of " a day which most of us dared not hope to see, — an event worth the dreadful war, worth its costs and uncertainties."

From the " Remarks " at the funeral services for Abraham Lincoln, held in Concord on the 19th of April, 1865, I extract this admirably drawn character of the man : —

" He is the true history of the American people in his time. Step by step he walked before them ; slow with their slowness, quickening his march by theirs, the true representative of this continent ; an entirely public man ; father of his country, the pulse of twenty millions throbbing in his heart, the thought of their minds articulated by his tongue."

The following are the titles of the remaining contents of this volume : " Harvard Commemoration Speech ; " " Editor's Address : Massachusetts Quarterly Review ; " " Woman ; " " Address to Kossuth ; " " Robert Burns ; " " Walter Scott ; " " Remarks at the Organization of the Free Religious Association ; " " Speech at the Annual Meeting of the Free Religious Association ; " " The Fortune of the Republic."

In treating of the " Woman Question," Emerson speaks temperately, delicately, with perfect fairness, but leaves it in the hands of the women themselves to determine whether they shall have an equal part in public affairs. " The new movement," he says, " is only a tide shared by the spirits of man and woman; and you may proceed in the faith that whatever the woman's heart is prompted to desire, the man's mind is simultaneously prompted to accomplish."

It is hard to turn a leaf in any book of Emerson's writing without finding some pithy remark or some striking image or witty comment which illuminates the page where we find it and tempts us to seize upon it for an extract. But I must content myself with these few sentences from " The Fortune of the Republic," the last address he ever delivered, in which his belief in America and her institutions, and his trust in the Providence which overrules all nations and all worlds, have found fitting utterance : —

" Let the passion for America cast out the passion for Europe. Here let there be what the earth waits for, — exalted manhood. What this country longs for is personalities, grand persons, to counteract its materialities. For it is the rule of the universe that corn shall serve man, and not man corn.

" They who find America insipid, — they for whom London and Paris have spoiled their own homes, can be spared to return to those cities. I not only see a career at home for more genius than we have, but for more than there is in the world.

"Our helm is given up to a better guidance than our own; the course of events is quite too strong for any helmsman, and our little wherry is taken in tow by the ship of the great Admiral which knows the way, and has the force to draw men and states and planets to their good."

With this expression of love and respect for his country and trust in his country's God, we may take leave of Emerson's prose writings.

CHAPTER XIV.

EMERSON'S POEMS.

THE following " Prefatory Note " by Mr. Cabot introduces the ninth volume of the series of Emerson's collected works : —

"This volume contains nearly all the pieces included in the POEMS and MAY-DAY of former editions. In 1876 Mr. Emerson published a selection from his poems, adding six new ones, and omitting many. Of those omitted, several are now restored, in accordance with the expressed wishes of many readers and lovers of them. Also some pieces never before published are here given in an Appendix, on various grounds. Some of them appear to have had Emerson's approval, but to have been withheld because they were unfinished. These it seemed best not to suppress, now that they can never receive their completion. Others, mostly of an early date, remained unpublished doubtless because of their personal and private nature. Some of these seem to have an autobiographic interest sufficient to justify their publication. Others again, often mere fragments, have been admitted as characteristic, or as expressing in poetic form thoughts found in the Essays.

"In coming to a decision in these cases, it seemed on the whole preferable to take the risk of including too much rather than the opposite, and to leave the task of further winnowing to the hands of time.

"As was stated in the Preface to the first volume of this edition of Mr. Emerson's writings, the readings adopted by him in the "Selected Poems" have not always been followed here, but in some cases preference has been given to corrections made by him when he was in fuller strength than at the time of the last revision.

"A change in the arrangement of the stanzas of "May-Day," in the part representative of the march of Spring, received his sanction as bringing them more nearly in accordance with the events in Nature."

Emerson's verse has been a fertile source of discussion. Some have called him a poet and nothing but a poet, and some have made so much of the palpable defects of his verse that they have forgotten to recognize its true claims. His prose is often highly poetical, but his verse is something more than the most imaginative and rhetorical passages of his prose. An illustration presently to be given will make this point clear.

Poetry is to prose what the so-called full dress of the ball-room is to the plainer garments of the household and the street. Full dress, as we call it, is so full of beauty that it cannot hold it all, and the redundancy of nature overflows the narrowed margin of satin or velvet.

It reconciles us to its approach to nudity by the richness of its drapery and ornaments. A pearl or diamond necklace or a blushing bouquet excuses the liberal allowance of undisguised nature. We expect from the fine lady in her brocades and laces a generosity of display which we should reprimand with the virtuous severity of Tartuffe if ventured upon by the waiting-maid in her calicoes. So the poet reveals himself under the protection of his imaginative and melodious phrases, — the flowers and jewels of his vocabulary.

Here is a prose sentence from Emerson's "Works and Days:" —

"The days are ever divine as to the first Aryans. They come and go like muffled and veiled figures, sent from a distant friendly party; but they say nothing, and if we do not use the gifts they bring, they carry them as silently away."

Now see this thought in full dress, and then ask what is the difference between prose and poetry: —

"DAYS.

"Daughters of Time, the hypocritic Days,
  Muffled and dumb like barefoot dervishes,
  And marching single in an endless file,
  Bring diadems and fagots in their hands.
  To each they offer gifts after his will,

> Bread, kingdom, stars, and sky that holds them all.
> I, in my pleachéd garden watched the pomp,
> Forgot my morning wishes, hastily
> Took a few herbs and apples, and the Day
> Turned and departed silent.   I too late
> Under her solemn fillet saw the scorn."

— Cinderella at the fireside, and Cinderella at the prince's ball! The full dress version of the thought is glittering with new images like bracelets and brooches and ear-rings, and fringed with fresh adjectives like edges of embroidery. That one word *pleachéd*, an heir-loom from Queen Elizabeth's day, gives to the noble sonnet an antique dignity and charm like the effect of an ancestral jewel. But mark that now the poet reveals himself as he could not in the prosaic form of the first extract. It is his own neglect of his great opportunity of which he now speaks, and not merely the indolent indifference of others. It is himself who is the object of scorn. Self-revelation of beauty embellished by ornaments is the privilege of full dress; self-revelation in the florid costume of verse is the divine right of the poet. Passion that must express itself longs always for the freedom of rhythmic utterance. And in spite of the exaggeration and extravagance which shield themselves under the claim of poetic license, I venture to affirm that "*In* vino *veritas*" is not truer than *In* carmine *veritas*.

As a further illustration of what has just been said of the self-revelations to be looked for in verse, and in Emerson's verse more especially, let the reader observe how freely he talks about his bodily presence and infirmities in his poetry, — subjects he never referred to in prose, except incidentally, in private letters.

Emerson is so essentially a poet that whole pages of his are like so many litanies of alternating chants and recitations. His thoughts slip on and off their light rhythmic robes just as the mood takes him, as was shown in the passage I have quoted in prose and in verse. Many of the metrical preludes to his lectures are a versified and condensed abstract of the leading doctrine of the discourse. They are a curious instance of survival; the lecturer, once a preacher, still wants his text; and finds his scriptural motto in his own rhythmic inspiration.

Shall we rank Emerson among the great poets or not?

"The great poets are judged by the frame of mind they induce; and to them, of all men, the severest criticism is due."

These are Emerson's words in the Preface to "Parnassus."

His own poems will stand this test as well as

any in the language. They lift the reader into a higher region of thought and feeling. This seems to me a better test to apply to them than the one which Mr. Arnold cited from Milton. The passage containing this must be taken, not alone, but with the context. Milton had been speaking of "Logic" and of "Rhetoric," and spoke of poetry "as being less subtile and fine, but more simple, sensuous, and passionate." This relative statement, it must not be forgotten, is conditioned by what went before. If the terms are used absolutely, and not comparatively, as Milton used them, they must be very elastic if they would stretch widely enough to include all the poems which the world recognizes as masterpieces, nay, to include some of the best of Milton's own.

In spite of what he said about himself in his letter to Carlyle, Emerson was not only a poet, but a very remarkable one. Whether a great poet or not will depend on the scale we use and the meaning we affix to the term. The heat at eighty degrees of Fahrenheit is one thing and the heat at eighty degrees of Réaumur is a very different matter. The rank of poets is a point of very unstable equilibrium. From the days of Homer to our own, critics have been disputing about the place to be assigned to this or that member of the poetic hierarchy. It is not the most popular poet who is necessarily the greatest; Wordsworth never had half the popularity of Scott or Moore. It is not the multitude of remembered passages which settles the rank of a metrical composition as poetry. Gray's "Elegy," it is true, is full of lines we all remember, and is a great poem, if that term can be applied to any piece of verse of that length. But what shall we say to the "Ars Poetica" of Horace? It is crowded with lines worn smooth as old sesterces by constant quotation. And yet we should rather call it a versified criticism than a poem in the full sense of that word. And what shall we do with Pope's "Essay on Man," which has furnished more familiar lines than "Paradise Lost" and "Paradise Regained" both together? For all that, we know there is a school of writers who will not allow that Pope deserves the name of poet.

It takes a generation or two to find out what are the passages in a great writer which are to become commonplaces in literature and conversation. It is to be remembered that Emerson is one of those authors whose popularity must diffuse itself from above downwards. And after all, few will dare assert that "The Vanity of Human Wishes" is greater as a poem than Shelley's "Ode to the West Wind," or Keats's "Ode to a Nightingale," because no

line in either of these poems is half so often
quoted as

      " To point a moral or adorn a tale."

We cannot do better than begin our consideration of Emerson's poetry with Emerson's
own self-estimate. He says in a fit of humility,
writing to Carlyle : —

"I do not belong to the poets, but only to a low
department of literature, the reporters, suburban
men."

But Miss Peabody writes to Mr. Ireland : —

"He once said to me, 'I am not a great poet —
but whatever is of me *is a poet.*'"

These opposite feelings were the offspring of
different moods and different periods.

Here is a fragment, written at the age of
twenty-eight, in which his self-distrust and his
consciousness of the " vision," if not " the faculty,
divine," are revealed with the brave nudity of
the rhythmic confessional : —

    " A dull uncertain brain,
      But gifted yet to know
      That God has cherubim who go
      Singing an immortal strain,
      Immortal here below.
      I know the mighty bards,
      I listen while they sing,
      And now I know
      The secret store

> Which these explore
> When they with torch of genius pierce
> The tenfold clouds that cover
> The riches of the universe
> From God's adoring lover.
> And if to me it is not given
> To fetch one ingot thence
> Of that unfading gold of Heaven
> His merchants may dispense,
> Yet well I know the royal mine
>   And know the sparkle of its ore,
> Know Heaven's truth from lies that shine, —
>   Explored, they teach us to explore."

These lines are from "The Poet," a series of fragments given in the "Appendix," which, with his first volume, "Poems," his second, "May-Day, and other Pieces," form the complete ninth volume of the new series. These fragments contain some of the loftiest and noblest passages to be found in his poetical works, and if the reader should doubt which of Emerson's self-estimates in his two different moods spoken of above had most truth in it, he could question no longer after reading "The Poet."

Emerson has the most exalted ideas of the true poetic function, as this passage from "Merlin" sufficiently shows : —

> "Thy trivial harp will never please
>   Or fill my craving ear ;
>   Its chords should ring as blows the breeze,
>   Free, peremptory, clear.

No jingling serenader's art
Nor tinkling of piano-strings
Can make the wild blood start
In its mystic springs ;
The kingly bard
Must smite the chords rudely and **hard,**
As with hammer or with mace ;
That they may render back
Artful thunder, which conveys
Secrets of the solar track,
Sparks of the supersolar blaze.
. . . .
Great is the art,
Great be the manners of the bard.
He shall not his brain encumber
With the coil of rhythm and number ;
But leaving rule and pale forethought
He shall aye climb
For his rhyme.
' Pass in, pass in,' the angels say,
' In to the upper doors,
Nor count compartments of the floors,
But mount to paradise
By the stairway of surprise.' "

And here is another passage from " The Poet,"
mentioned in the quotation before the last, in
which the bard is spoken of as performing greater
miracles than those ascribed to Orpheus : —

" A Brother of the world, his song
Sounded like a tempest strong
Which tore from oaks their branches broad,
And stars from the ecliptic road.
Time wore he as his clothing-weeds,

He sowed the sun and moon for seeds.
As melts the iceberg in the seas,
As clouds give rain to the eastern breeze,
As snow-banks thaw in April's beam,
The solid kingdoms like a dream
Resist in vain his motive strain,
They totter now and float amain.
For the Muse gave special charge
His learning should be deep and large,
And his training should not scant
The deepest lore of wealth or want :
His flesh should feel, his eyes should read
Every maxim of dreadful Need ;
In its fulness he should taste
Life's honeycomb, but not too fast ;
Full fed, but not intoxicated ;
He should be loved ; he should be hated ;
A blooming child to children dear,
His heart should palpitate with fear."

We look naturally to see what poets were
Emerson's chief favorites. In his poems "The
Test" and "The Solution," we find that the
five whom he recognizes as defying the powers
of destruction are Homer, Dante, Shakespeare,
Swedenborg, Goethe.

Here are a few of his poetical characterizations
from "The Harp : "—

" And this at least I dare affirm,
Since genius too has bound and term,
There is no bard in all the choir,
Not Homer's self, the poet-sire,
Wise Milton's odes of pensive pleasure,

> Or Shakespeare whom no mind can measure,
> Nor Collins' verse of tender pain,
> Nor Byron's clarion of disdain,
> Scott, the delight of generous boys,
> Or Wordsworth, Pan's recording voice, —
> Not one of all can put in verse,
> Or to this presence could rehearse
> The sights and voices ravishing
> The boy knew on the hills in spring." —

In the notice of "Parnassus" some of his preferences have been already mentioned.

Comparisons between men of genius for the sake of aggrandizing the one at the expense of the other are the staple of the meaner kinds of criticism. No lover of art will clash a Venetian goblet against a Roman amphora to see which is strongest; no lover of nature undervalues a violet because it is not a rose. But comparisons used in the way of description are not odious.

The difference between Emerson's poetry and that of the contemporaries with whom he would naturally be compared is that of algebra and arithmetic. He deals largely in general symbols, abstractions, and infinite series. He is always seeing the universal in the particular. The great multitude of mankind care more for two and two, something definite, a fixed quantity, than for $a + b$'s and x^{2}'s, — symbols used for undetermined amounts and indefinite possibili-

21

ties. Emerson is a citizen of the universe who
has taken up his residence for a few days and
nights in this travelling caravansary between
the two inns that hang out the signs of Venus
and Mars. This little planet could not provin-
cialize such a man. The multiplication-table is
for the every day use of every day earth-people,
but the symbols he deals with are too vast, sometimes, we must own, too vague, for the unillumi-
nated terrestrial and arithmetical intelligence.
One cannot help feeling that he might have
dropped in upon us from some remote centre of
spiritual life, where, instead of addition and sub-
traction, children were taught quaternions, and
where the fourth dimension of space was as familiarly known to everybody as a foot-measure or a
yard-stick is to us. Not that he himself dealt
in the higher or the lower mathematics, but he
saw the hidden spiritual meaning of things as
Professor Cayley or Professor Sylvester see the
meaning of their mysterious formulæ. Without
using the Rosetta-stone of Swedenborg, Emerson finds in every phenomenon of nature a hiero-
glyphic. Others measure and describe the monuments, — he reads the sacred inscriptions. How
alive he makes Monadnoc! Dinocrates under-
took to "hew Mount Athos to the shape of
man" in the likeness of Alexander the Great.
Without the help of tools or workmen, Emerson

makes "Cheshire's haughty hill" stand before us an impersonation of kingly humanity, and talk with us as a god from Olympus might have talked.

This is the fascination of Emerson's poetry; it moves in a world of universal symbolism. The sense of the infinite fills it with its majestic presence. It shows, also, that he has a keen delight in the every-day aspects of nature. But he looks always with the eye of a poet, never with that of the man of science. The law of association of ideas is wholly different in the two. The scientific man connects objects in sequences and series, and in so doing is guided by their collective resemblances. His aim is to classify and index all that he sees and contemplates so as to show the relations which unite, and learn the laws that govern, the subjects of his study. The poet links the most remote objects together by the slender filament of wit, the flowery chain of fancy, or the living, pulsating cord of imagination, always guided by his instinct for the beautiful. The man of science clings to his object, as the marsupial embryo to its teat, until he has filled himself as full as he can hold; the poet takes a sip of his dew-drop, throws his head up like a chick, rolls his eyes around in contemplation of the heavens above him and the universe in general, and never thinks of asking a Linnæan question as to the flower that furnished him his dew-drop. The poetical and scientific natures rarely coexist; Haller and Goethe are examples which show that such a union may occur, but as a rule the poet is contented with the colors of the rainbow and leaves the study of Fraunhofer's lines to the man of science.

Though far from being a man of science, Emerson was a realist in the best sense of that word. But his realities reached to the highest heavens: like Milton, —

> " He passed the flaming bounds of place and time ;
> The living throne, the sapphire blaze
> Where angels tremble while they gaze,
> HE SAW "—

Everywhere his poetry abounds in celestial imagery. If Galileo had been a poet as well as an astronomer, he would hardly have sowed his verse thicker with stars than we find them in the poems of Emerson.

Not less did Emerson clothe the common aspects of life with the colors of his imagination. He was ready to see beauty everywhere : —

> " Thou can'st not wave thy staff in air,
> Or dip thy paddle in the lake,
> But it carves the bow of beauty there,
> And the ripples in rhyme the oar forsake."

He called upon the poet to

> " Tell men what they knew before ;
> Paint the prospect from their door."

And his practice was like his counsel. He saw our plain New England life with as honest New England eyes as ever looked at a huckleberry-bush or into a milking-pail.

This noble quality of his had its dangerous side. In one of his exalted moods he would have us

"Give to barrows, trays and pans
Grace and glimmer of romance."

But in his Lecture on "Poetry and Imagination," he says: —

"What we once admired as poetry has long since come to be a sound of tin pans; and many of our later books we have outgrown. Perhaps Homer and Milton will be tin pans yet."

The "grace and glimmer of romance" which was to invest the tin pan are forgotten, and he uses it as a belittling object for comparison. He himself was not often betrayed into the mistake of confounding the prosaic with the poetical, but his followers, so far as the "realists" have taken their hint from him, have done it most thoroughly. Mr. Whitman enumerates all the objects he happens to be looking at as if they were equally suggestive to the poetical mind, furnishing his reader a large assortment on which he may exercise the fullest freedom of selection. It is only giving him the same liberty that Lord Timothy Dexter allowed his readers in the matter of punctuation, by leaving all stops out of his sentences, and printing at the end of his book a page of commas, semicolons, colons, periods, notes of interrogation and exclamation, with which the reader was expected to "pepper" the pages as he might see fit.

French realism does not stop at the tin pan, but must deal with the slop-pail and the wash-tub as if it were literally true that

> " In the mud and scum of things
> There alway, alway something sings."

Happy were it for the world if M. Zola and his tribe would stop even there; but when they cross the borders of science into its infected districts, leaving behind them the reserve and delicacy which the genuine scientific observer never forgets to carry with him, they disgust even those to whom the worst scenes they describe are too wretchedly familiar. The true realist is such a man as Parent du Chatelet; exploring all that most tries the senses and the sentiments, and reporting all truthfully, but soberly, chastely, without needless circumstance, or picturesque embellishment, for a useful end, and not for a mere sensational effect.

What a range of subjects from " The Problem " and " Uriel " and " Forerunners " to " The Humble-Bee " and " The Titmouse ! " Nor let the reader who thinks the poet must go far to find a fitting theme fail to read the singularly impressive home-poem, " Hamatreya," beginning with the names of the successive owners of a piece of land in Concord, — probably the same he owned after the last of them : —

"Bulkeley, Hunt, Willard, Hosmer, Meriam, Flint,"

and ending with the austere and solemn " Earth-Song."

Full of poetical feeling, and with a strong desire for poetical expression, Emerson experienced a difficulty in the mechanical part of metrical composition. His muse picked her way as his speech did in conversation and in lecturing. He made desperate work now and then with rhyme and rhythm, showing that though a born poet he was not a born singer. Think of making " feeble " rhyme with " people," " abroad " with " Lord," and contemplate the following couplet which one cannot make rhyme without actual verbicide : —

" Where feeds the moose, and walks the surly bear,
    And up the tall mast runs the woodpeck "- are !

And how could prose go on all-fours more unmetrically than this ?

" In Adirondac lakes
    At morn or noon the guide rows bare-headed."

It was surely not difficult to say —

" At morn or noon bare-headed rows the guide."

And yet while we note these blemishes, many of us will confess that we like his uncombed verse better, oftentimes, than if it were trimmed more neatly and disposed more nicely. When he is at his best, his lines flow with careless ease, as a mountain stream tumbles, sometimes rough and sometimes smooth, but all the more interesting for the rocks it runs against and the grating of the pebbles it rolls over.

There is one trick of verse which Emerson occasionally, not very often, indulges in. This is the crowding of a redundant syllable into a line. It is a liberty which is not to be abused by the poet. Shakespeare, the supreme artist, and Milton, the " mighty-mouth'd inventor of harmonies," knew how to use it effectively. Shelley employed it freely. Bryant indulged in it occasionally, and wrote an article in an early number of the "North American Review" in defence of its use. Willis was fond of it. As a relief to monotony it may be now and then allowed, — may even have an agreeable effect in breaking the monotony of too formal verse. But it may easily become a deformity and a cause of aversion. A humpback may add picturesqueness to a procession, but if there are too many humpbacks in line we turn away from the sight of them. Can any ear reconcile itself to the last of these three lines of Emerson's?

"Oh, what is Heaven but the fellowship
 Of minds that each can stand against the world
 By its own meek and incorruptible will?"

These lines that lift their backs up in the middle — span-worm lines, we may call them — are not to be commended for common use because some great poets have now and then admitted them. They have invaded some of our recent poetry as the canker-worms gather on our elms in June. Emerson has one or two of them here and there, but they never swarm on his leaves so as to frighten us away from their neighborhood.

As for the violently artificial rhythms and rhymes which have reappeared of late in English and American literature, Emerson would as soon have tried to ride three horses at once in a circus as to shut himself up in triolets, or attempt any cat's - cradle tricks of rhyming sleight of hand.

If we allow that Emerson is not a born singer, that he is a careless versifier and rhymer, we must still recognize that there is something in his verse which belongs, indissolubly, sacredly, to his thought. Who would decant the wine of his poetry from its quaint and antique-looking *lagena?* — Read his poem to the Æolian harp ("The Harp") and his model betrays itself: —

> " These syllables that Nature spoke,
>   And thé thoughts that in him woke
> Can adequately utter none
> Save to his ear the wind-harp lone.
> Therein I hear the Parcæ reel
> The threads of man at their humming wheel,
> The threads of life and power and pain,
> So sweet and mournful falls the strain.
> And best can teach its Delphian chord
> How Nature to the soul is moored,
> If once again that silent string,
> As erst it wont, would thrill and ring."

There is no need of quoting any of the poems which have become familiar to most true lovers of poetry. Emerson saw fit to imitate the Egyptians by placing " The Sphinx " at the entrance of his temple of song. This poem was not fitted to attract worshippers. It is not easy of comprehension, not pleasing in movement. As at first written it had one verse in it which sounded so much like a nursery rhyme that Emerson was prevailed upon to omit it in the later versions. There are noble passages in it, but they are for the adept and not for the beginner. A commonplace young person taking up the volume and puzzling his or her way along will come by and by to the verse : —

> " Have I a lover
>   Who is noble and free ? —
> I would he were nobler
>   Than to love me."

The commonplace young person will be apt to
say or think *c'est magnifique, mais ce n'est pas
— l'amour.*

The third poem in the volume, " The Problem," should have stood first in order. This
ranks among the finest of Emerson's poems.
All his earlier verse has a certain freshness
which belongs to the first outburst of song in a
poetic nature. " Each and All," " The Humble-
Bee," " The Snow-Storm," should be read before
" Uriel," " The World-Soul," or " Mithridates."
" Monadnoc " will be a good test of the reader's taste for Emerson's poetry, and after this
" Woodnotes."

In studying his poems we must not overlook
the delicacy of many of their descriptive portions. If in the flights of his imagination he
is like the strong-winged bird of passage, in his
exquisite choice of descriptive epithets he reminds me of the *tenui-rostrals.* His subtle selective instinct penetrates the vocabulary for the
one word he wants, as the long, slender bill of
those birds dives deep into the flower for its
drop of honey. Here is a passage showing admirably the two different conditions : wings closed
and the selective instinct picking out its descriptive expressions ; then suddenly wings flash-
ing open and the imagination in the firmament,
where it is always at home. Follow the pitiful

inventory of insignificances of the forlorn being
he describes with a pathetic humor more likely
to bring a sigh than a smile, and then mark the
grand hyperbole of the last two lines. The passage is from the poem called " Destiny " : —

> " Alas ! that one is born in blight,
>   Victim of perpetual slight :
>   When thou lookest on his face,
>   Thy heart saith ' Brother, go thy ways !
>   None shall ask thee what thou doest,
>   Or care a rush for what thou knowest,
>   Or listen when thou repliest,
>   Or remember where thou liest,
>   Or how thy supper is sodden ; '
>   And another is born
>   To make the sun forgotten."

Of all Emerson's poems the " Concord Hymn "
is the most nearly complete and faultless, — but
it is not distinctively Emersonian.   It is such
a poem as Collins might have written, — it has
the very movement and melody of the " Ode
on the Death of Mr. Thomson," and of the
" Dirge in Cymbeline," with the same sweetness
and tenderness of feeling.   Its one conspicuous
line,

> " And fired the shot heard round the world,"

must not take to itself all the praise deserved
by this perfect little poem, a model for all of
its kind.   Compact, expressive, serene, solemn,
musical, in four brief stanzas it tells the story of

the past, records the commemorative act of the passing day, and invokes the higher Power that governs the future to protect the Memorial-stone sacred to Freedom and her martyrs.

These poems of Emerson's find the readers that must listen to them and delight in them, as the "Ancient Mariner" fastened upon the man who must hear him. If any doubter wishes to test his fitness for reading them, and if the poems already mentioned are not enough to settle the question, let him read the paragraph of "May-Day," beginning, —

"I saw the bud-crowned Spring go forth,"

"Sea-shore," the fine fragments in the "Appendix" to his published works, called, collectively, "The Poet," blocks bearing the mark of poetic genius, but left lying round for want of the structural instinct, and last of all, that which is, in many respects, first of all, the "Threnody," a lament over the death of his first-born son. This poem has the dignity of "Lycidas" without its refrigerating classicism, and with all the tenderness of Cowper's lines on the receipt of his mother's picture. It may well compare with others of the finest memorial poems in the language, — with Shelley's "Adonais," and Matthew Arnold's "Thyrsis," leaving out of view Tennyson's "In Memoriam" as of wider scope and larger pattern.

Many critics will concede that there is much truth in Mr. Arnold's remark on the want of " evolution " in Emerson's poems. One is struck with the fact that a great number of fragments lie about his poetical workshop: poems begun and never finished; scraps of poems, chips of poems, paving the floor with intentions never carried out. One cannot help remembering Coleridge with his incomplete " Christabel," and his " Abyssinian Maid," and her dulcimer which she never got a tune out of. We all know there was good reason why Coleridge should have been infirm of purpose. But when we look at that great unfinished picture over which Allston labored with the hopeless ineffectiveness of Sisyphus; when we go through a whole gallery of pictures by an American artist in which the backgrounds are slighted as if our midsummer heats had taken away half the artist's life and vigor; when we walk round whole rooms full of sketches, impressions, effects, symphonies, invisibilities, and other apologies for honest work, it would not be strange if it should suggest a painful course of reflections as to the possibility that there may be something in our climatic or other conditions which tends to scholastic and artistic anæmia and insufficiency, — the opposite of what we find showing itself in the full-blooded verse of poets like Browning and on the flaming

canvas of painters like Henri Regnault. Life
seemed lustier in Old England than in New
England to Emerson, to Hawthorne, and to that
admirable observer, Mr. John Burroughs. Perhaps we require another century or two of accli-
mation.

Emerson never grappled with any considerable
metrical difficulties. He wrote by preference in
what I have ventured to call the normal respiratory measure, — octosyllabic verse, in which
one common expiration is enough and not too
much for the articulation of each line. The
"fatal facility" for which this verse is noted
belongs to it as recited and also as written, and
it implies the need of only a minimum of skill
and labor. I doubt if Emerson would have written a verse of poetry if he had been obliged to
use the Spenserian stanza. In the simple measures he habitually employed he found least
hindrance to his thought.

Every true poet has an atmosphere as much
as every great painter. The golden sunshine of
Claude and the pearly mist of Corot belonged
to their way of looking at nature as much as the
color of their eyes and hair belonged to their
personalities. So with the poets; for Wordsworth the air is always serene and clear, for
Byron the sky is uncertain between storm and
sunshine. Emerson sees all nature in the same

pearly mist that wraps the willows and the streams of Corot. Without its own character-istic atmosphere, illuminated by

> " The light that never was on sea or land,"

we may have good verse but no true poem. In his poetry there is not merely this atmosphere, but there is always a mirage in the horizon.

Emerson's poetry is eminently subjective, — if Mr. Ruskin, who hates the word, will pardon me for using it in connection with a reference to two of his own chapters in his " Modern Painters." These are the chapter on " The Pathetic Fallacy," and the one which follows it " On Classical Landscape." In these he treats of the transfer of a writer's mental or emotional conditions to the external nature which he con-templates. He asks his readers to follow him in a long examination of what he calls by the sin-gular name mentioned, " the pathetic fallacy," because, he says, " he will find it eminently characteristic of the modern mind ; and in the landscape, whether of literature or art, he will also find the modern painter endeavoring to express something which he, as a living creature, imagines in the lifeless object, while the classical and mediæval painters were content with ex-pressing the unimaginary and actual qualities of the object itself."

Illustrations of Mr. Ruskin's "pathetic fallacy" may be found almost anywhere in Emerson's poems. Here is one which offers itself without search : —

> " Daily the bending skies solicit man,
>   The seasons chariot him from this exile,
>   The rainbow hours bedeck his glowing wheels,
>   The storm-winds urge the heavy weeks along,
>   Suns haste to set, that so remoter lights
>   Beckon the wanderer to his vaster home."

The expression employed by Ruskin gives the idea that he is dealing with a defect. If he had called the state of mind to which he refers the *sympathetic illusion*, his readers might have looked upon it more justly.

It would be a pleasant and not a difficult task to trace the resemblances between Emerson's poetry and that of other poets. Two or three such resemblances have been incidentally referred to, a few others may be mentioned.

In his contemplative study of Nature he reminds us of Wordsworth, at least in certain brief passages, but he has not the staying power of that long-breathed, not to say long-winded, lover of landscapes. Both are on the most intimate terms with Nature, but Emerson contemplates himself as belonging to her, while Wordsworth feels as if she belonged to him.

22

"Good-by, proud world,"

recalls Spenser and Raleigh. "The Humble-Bee" is strongly marked by the manner and thought of Marvell. Marvell's

> "Annihilating all that's made
> To a green thought in a green shade,"

may well have suggested Emerson's

> "The green silence dost displace
> With thy mellow, breezy bass."

"The Snow-Storm" naturally enough brings to mind the descriptions of Thomson and of Cowper, and fragment as it is, it will not suffer by comparison with either.

"Woodnotes," one of his best poems, has passages that might have been found in Milton's "Comus;" this, for instance: —

> "All constellations of the sky
> Shed their virtue through his eye.
> Him Nature giveth for defence
> His formidable innocence."

Of course his Persian and Indian models betray themselves in many of his poems, some of which, called translations, sound as if they were original.

So we follow him from page to page and find him passing through many moods, but with one pervading spirit: —

"Melting matter into dreams,
Panoramas which I saw,
And whatever glows or seems
Into substance, into Law."

We think in reading his "Poems" of these words of Sainte-Beuve : —

"The greatest poet is not he who has done the best ; it is he who suggests the most ; he, not all of whose meaning is at first obvious, and who leaves you much to desire, to explain, to study ; much to complete in your turn."

Just what he shows himself in his prose, Emerson shows himself in his verse. Only when he gets into rhythm and rhyme he lets us see more of his personality, he ventures upon more audacious imagery, his flight is higher and swifter, his brief crystalline sentences have dissolved and pour in continuous streams. Where they came from, or whither they flow to empty themselves, we cannot always say, — it is enough to enjoy them as they flow by us.

Incompleteness — want of beginning, middle, and end, — is their too common fault. His pages are too much like those artists' studios all hung round with sketches and "bits" of scenery. "The Snow-Storm" and "Sea-Shore" are "bits" out of a landscape that was never painted, admirable, so far as they go, but forcing us to ask, "Where is the painting for which these scraps

are studies ? " or "Out of what great picture have
these pieces been cut ?"

We do not want his fragments to be made
wholes, — if we did, what hand could be found
equal to the task ? We do not want his rhythms
and rhymes smoothed and made more melodious.
They are as honest as Chaucer's, and we like
them as they are, not modernized or manipulated
by any versifying drill-sergeant, — if we wanted
them reshaped whom could we trust to meddle
with them ?

His poetry is elemental; it has the rock beneath it in the eternal laws on which it rests;
the roll of deep waters in its grander harmonies;
its air is full of Æolian strains that waken and
die away as the breeze wanders over them ; and
through it shines the white starlight, and from
time to time flashes a meteor that startles us
with its sudden brilliancy.

After all our criticisms, our selections, our
analyses, our comparisons, we have to recognize
that there is a charm in Emerson's poems which
cannot be defined any more than the fragrance
of a rose or a hyacinth, — any more than the
tone of a voice which we should know from all
others if all mankind were to pass before us, and
each of its articulating representatives should
call us by name.

All our crucibles and alembics leave unaccounted for the great mystery of *style*. "The style is of [a part of] the man himself," said Buffon, and this saying has passed into the stronger phrase, "The style is the man."

The "personal equation" which differentiates two observers is not confined to the tower of the astronomer. Every human being is individualized by a new arrangement of elements. His mind is a safe with a lock to which only certain letters are the key. His ideas follow in an order of their own. His words group themselves together in special sequences, in peculiar rhythms, in unlooked-for combinations, the total effect of which is to stamp all that he says or writes with his individuality. We may not be able to assign the reason of the fascination the poet we have been considering exercises over us. But this we can say, that he lives in the highest atmosphere of thought; that he is always in the presence of the infinite, and ennobles the accidents of human existence so that they partake of the absolute and eternal while he is looking at them; that he unites a royal dignity of manner with the simplicity of primitive nature; that his words and phrases arrange themselves, as if by an elective affinity of their own, with a *curiosa felicitas* which captivates and enthrals the reader who comes fully under its influence, and that through all he sings as in all he says for us we recognize the same serene, high, pure intelligence and moral nature, infinitely precious to us, not only in themselves, but as a promise of what the transplanted life, the air and soil and breeding of this western world may yet educe from their potential virtues, shaping themselves, at length, in a literature as much its own as the Rocky Mountains and the Mississippi.

CHAPTER XV.

Recollections of Emerson's Last Years. — Mr. Conway's
Visits. — Extracts from Mr. Whitman's Journal. — Dr. Le
Baron Russell's Visit. — Dr. Edward Emerson's Account.
— Illness and Death. — Funeral Services.

MR. CONWAY gives the following account of
two visits to Emerson after the decline of his
faculties had begun to make itself obvious : —

"In 1875, when I stayed at his house in Concord for
a little time, it was sad enough to find him sitting as a
listener before those who used to sit at his feet in
silence. But when alone with him he conversed in the
old way, and his faults of memory seemed at times to
disappear. There was something striking in the kind
of forgetfulness by which he suffered. He remembered the realities and uses of things when he could
not recall their names. He would describe what he
wanted or thought of ; when he could not recall
'chair' he could speak of that which supports the
human frame, and 'the implement that cultivates the
soil' must do for plough. —

"In 1880, when I was last in Concord, the trouble had made heavy strides. The intensity of his
silent attention to every word that was said was
painful, suggesting a concentration of his powers

to break through the invisible walls closing around them. Yet his face was serene; he was even cheerful, and joined in our laughter at some letters his eldest daughter had preserved, from young girls, trying to coax autograph letters, and in one case asking for what price he would write a valedictory address she had to deliver at college. He was still able to joke about his 'naughty memory;' and no complaint came from him when he once rallied himself on living too long. Emerson appeared to me strangely beautiful at this time, and the sweetness of his voice, when he spoke of the love and providence at his side, is quite indescribable." —

One of the later glimpses we have of Emerson is that preserved in the journal of Mr. Whitman, who visited Concord in the autumn of 1881. Mr. Ireland gives a long extract from this journal, from which I take the following: —

"On entering he had spoken very briefly, easily and politely to several of the company, then settled himself in his chair, a trifle pushed back, and, though a listener and apparently an alert one, remained silent through the whole talk and discussion. And so, there Emerson sat, and I looking at him. A good color in his face, eyes clear, with the well-known expression of sweetness, and the old clear-peering aspect quite the same."

Mr. Whitman met him again the next day, Sunday, September 18th, and records: —

"As just said, a healthy color in the cheeks, and

good light in the eyes, cheery expression, and just the amount of talking that best suited, namely, a word or short phrase only where needed, and almost always with a smile."

Dr. Le Baron Russell writes to me of Emerson at a still later period : —

"One incident I will mention which occurred at my last visit to Emerson, only a few months before his death. I went by Mrs. Emerson's request to pass a Sunday at their house at Concord towards the end of June. His memory had been failing for some time, and his mind as you know was clouded, but the old charm of his voice and manner had never left him. On the morning after my arrival Mrs. Emerson took us into the garden to see the beautiful roses in which she took great delight. One red rose of most brilliant color she called our attention to especially ; its 'hue' was so truly 'angry and brave' that I involuntarily repeated Herbert's line, —

'Bids the rash gazer wipe his eye,' —

from the verses which Emerson had first repeated to me so long ago. Emerson looked at the rose admiringly, and then as if by a sudden impulse lifted his hat gently, and said with a low bow, 'I take off my hat to it.'"

Once a poet, always a poet. It was the same reverence for the beautiful that he had shown in the same way in his younger days on entering the wood, as Governor Rice has told us the story, given in an earlier chapter.

I do not remember Emerson's last time of at tendance at the "Saturday Club," but I recollect that he came after the trouble in finding words had become well marked. "My memory hides itself," he said. The last time I saw him, living, was at Longfellow's funeral. I was sitting op posite to him when he rose, and going to the side of the coffin, looked intently upon the face of the dead poet. A few minutes later he rose again and looked once more on the familiar features, not apparently remembering that he had just done so. Mr. Conway reports that he said to a friend near him, "That gentleman was a sweet, beautiful soul, but I have entirely forgotten his name."

Dr. Edward Emerson has very kindly fur nished me, in reply to my request, with informa tion regarding his father's last years which will interest every one who has followed his life through its morning and midday to the hour of evening shadows.

"May-Day," which was published in 1867, was made up of the poems written since his first volume appeared. After this he wrote no poems, but with some difficulty fitted the refrain to the poem "Boston," which had remained unfinished since the old Anti-slavery days. "Greatness,"

and the " Phi Beta Kappa Oration" of 1867,
were among his last pieces of work. His College Lectures, " The Natural History of the Intellect," were merely notes recorded years before,
and now gathered and welded together. In
1876 he revised his poems, and made the selections from them for the " Little Classic" edition
of his works, then called " Selected Poems."
In that year he gave his " Address to the
Students of the University of Virginia." This
was a paper written long before, and its revision,
with the aid of his daughter Ellen, was accomplished with much difficulty.

The year 1867 was about the limit of his
working life. During the last five years he
hardly answered a letter. Before this time it
had become increasingly hard for him to do so,
and he always postponed and thought he should
feel more able the next day, until his daughter
Ellen was compelled to assume the correspondence. He did, however, write some letters in
1876, as, for instance, the answer to the invitation of the Virginia students.

Emerson left off going regularly to the " Saturday Club" probably in 1875. He used to depend on meeting Mr. Cabot there, but after Mr.
Cabot began to come regularly to work on " Letters and Social Aims," Emerson, who relied
on his friendly assistance, ceased attending the

meetings. The trouble he had in finding the word he wanted was a reason for his staying away from all gatherings where he was called upon to take a part in conversation, though he the more willingly went to lectures and readings and to church. His hearing was very slightly impaired, and his sight remained pretty good, though he sometimes said letters doubled, and that " M's " and " N's " troubled him to read. He recognized the members of his own family and his *old* friends ; but, as I infer from this statement, he found a difficulty in remembering the faces of new acquaintances, as is common with old persons.

He continued the habit of reading, — read through all his printed works with much interest and surprise, went through all his manuscripts, and endeavored, unsuccessfully, to index them. In these Dr. Emerson found written " Examined 1877 or 1878," but he found no later date.

In the last year or two he read anything which he picked up on his table, but he read the same things over, and whispered the words like a child. He liked to look over the " Advertiser," and was interested in the " Nation." He enjoyed pictures in books and showed them with delight to guests.

All this with slight changes and omissions is from the letter of Dr. Emerson in answer to my questions. The twilight of a long, bright day of life may be saddening, but when the shadow falls so gently and gradually, with so little that is painful and so much that is soothing and comforting, we do not shrink from following the imprisoned spirit to the very verge of its earthly existence.

But darker hours were in the order of nature very near at hand. From these he was saved by his not untimely release from the imprisonment of the worn-out bodily frame.

In April, 1882, Emerson took a severe cold, and became so hoarse that he could hardly speak. When his son, Dr. Edward Emerson, called to see him, he found him on the sofa, feverish, with more difficulty of expression than usual, dull, but not uncomfortable. As he lay on his couch he pointed out various objects, among others a portrait of Carlyle "the good man, — my friend." His son told him that he had seen Carlyle, which seemed to please him much. On the following day the unequivocal signs of pneumonia showed themselves, and he failed rapidly. He still recognized those around him, among the rest Judge Hoar, to whom he held out his arms for a last embrace. A sharp pain coming on, ether was administered with relief. And in a little time, surrounded by those who loved him and whom he loved, he passed quietly away. He lived very nearly to the completion of his eightieth year, having been born May 25, 1803, and his death occurring on the 27th of April, 1882.

Mr. Ireland has given a full account of the funeral, from which are, for the most part, taken the following extracts: —

"The last rites over the remains of Ralph Waldo Emerson took place at Concord on the 30th of April. A special train from Boston carried a large number of people. Many persons were on the street, attracted by the services, but were unable to gain admission to the church where the public ceremonies were held. Almost every building in town bore over its entrance-door a large black and white rosette with other sombre draperies. The public buildings were heavily draped, and even the homes of the very poor bore outward marks of grief at the loss of their friend and fellow-townsman.

"The services at the house, which were strictly private, occurred at 2.30, and were conducted by Rev. W. H. Furness of Philadelphia, a kindred spirit and an almost life-long friend. They were simple in character, and only Dr. Furness took part in them. The body lay in the front northeast room, in which were gathered the family and close friends of the deceased. The only flowers were contained in three vases on the mantel, and were lilies of the valley, red and white roses, and arbutus. The adjoining room and hall were filled with friends and neighbors.

"At the church many hundreds of persons were awaiting the arrival of the procession, and all the space, except the reserved pews, was packed. In front of the pulpit were simple decorations, boughs of pine covered the desk, and in their centre was a harp of yellow jonquils, the gift of Miss Louisa M. Alcott. Among the floral tributes was one from the teachers and scholars in the Emerson school. By the sides of the pulpit were white and scarlet geraniums and pine boughs, and high upon the wall a laurel wreath.

"Before 3.30 the pall-bearers brought in the plain black walnut coffin, which was placed before the pulpit. The lid was turned back, and upon it was put a cluster of richly colored pansies and a small bouquet of roses. While the coffin was being carried in, 'Pleyel's Hymn' was rendered on the organ by request of the family of the deceased. Dr. James Freeman Clarke then entered the pulpit. Judge E. Rockwood Hoar remained by the coffin below, and when the congregation became quiet, made a brief and pathetic address, his voice many times trembling with emotion."

I subjoin this most impressive "Address" entire, from the manuscript with which Judge Hoar has kindly favored me : —

"The beauty of Israel is fallen in its high place! Mr. Emerson has died; and we, his friends and neighbors, with this sorrowing company, have turned aside the procession from his home to his grave, — to this temple of his fathers, that we may here unite in our parting tribute of memory and love.

" There is nothing to mourn for him. That brave
and manly life was rounded out to the full length
of days. That dying pillow was softened by the
sweetest domestic affection ; and as he lay down to
the sleep which the Lord giveth his beloved, his face
was as the face of an angel, and his smile seemed to
give a glimpse of the opening heavens.

" Wherever the English language is spoken throughout the world his fame is established and secure.
Throughout this great land and from beyond the sea
will come innumerable voices of sorrow for this great
public loss. But we, his neighbors and townsmen,
feel that he was *ours.* He was descended from the
founders of the town. He chose our village as the
place where his lifelong work was to be done. It
was to our fields and orchards that his presence gave
such value ; it was our streets in which the children
looked up to him with love, and the elders with reverence. He was our ornament and pride.

> " ' He is gone — is dust, —
> He the more fortunate ! Yea, he hath finished !
> For him there is no longer any future.
> His life is bright — bright without spot it was
> And cannot cease to be.   No ominous hour
> Knocks at his door with tidings of mishap.
> Far off is he, above desire and fear ;
> No more submitted to the change and chance
> Of the uncertain planets. —

> " ' The bloom is vanished from my life,
> For, oh ! he stood beside me like my youth ;
> Transformed for me the real to a dream,

Clothing the palpable and the familiar
With golden exhalations of the dawn.
Whatever fortunes wait my future toils,
The *beautiful* is vanished and returns not.'

"That lofty brow, the home of all wise thoughts and high aspirations, — those lips of eloquent music, — that great soul, which trusted in God and never let go its hope of immortality,— that large heart, to which everything that belonged to man was welcome, — that hospitable nature, loving and tender and generous, having no repulsion or scorn for anything but meanness and baseness,— oh, friend, brother, father, lover, teacher, inspirer, guide! is there no more that we can do now than to give thee this our hail and farewell!"

Judge Hoar's remarks were followed by the congregation singing the hymns, " Thy will be done," "I will not fear the fate provided by Thy love." The Rev. Dr. Furness then read selections from the Scriptures.

The Rev. James Freeman Clarke then delivered an "Address," from which I extract two eloquent and inspiring passages, regretting to omit any that fell from lips so used to noble utterances and warmed by their subject, — for there is hardly a living person more competent to speak or write of Emerson than this high-minded and brave-souled man, who did not wait until he was famous to be his admirer and champion.

23

" The saying of the Liturgy is true and wise, that 'in the midst of life we are in death.' But it is still more true that in the midst of death we are in life. Do we ever believe so much in immortality as when we look on such a dear and noble face, now so still, which a few hours ago was radiant with thought and love? 'He is not here: he is risen.' That power which we knew, — that soaring intelligence, that soul of fire, that ever-advancing spirit, — *that* cannot have been suddenly annihilated with the decay of these earthly organs. It has left its darkened dust behind. It has outsoared the shadow of our night. God does not trifle with his creatures by bringing to nothing the ripe fruit of the ages by the lesion of a cerebral cell, or some bodily tissue. Life does not die, but matter dies off from it. The highest energy we know, the soul of man, the unit in which meet intelligence, imagination, memory, hope, love, purpose, insight, — this agent of immense resource and boundless power, — this has not been subdued by its instrument. When we think of such an one as he, we can only think of life, never of death.

" Such was his own faith, as expressed in his paper on 'Immortality.' But he himself was the best argument for immortality. Like the greatest thinkers, he did not rely on logical proof, but on the higher evidence of universal instincts, — the vast streams of belief which flow through human thought like currents in the ocean; those shoreless rivers which forever roll along their paths in the Atlantic and Pacific, not restrained by banks, but guided by the revolutions of the globe and the attractions of the sun."

. . . .

  " Let us then ponder his words : —

  " ' Wilt thou not ope thy heart to know
      What rainbows teach and sunsets show ?
      Voice of earth to earth returned,
      Prayers of saints that inly burned,
      Saying, *What is excellent
      As God lives, is permanent ;
      Hearts are dust, hearts' loves remain ;
      Hearts' love will meet thee again.*

. . . . . .

      House and tenant go to ground
      Lost in God, in Godhead found.' "

After the above address a feeling prayer was
offered by Rev. Howard M. Brown, of Brookline, and the benediction closed the exercises in
the church. Immediately before the benediction,
Mr. Alcott recited the following sonnet, which he
had written for the occasion : —

  " His harp is silent : shall successors rise,
      Touching with venturous hand the trembling string,
      Kindle glad raptures, visions of surprise,
      And wake to ecstasy each slumbering thing ?
      Shall life and thought flash new in wondering eyes,
      As when the seer transcendent, sweet, and wise,
      World-wide his native melodies did sing,
      Flushed with fair hopes and ancient memories ?
      Ah, no ! That matchless lyre shall silent lie :
      None hath the vanished minstrel's wondrous skill
      To touch that instrument with art and will.
      With him, winged poesy doth droop and die ;
      While our dull age, left voiceless, must lament
      The bard high heaven had for its service sent."

"Over an hour was occupied by the passing files of neighbors, friends, and visitors looking for the last time upon the face of the dead poet. The body was robed completely in white, and the face bore a natural and peaceful expression. From the church the procession took its way to the cemetery. The grave was made beneath a tall pine-tree upon the hill-top of Sleepy Hollow, where lie the bodies of his friends Thoreau and Hawthorne, the upturned sod being concealed by strewings of pine boughs. A border of hemlock spray surrounded the grave and completely lined its sides. The services here were very brief, and the casket was soon lowered to its final resting-place.

"The Rev. Dr. Haskins, a cousin of the family, an Episcopal clergyman, read the Episcopal Burial Service, and closed with the Lord's Prayer, ending at the words, 'and deliver us from evil.' In this all the people joined. Dr. Haskins then pronounced the benediction. After it was over the grandchildren passed the open grave and threw flowers into it."

So vanished from human eyes the bodily presence of Ralph Waldo Emerson, and his finished record belongs henceforth to memory.

CHAPTER XVI.

EMERSON. — A RETROSPECT.

EMERSON'S earthly existence was in the estimate of his own philosophy so slight an occur-
rence in his career of being that his relations to
the accidents of time and space seem quite secondary matters to one who has been long living
in the companionship of his thought. Still, he
had to be born, to take in his share of the atmosphere in which we are all immersed, to have
dealings with the world of phenomena, and at
length to let them all " soar and sing " as he left
his earthly half-way house. It is natural and
pardonable that we should like to know the details of the daily life which the men whom we

admire have shared with common mortals, ourselves among the rest. But Emerson has said truly " Great geniuses have the shortest biographies. Their cousins can tell you nothing about them. They lived in their writings, and so their home and street life was trivial and commonplace."

The reader has had many extracts from Emerson's writings laid before him. It was no easy task to choose them, for his paragraphs are so condensed, so much in the nature of abstracts, that it is like distilling absolute alcohol to attempt separating the spirit of what he says from his undiluted thought. His books are all so full of his life to their last syllable that we might letter every volume *Emersoniana*, by Ralph Waldo Emerson.

From the numerous extracts I have given from Emerson's writings it may be hoped that the reader will have formed an idea for himself of the man and of the life which have been the subjects of these pages. But he may probably expect something like a portrait of the poet and moralist from the hand of his biographer, if the author of this Memoir may borrow the name which will belong to a future and better equipped laborer in the same field. He may not unreasonably look for some general estimate of the life-work of the scholar and thinker of whom he has

been reading. He will not be disposed to find
fault with the writer of the Memoir if he mentions many things which would seem very trivial
but for the interest they borrow from the individual to whom they relate.

Emerson's personal appearance was that of a
scholar, the descendant of scholars. He was tall
and slender, with the complexion which is bred
in the alcove and not in the open air. He used
to tell his son Edward that he measured six feet
in his shoes, but his son thinks he could hardly
have straightened himself to that height in his
later years. He was very light for a man of
his stature. He got on the scales at Cheyenne,
on his trip to California, comparing his weight
with that of a lady of the party. A little while
afterwards he asked of his fellow-traveller, Professor Thayer, "How much did I weigh? A
hundred and forty?" "A hundred and forty
and a half," was the answer. "Yes, yes, a hundred and forty and a half! That *half* I prize ;
it is an index of better things!"

Emerson's head was not such as Schopenhauer insists upon for a philosopher. He wore
a hat measuring six and seven eighths on the
cephalometer used by hatters, which is equiva-
lent to twenty-one inches and a quarter of circumference. The average size is from seven to
seven and an eighth, so that his head was quite

small in that dimension.   It was long and narrow, but lofty, almost symmetrical, and of more nearly equal breadth in its anterior and posterior regions than many or most heads.

His shoulders sloped so much as to be commented upon for this peculiarity by Mr. Gilfillan, and like "Ammon's great son," he carried one shoulder a little higher than the other.   His face was thin, his nose somewhat accipitrine, casting a broad shadow; his mouth rather wide, well formed and well closed, carrying a question and an assertion in its finely finished curves; the lower lip a little prominent, the chin shapely and firm, as becomes the corner-stone of the countenance.   His expression was calm, sedate, kindly, with that look of refinement, centring about the lips, which is rarely found in the male New Englander, unless the family features have been for two or three cultivated generations the battle-field and the playground of varied thoughts and complex emotions as well as the sensuous and nutritive port of entry.   His whole look was irradiated by an ever active inquiring intelligence. His manner was noble and gracious.   Few of our fellow-countrymen have had larger opportunities of seeing distinguished personages than our present minister at the Court of St. James.   In a recent letter to myself, which I trust Mr. Lowell will pardon my quoting, he says of Emerson : —

" There was a majesty about him beyond all other men I have known, and he habitually dwelt in that ampler and diviner air to which most of us, if ever, only rise in spurts."

From members of his own immediate family I have derived some particulars relating to his personality and habits which are deserving of record.

His hair was brown, quite fine, and, till he was fifty, very thick. His eyes were of the " strongest and brightest blue." The member of the family who tells me this says : —

" My sister and I have looked for many years to see whether any one else had such absolutely blue eyes, and have never found them except in sea-captains. I have seen three sea-captains who had them."

He was not insensible to music, but his gift in that direction was very limited, if we may judge from this family story. When he was in College, and the singing-master was gathering his pupils, Emerson presented himself, intending to learn to sing. The master received him, and when his turn came, said to him, " Chord ! " " What ? " said Emerson. " Chord ! Chord ! I tell you," repeated the master. " I don't know what you mean," said Emerson. " Why, sing ! Sing a note." " So I made some kind of a noise, and the singing-master said, ' That will do, sir. You need not come again.' "

Emerson's mode of living was very simple: coffee in the morning, tea in the evening, animal food by choice only once a day, wine only when with others using it, but always *pie* at breakfast. "It stood before him and was the first thing eaten." Ten o'clock was his bed-time, six his hour of rising until the last ten years of his life, when he rose at seven. Work or company sometimes led him to sit up late, and this he could do night after night. He never was hungry, — could go any time from breakfast to tea without food and not know it, but was always ready for food when it was set before him.

He always walked from about four in the afternoon till tea-time, and often longer when the day was fine, or he felt that he should work the better.

It is plain from his writings that Emerson was possessed all his life long with the idea of his constitutional infirmity and insufficiency. He hated invalidism, and had little patience with complaints about ill-health, but in his poems, and once or twice in his letters to Carlyle, he expresses himself with freedom about his own bodily inheritance. In 1827, being then but twenty-four years old, he writes: —

> "I bear in youth the sad infirmities
> That use to undo the limb and sense of age."

Four years later : —

> "Has God on thee conferred
>   A bodily presence mean as Paul's,
> Yet made thee bearer of a word
>   Which sleepy nations as with trumpet calls ? "

and again, in the same year : —

> "Leave me, Fear, thy throbs are base,
>   Trembling for the body's sake." —

Almost forty years from the first of these dates we find him bewailing in "Terminus" his inherited weakness of organization.

And in writing to Carlyle, he says : —

"You are of the Anakim and know nothing of the debility and postponement of the blonde constitution."

Again, "I am the victim of miscellany — miscellany of designs, vast debility and procrastination."

He thought too much of his bodily insufficiencies, which, it will be observed, he refers to only in his private correspondence, and in that semi-nudity of self-revelation which is the privilege of poetry. His presence was fine and impressive, and his muscular strength was enough to make him a rapid and enduring walker.

Emerson's voice had a great charm in conversation, as in the lecture-room. It was never loud, never shrill, but singularly penetrating. He was apt to hesitate in the course of a sentence, so as to be sure of the exact word he wanted; picking his way through his vocabulary, to get at the best expression of his thought, as a well-dressed woman crosses the muddy pavement to reach the opposite sidewalk. It was this natural slight and not unpleasant semicolon pausing of the memory which grew upon him in his years of decline, until it rendered conversation laborious and painful to him.

He never laughed loudly. When he laughed it was under protest, as it were, with closed doors, his mouth shut, so that the explosion had to seek another respiratory channel, and found its way out quietly, while his eyebrows and nostrils and all his features betrayed the " ground swell," as Professor Thayer happily called it, of the half-suppressed convulsion. He was averse to loud laughter in others, and objected to Margaret Fuller that she made him laugh too much.

Emerson was not rich in some of those natural gifts which are considered the birthright of the New Englander. He had not the mechanical turn of the whittling Yankee. I once questioned him about his manual dexterity, and he told me he could split a shingle four ways with one nail, — which, as the intention is not to split it at all in fastening it to the roof of a house or elsewhere, I took to be a confession of inaptitude for mechanical works. He does not seem to have

been very accomplished in the handling of agricultural implements either, for it is told in the
family that his little son, Waldo, seeing him at
work with a spade, cried out, " Take care, papa,
— you will dig your leg."

He used to regret that he had no ear for music.
I have said enough about his verse, which often
jars on a sensitive ear, showing a want of the
nicest perception of harmonies and discords in
the arrangement of the words.

There are stories which show that Emerson
had a retentive memory in the earlier part of his
life. It is hard to say from his books whether
he had or not, for he jotted down such a multitude of things in his diary that this was a kind
of mechanical memory which supplied him with
endless materials of thought and subjects for his
pen.

Lover and admirer of Plato as Emerson was,
the doors of the academy, over which was the
inscription μηδὲις ἀγεωμέτρητος ἔσειτω, — Let no
one unacquainted with geometry enter here, —
would have been closed to him. All the exact
sciences found him an unwilling learner. He
says of himself that he cannot multiply seven
by twelve with impunity.

In an unpublished manuscript kindly sub-
mitted to me by Mr. Frothingham, Emerson is
reported as saying, " God has given me the

seeing eye, but not the working hand." His gift
was insight: he saw the germ through its en-
velop; the particular in the light of the universal; the fact in connection with the principle;
the phenomenon as related to the law; all this
not by the slow and sure process of science, but
by the sudden and searching flashes of imaginative double vision. He had neither the patience
nor the method of the inductive reasoner; he
passed from one thought to another not by logical steps but by airy flights, which left no foot-
prints. This mode of intellectual action when
found united with natural sagacity becomes poetry, philosophy, wisdom, or prophecy in its various
forms of manifestation. Without that gift of
natural sagacity (*odoratio quædam venatica*), —
a good scent for truth and beauty, — it appears
as extravagance, whimsicality, eccentricity, or
insanity, according to its degree of aberration.
Emerson was eminently sane for an idealist. He
carried the same sagacity into the ideal world
that Franklin showed in the affairs of common
life.

He was constitutionally fastidious, and had
to school himself to become able to put up with
the terrible inflictions of uncongenial fellow-
ships. We must go to his poems to get at his
weaknesses. The clown of the first edition of
" Monadnoc " " with heart of cat and eyes of

bug," disappears in the after-thought of the later
version of the poem, but the eye that recognized
him and the nature that recoiled from him were
there still. What must he not have endured
from the persecutions of small-minded worshippers who fastened upon him for the interminable
period between the incoming and the outgoing
railroad train! He was a model of patience and
good temper. We might have feared that he
lacked the sensibility to make such intrusions and
offences an annoyance. But when Mr. Frothingham gratifies the public with those most interesting personal recollections which I have had
the privilege of looking over, it will be seen that
his equanimity, admirable as it was, was not in-
capable of being disturbed, and that on rare
occasions he could give way to the feeling which
showed itself of old in the doom pronounced on
the barren fig-tree.

Of Emerson's affections his home-life, and
those tender poems in memory of his brothers
and his son, give all the evidence that could be
asked or wished for. His friends were all who
knew him, for none could be his enemy; and his
simple graciousness of manner, with the sincerity
apparent in every look and tone, hardly admitted
indifference on the part of any who met him,
were it but for a single hour. Even the little
children knew and loved him, and babes in arms

returned his angelic smile. Of the friends who were longest and most intimately associated with him, it is needless to say much in this place. Of those who are living, it is hardly time to speak; of those who are dead, much has already been written. Margaret Fuller, — I must call my early schoolmate as I best remember her, — leaves her life pictured in the mosaic of five artists, — Emerson himself among the number; Thoreau is faithfully commemorated in the loving memoir by Mr. Sanborn; Theodore Parker lives in the story of his life told by the eloquent Mr. Weiss; Hawthorne awaits his portrait from the master-hand of Mr. Lowell.

How nearly any friend, other than his brothers Edward and Charles, came to him, I cannot say, indeed I can hardly guess. That "majesty" Mr. Lowell speaks of always seemed to hedge him round like the divinity that doth hedge a king. What man was he who would lay his hand familiarly upon his shoulder and call him Waldo? No disciple of Father Mathew would be likely to do such a thing. There may have been such irreverent persons, but if any one had so ventured at the "Saturday Club," it would have produced a sensation like Brummel's "George, ring the bell," to the Prince Regent. His ideas of friendship, as of love, seem almost too exalted for our earthly conditions, and sug-

gest the thought as do many others of his characteristics, that the spirit which animated his
mortal frame had missed its way on the shining path to some brighter and better sphere of
being.

Not so did Emerson appear among the plain
working farmers of the village in which he lived.
He was a good, unpretending fellow-citizen who
put on no airs, who attended town-meetings, took
his part in useful measures, was no great hand
at farming, but was esteemed and respected, and
felt to be a principal source of attraction to Concord, for strangers came flocking to the place as
if it held the tomb of Washington.

What was the errand on which he visited our
earth, — the message with which he came com-
missioned from the Infinite source of all life?

Every human soul leaves its port with sealed
orders. These may be opened earlier or later
on its voyage, but until they are opened no one
can tell what is to be his course or to what harbor he is bound.

Emerson inherited the traditions of the Boston pulpit, such as they were, damaged, in the
view of the prevailing sects of the country,
perhaps by too long contact with the " Sons of
Liberty," and their revolutionary notions. But
the most " liberal " Boston pulpit still held to

24

many doctrines, forms, and phrases open to the challenge of any independent thinker.

In the year 1832 this young priest, then a settled minister, "began," as was said of another, — "to be about thirty years of age." He had opened his sealed orders and had read therein :

Thou shalt not profess that which thou dost not believe.

Thou shalt not heed the voice of man when it agrees not with the voice of God in thine own soul.

Thou shalt study and obey the laws of the Universe and they will be thy fellow-servants.

Thou shalt speak the truth as thou seest it, without fear, in the spirit of kindness to all thy fellow-creatures, dealing with the manifold interests of life and the typical characters of history.

Nature shall be to thee as a symbol. The life of the soul, in conscious union with the Infinite, shall be for thee the only real existence.

This pleasing show of an external world through which thou art passing is given thee to interpret by the light which is in thee. Its least appearance is not unworthy of thy study. Let thy soul be open and thine eyes will reveal to thee beauty everywhere.

Go forth with thy message among thy fellow-

creatures; teach them they must trust themselves as guided by that inner light which dwells
with the pure in heart, to whom it was promised
of old that they shall see God.

Teach them that each generation begins the
world afresh, in perfect freedom; that the present is not the prisoner of the past, but that to-
day holds captive all yesterdays, to compare, to
judge, to accept, to reject their teachings, as
these are shown by its own morning's sun.

To thy fellow-countrymen thou shalt preach
the gospel of the New World, that here, here in
our America, is the home of man; that here is
the promise of a new and more excellent social
state than history has recorded.

Thy life shall be as thy teachings, brave,
pure, truthful, beneficent, hopeful, cheerful, hospitable to all honest belief, all sincere thinkers,
and active according to thy gifts and opportunities.

He was true to the orders he had received.
Through doubts, troubles, privations, opposition,
he would not

> "bate a jot
> Of heart or hope, but still bear up and steer
> Right onward."

All through the writings of Emerson the spirit
of these orders manifests itself. His range of

subjects is very wide, ascending to the highest sphere of spiritual contemplation, bordering on that "intense inane" where thought loses itself in breathless ecstasy, and stooping to the homeliest maxims of prudence and the every-day lessons of good manners. And all his work was done, not so much

> "As ever in his great Taskmaster's eye,"

as in the ever-present sense of divine companionship.

He was called to sacrifice his living, his position, his intimacies, to a doubt, and he gave them all up without a murmur. He might have been an idol, and he broke his own pedestal to attack the idolatry which he saw all about him. He gave up a comparatively easy life for a toilsome and trying one; he accepted a precarious employment, which hardly kept him above poverty, rather than wear the golden padlock on his lips which has held fast the conscience of so many pulpit Chrysostoms. Instead of a volume or two of sermons, bridled with a text and harnessed with a confession of faith, he bequeathed us a long series of Discourses and Essays in which we know we have his honest thoughts, free from that professional bias which tends to make the pulpit teaching of the fairest-minded preacher follow a diagonal of two forces, — the promptings of his personal and his ecclesiastical opinions.

Without a church or a pulpit, he soon had a congregation. It was largely made up of young persons of both sexes, young by nature, if not in years, who, tired of routine and formulæ, and full of vague aspirations, found in his utterances the oracles they sought. To them, in the words of his friend and neighbor Mr. Alcott, he

"Sang his full song of hope and lofty cheer."

Nor was it only for a few seasons that he drew his audiences of devout listeners around him. Another poet, his Concord neighbor, Mr. Sanborn, who listened to him many years after the first flush of novelty was over, felt the same enchantment, and recognized the same inspiring life in his words, which had thrilled the souls of those earlier listeners.

" His was the task and his the lordly gift
     Our eyes, our hearts, bent earthward, to uplift."

This was his power, — to inspire others, to make life purer, loftier, calmer, brighter. Optimism is what the young want, and he could no more help taking the hopeful view of the universe and its future than Claude could help flooding his landscapes with sunshine.

"Nature," published in 1836, " the first clear manifestation of his genius," as Mr. Norton calls it, revealed him as an idealist and a poet, with a tendency to mysticism. If he had been independent in circumstances, he would doubtless have developed more freely in these directions. But he had his living to get and a family to support, and he must look about him for some paying occupation. The lecture-room naturally presented itself to a scholar accustomed to speaking from the pulpit. This medium of communicating thought was not as yet very popular, and the rewards it offered were but moderate. Emerson was of a very hopeful nature, however, and believed in its possibilities.

— " I am always haunted with brave dreams of what might be accomplished in the lecture-room, — so free and so unpretending a platform, — a Delos not yet made fast. I imagine an eloquence of infinite variety, rich as conversation can be, with anecdote, joke, tragedy, epics and pindarics, argument and confession." So writes Emerson to Carlyle in 1841.

It would be as unfair to overlook the special form in which Emerson gave most of his thoughts to the world, as it would be to leave out of view the calling of Shakespeare in judging his literary character. Emerson was an essayist and a lecturer, as Shakespeare was a dramatist and a play-actor.

The exigencies of the theatre account for

much that is, as it were, accidental in the writings of Shakespeare. The demands of the lecture-room account for many peculiarities which
are characteristic of Emerson as an author.
The play must be in five acts, each of a given
length. The lecture must fill an hour and not
overrun it. Both play and lecture must be
vivid, varied, picturesque, stimulating, or the
audience would tire before the allotted time was
over.

Both writers had this in common : they were
poets and moralists. They reproduced the conditions of life in the light of penetrative observation and ideal contemplation ; they illustrated
its duties in their breach and in their observance, by precepts and well-chosen portraits of
character. The particular form in which they
wrote makes little difference when we come upon
the utterance of a noble truth or an elevated
sentiment.

It was not a simple matter of choice with the
dramatist or the lecturer in what direction they
should turn their special gifts. The actor had
learned his business on the stage ; the lecturer
had gone through his apprenticeship in the pulpit. Each had his bread to earn, and he must
work, and work hard, in the way open before
him. For twenty years the playwright wrote
dramas, and retired before middle age with a

good estate to his native town. For forty years
Emerson lectured and published lectures, and
established himself at length in competence in
the village where his ancestors had lived and
died before him. He never became rich, as
Shakespeare did. He was never in easy circumstances until he was nearly seventy years old.
Lecturing was hard work, but he was under the
"base necessity," as he called it, of constant
labor, writing in summer, speaking everywhere
east and west in the trying and dangerous winter season.

He spoke in great cities to such cultivated
audiences as no other man could gather about
him, and in remote villages where he addressed
plain people whose classics were the Bible and
the "Farmer's Almanac." Wherever he appeared in the lecture-room, he fascinated his
listeners by his voice and manner; the music of
his speech pleased those who found his thought
too subtle for their dull wits to follow.

When the Lecture had served its purpose, it
came before the public in the shape of an Essay.
But the Essay never lost the character it borrowed from the conditions under which it was
delivered; it was a lay sermon, — *concio ad pop-
ulum.* We must always remember what we are
dealing with. "Expect nothing more of my
power of construction, — no ship-building, no

clipper, smack, nor skiff even, only boards and logs tied together." — " Here I sit and read and write, with very little system, and, as far as regards composition, with the most fragmentary result: paragraphs incompressible, each sentence an infinitely repellent particle." We have then a moralist and a poet appearing as a Lecturer and an Essayist, and now and then writing in verse. He liked the freedom of the platform. "I preach in the Lecture-room," he says, "and there it tells, for there is no prescription. You may laugh, weep, reason, sing, sneer, or pray, according to your genius." In England, he says, "I find this lecturing a key which opens all doors." But he did not tend to overvalue the calling which from "base necessity" he followed so diligently. "Incorrigible spouting Yankee," he calls himself; and again, "I peddle out all the wit I can gather from Time or from Nature, and am pained at heart to see how thankfully that little is received." Lecture-peddling was a hard business and a poorly paid one in the earlier part of the time when Emerson was carrying his precious wares about the country and offering them in competition with the cheapest itinerants, with shilling concerts and negro-minstrel entertainments. But one could get a kind of living out of it if he had invitations enough. I remember Emerson's coming to my house to know if I could fill his place at a certain Lyceum so that he might accept a very advantageous invitation in another direction. I told him that I was unfortunately engaged for the evening mentioned. He smiled serenely, saying that then he supposed he must give up the new stove for that season.

No man would accuse Emerson of parsimony of ideas. He crams his pages with the very marrow of his thought. But in weighing out a lecture he was as punctilious as Portia about the pound of flesh. His utterance was deliberate and spaced with not infrequent slight delays. Exactly at the end of the hour the lecture stopped. Suddenly, abruptly, but quietly, without peroration of any sort, always with "a gentle shock of mild surprise" to the unprepared listener. He had weighed out the full measure to his audience with perfect fairness.

> ὥστε τάλαντα γυνὴ χερνῆτις ἀληθὴς
> Ἥτε σταθμὸν ἔχουσα καὶ εἴριον, ἀμφὶς ἀνέλκει
> Ἰσάζους, ἵνα παισὶν ἀεικέα μισθὸν ἄρηται,

or, in Bryant's version,

> "as the scales
> Are held by some just woman, who maintains
> By spinning wool her household, — carefully
> She poises both the wool and weights, to make
> The balance even, that she may provide
> A pittance for her babes." —

As to the charm of his lectures all are agreed. It is needless to handle this subject, for Mr. Lowell has written upon it. Of their effect on his younger listeners he says, " To some of us that long past experience remains the most marvellous and fruitful we have ever had. Emerson awakened us, saved us from the body of this death. It is the sound of the trumpet that the young soul longs for, careless of what breath may fill it. Sidney heard it in the ballad of ' Chevy Chase,' and we in Emerson. Nor did it blow retreat, but called us with assurance of victory."

There was, besides these stirring notes, a sweet seriousness in Emerson's voice that was infinitely soothing. So might " Peace, be still," have sounded from the lips that silenced the storm. I remember that in the dreadful war-time, on one of the days of anguish and terror, I fell in with Governor Andrew, on his way to a lecture of Emerson's, where he was going, he said, to relieve the strain upon his mind. An hour passed in listening to that flow of thought, calm and clear as the diamond drops that distil from a mountain rock, was a true nepenthe for a care-worn soul.

An author whose writings are like mosaics must have borrowed from many quarries. Emerson had read more or less thoroughly through a very wide range of authors. I shall presently show how extensive was his reading. No doubt he had studied certain authors diligently, a few, it would seem, thoroughly. But let no one be frightened away from his pages by the terrible names of Plotinus and Proclus and Porphyry, of Behmen or Spinoza, or of those modern German philosophers with whom it is not pretended that he had any intimate acquaintance. Mr. George Ripley, a man of erudition, a keen critic, a lover and admirer of Emerson, speaks very plainly of his limitations as a scholar.

" As he confesses in the Essay on ' Books,' his learning is second hand; but everything sticks which his mind can appropriate. He defends the use of translations, and I doubt whether he has ever read ten pages of his great authorities, Plato, Plutarch, Montaigne, or Goethe, in the original. He is certainly no friend of profound study any more than of philosophical speculation. Give him a few brilliant and suggestive glimpses, and he is content."

One correction I must make to this statement. Emerson says he has " contrived to read " almost every volume of Goethe, and that he has fifty-five of them, but that he has read nothing else in German, and has not looked into him for a long time. This was in 1840, in a letter to

Carlyle. It was up-hill work, it may be suspected, but he could not well be ignorant of his
friend's great idol, and his references to Goethe
are very frequent.

Emerson's quotations are like the miraculous
draught of fishes. I hardly know his rivals
except Burton and Cotton Mather. But no one
would accuse him of pedantry. Burton quotes
to amuse himself and his reader; Mather quotes
to show his learning, of which he had a vast
conceit; Emerson quotes to illustrate some original thought of his own, or because another writer's way of thinking falls in with his own, —
never with a trivial purpose. Reading as he
did, he must have unconsciously appropriated a
great number of thoughts from others. But he
was profuse in his references to those from
whom he borrowed, — more profuse than many
of his readers would believe without taking the
pains to count his authorities. This I thought
it worth while to have done, once for all, and
I will briefly present the results of the examination. The named references, chiefly to authors,
as given in the table before me, are three thousand three hundred and ninety-three, relating to
eight hundred and sixty-eight different individuals. Of these, four hundred and eleven are
mentioned more than once; one hundred and
fifty-five, five times or more; sixty-nine, ten

times or more; thirty-eight, fifteen times or
more; and twenty-seven, twenty times or more.
These twenty-seven names alone, the list of
which is here given, furnish no less than one
thousand and sixty-five references.

Authorities.	Number of times mentioned.
Shakespeare	112
Napoleon	84
Plato	81
Plutarch	70
Goethe	62
Swift	49
Bacon	47
Milton	46
Newton	43
Homer	42
Socrates	42
Swedenborg	40
Montaigne	30
Saadi	30
Luther	30

Authorities.	Number of times mentioned.
Webster	27
Aristotle	25
Hafiz	25
Wordsworth	25
Burke	24
Saint Paul	24
Dante	22
Shattuck (Hist. of Concord)	21
Chaucer	20
Coleridge	20
Michael Angelo	20
The name of Jesus occurs fifty-four times.	

It is interesting to observe that Montaigne,
Franklin, and Emerson all show the same fondness for Plutarch.

Montaigne says, " I never settled myself to
the reading of any book of solid learning but
Plutarch and Seneca."

Franklin says, speaking of the books in his
father's library, " There was among them Plutarch's Lives, which I read abundantly, and I
still think that time spent to great advantage."

Emerson says, " I must think we are more

deeply indebted to him than to all the ancient writers."

Studies of life and character were the delight of all these four moralists. As a judge of character, Dr. Hedge, who knew Emerson well, has spoken to me of his extraordinary gift, and no reader of "English Traits" can have failed to mark the formidable penetration of the intellect which looked through those calm cerulean eyes.

Noscitur a sociis is as applicable to the books a man most affects as well as to the companions he chooses. It is with the kings of thought that Emerson most associates. As to borrowing from his royal acquaintances his ideas are very simple and expressed without reserve.

"All minds quote. Old and new make the warp and woof of every moment. There is no thread that is not a twist of these two strands. By necessity, by proclivity, and by delight, we all quote."

What Emerson says of Plutarch applies very nearly to himself.

"In his immense quotation and allusion we quickly cease to discriminate between what he quotes and what he invents. We sail on his memory into the ports of every nation, enter into every private property, and do not stop to discriminate owners, but give him the praise of all."

Mr. Ruskin and Lord Tennyson have thought it worth their while to defend themselves from the charge of plagiarism. Emerson would never have taken the trouble to do such a thing. His mind was overflowing with thought as a river in the season of flood, and was full of floating fragments from an endless variety of sources. He drew ashore whatever he wanted that would serve his purpose. He makes no secret of his mode of writing. " I dot evermore in my endless journal, a line on every knowable in nature; but the arrangement loiters long, and I get a brick-kiln instead of a house." His journal is " full of disjointed dreams and audacities." Writing by the aid of this, it is natural enough that he should speak of his " lapidary style " and say " I build my house of boulders."

" It is to be remembered," says Mr. Ruskin, " that all men who have sense and feeling are continually helped : they are taught by every person they meet, and enriched by everything that falls in their way. The greatest is he who has been oftenest aided ; and if the attainments of all human minds could be traced to their real sources, it would be found that the world had been laid most under contribution by the men of most original powers, and that every day of their existence deepened their debt to their race, while it enlarged their gifts to it."

The reader may like to see a few coincidences between Emerson's words and thoughts and those of others.

Some sayings seem to be a kind of family property. " Scorn trifles " comes from Aunt Mary Moody Emerson, and reappears in her nephew, Ralph Waldo. — " What right have you, Sir, to your virtue ? Is virtue piecemeal? This is a jewel among the rags of a beggar." So writes Ralph Waldo Emerson in his Lecture " New England Reformers." — " Hiding the badges of royalty beneath the gown of the mendicant, and ever on the watch lest their rank be betrayed by the sparkle of a gem from under their rags." Thus wrote Charles Chauncy Emerson in the " Harvard Register " nearly twenty years before.

> " The hero is not fed on sweets,
> Daily his own heart he eats."

The image comes from Pythagoras *via* Plutarch.

Now and then, but not with any questionable frequency, we find a sentence which recalls Carlyle.

" The national temper, in the civil history, is not flashy or whiffling. The slow, deep English mass smoulders with fire, which at last sets all its borders in flame. The wrath of London is not French wrath, but has a long memory, and in hottest heat a register and rule."

Compare this passage from " English Traits " with the following one from Carlyle's " French Revolution " : —

" So long this Gallic fire, through its successive changes of color and character, will blaze over the face of Europe, and afflict and scorch all men : — till it provoke all men, till it kindle another kind of fire, the Teutonic kind, namely ; and be swallowed up, so to speak, in a day ! For there is a fire comparable to the burning of dry jungle and grass ; most sudden, high-blazing : and another fire which we liken to the burning of coal, or even of anthracite coal, but which no known thing will put out."

> " O what are heroes, prophets, men
>   But pipes through which the breath of man doth blow
>   A momentary music."

The reader will find a similar image in one of Burns's letters, again in one of Coleridge's poetical fragments, and long before any of them, in a letter of Leibnitz.

> " He builded better than he knew "

is the most frequently quoted line of Emerson. The thought is constantly recurring in our literature. It helps out the minister's sermon ; and a Fourth of July Oration which does not borrow it is like the " Address without a Phœnix " among the Drury Lane mock poems. Can we find any trace of this idea elsewhere?

In a little poem of Coleridge's, "William Tell," are these two lines:

> " On wind and wave the boy would toss
> Was great, nor knew how great he was."

The thought is fully worked out in the celebrated Essay of Carlyle called " Characteristics." It reappears in Emerson's poem " Fate."

> " Unknown to Cromwell as to me
> Was Cromwell's measure and degree ;
> Unknown to him as to his horse,
> If he than his groom is better or worse."

It is unnecessary to illustrate this point any further in this connection. In dealing with his poetry other resemblances will suggest themselves. All the best poetry the world has known is full of such resemblances. If we find Emerson's wonderful picture, " Initial Love" prefigured in the " Symposium" of Plato, we have only to look in the " Phædrus " and we we shall find an earlier sketch of Shakespeare's famous group, —

> " The lunatic, the lover, and the poet."

Sometimes these resemblances are nothing more than accidental coincidences ; sometimes the similar passages are unconsciously borrowed from another ; sometimes they are paraphrases, varia-

tions, embellished copies, *éditions de luxe* of
sayings that all the world knows are old, but
which it seems to the writer worth his while to
say over again. The more improved versions of
the world's great thoughts we have, the better,
and we look to the great minds for them. The
larger the river the more streams flow into it.
The wide flood of Emerson's discourse has a
hundred rivers and thousands of streamlets for
its tributaries.

It was not from books only that he gathered
food for thought and for his lectures and essays.
He was always on the lookout in conversation
for things to be remembered. He picked up
facts one would not have expected him to care
for. He once corrected me in giving Flora
Temple's time at Kalamazoo. I made a mistake
of a quarter of a second, and he set me right.
He was not always so exact in his memory, as
I have already shown in several instances. Another example is where he speaks of Quintus
Curtius, the historian, when he is thinking of Met-
tus Curtius, the self-sacrificing equestrian. Little inaccuracies of this kind did not concern
him much ; he was a wholesale dealer in illustrations, and could not trouble himself about a
trifling defect in this or that particular article.

Emerson was a man who influenced others
more than others influenced him. Outside of

his family connections, the personalities which can be most easily traced in his own are those of Carlyle, Mr. Alcott, and Thoreau. Carlyle's harsh virility could not be without its effect on his valid, but sensitive nature. Alcott's psychological and physiological speculations interested him as an idealist. Thoreau lent him a new set of organs of sense of wonderful delicacy. Emerson looked at nature as a poet, and his natural history, if left to himself, would have been as vague as that of Polonius. But Thoreau had a pair of eyes which, like those of the Indian deity, could see the smallest emmet on the blackest stone in the darkest night, — or come nearer to seeing it than those of most mortals. Emerson's long intimacy with him taught him to give an outline to many natural objects which would have been poetic nebulæ to him but for this companionship. A nicer analysis would detect many alien elements mixed with his individuality, but the family traits predominated over all the external influences, and the personality stood out distinct from the common family qualities. Mr. Whipple has well said: "Some traits of his mind and character may be traced back to his ancestors, but what doctrine of heredity can give us the genesis of his genius? Indeed the safest course to pursue is to quote his own words, and despairingly confess that it is the nature of gen-

ius ' to spring, like the rainbow daughter of
Wonder, from the invisible, to abolish the past
and refuse all history.' "

Emerson's place as a thinker is somewhat difficult to fix. He cannot properly be called a
psychologist. He made notes and even delivered lectures on the natural history of the intellect ; but they seem to have been made up,
according to his own statement, of hints and
fragments rather than of the results of systematic study. He was a man of intuition, of insight, a seer, a poet, with a tendency to mysticism. This tendency renders him sometimes
obscure, and once in a while almost, if not quite,
unintelligible. We can, for this reason, understand why the great lawyer turned him over to
his daughters, and Dr. Walter Channing complained that his lecture made his head ache.
But it is not always a writer's fault that he is
not understood. Many persons have poor heads
for abstractions ; and as for mystics, if they
understand themselves it is quite as much as can
be expected. But that which is mysticism to a
dull listener may be the highest and most inspiring imaginative clairvoyance to a brighter one.
It is to be hoped that no reader will take offence
at the following anecdote, which may be found
under the title " Diogenes," in the work of his

namesake, Diogenes Laertius. I translate from the Latin version.

"Plato was talking about ideas, and spoke of *mensality* and *cyathity* [*tableity*, and *gobletity*]. 'I can see a table and a goblet,' said the cynic, 'but I can see no such things as tableity and gobletity.' 'Quite so,' answered Plato, 'because you have the eyes to see a goblet and a table with, but you have not the brains to understand tableity and gobletity.'"

This anecdote may be profitably borne in mind in following Emerson into the spheres of intuition and mystical contemplation.

Emerson was an idealist in the Platonic sense of the word, a spiritualist as opposed to a materialist. He believes, he says, "as the wise Spenser teaches," that the soul makes its own body. This, of course, involves the doctrine of preëxistence; a doctrine older than Spenser, older than Plato or Pythagoras, having its cradle in India, fighting its way down through Greek philosophers and Christian fathers and German professors, to our own time, when it has found Pierre Leroux, Edward Beecher, and Brigham Young among its numerous advocates. Each has his fancies on the subject. The geography of an undiscovered country and the soundings of an ocean that has never been sailed over may belong to romance and poetry, but they do not belong to the realm of knowledge.

That the organ of the mind brings with it inherited aptitudes is a simple matter of observation. That it inherits truths is a different proposition. The eye does not bring landscapes into the world on its retina, — why should the brain bring thoughts? Poetry settles such questions very simply by saying it is so.

The poet in Emerson never accurately differentiated itself from the philosopher. He speaks of Wordsworth's Ode on the Intimations of Immortality as the high-water mark of the poetry of this century. It sometimes seems as if he had accepted the lofty rhapsodies of this noble Ode as working truths.

> " Not in entire forgetfulness,
>   And not in utter nakedness,
> But trailing clouds of glory do we come
>   From God, who is our home."

In accordance with this statement of a divine inheritance from a preëxisting state, the poet addresses the infant: —

> "Mighty prophet! Seer blest!
>   On whom those truths do rest
> Which we are toiling all our lives to find." —

These are beautiful fancies, but the philosopher will naturally ask the poet what are the truths which the child has lost between its cradle and the age of eight years, at which Wordsworth finds the little girl of whom he speaks in the lines, —

> " A simple child —
> That lightly draws its breath
> And feels its life in every limb, —
> What should it know of death ? "

What should it, sure enough, or of any other of
those great truths which Time with its lessons,
and the hardening of the pulpy brain can alone
render appreciable to the consciousness ? Undoubtedly every brain has its own set of moulds
ready to shape all material of thought into its
own individual set of patterns. If the mind
comes into consciousness with a good set of
moulds derived by " traduction," as Dryden
called it, from a good ancestry, it may be all
very well to give the counsel to the youth to
plant himself on his instincts. But the individual to whom this counsel is given probably has dangerous as well as wholesome instincts. He has also a great deal besides the
instincts to be considered. His instincts are
mixed up with innumerable acquired prejudices,
erroneous conclusions, deceptive experiences, partial truths, one-sided tendencies. The clearest
insight will often find it hard to decide what is
the real instinct, and whether the instinct itself
is, in theological language, from God or the devil.
That which was a safe guide for Emerson might
not work well with Lacenaire or Jesse Pomeroy.
The cloud of glory which the babe brings with

it into the world is a good set of instincts, which dispose it to accept moral and intellectual truths, — not the truths themselves. And too many children come into life trailing after them clouds which are anything but clouds of glory.

It may well be imagined that when Emerson proclaimed the new doctrine, — new to his young disciples, — of planting themselves on their instincts, consulting their own spiritual light for guidance, — trusting to intuition, — without reference to any other authority, he opened the door to extravagances in any unbalanced minds, if such there were, which listened to his teachings. Too much was expected out of the mouths of babes and sucklings. The children shut up by Psammetichus got as far as one word in their evolution of an original language, but *bekkos* was a very small contribution towards a complete vocabulary. " The Dial " was well charged with intuitions, but there was too much vagueness, incoherence, aspiration without energy, effort without inspiration, to satisfy those who were looking for a new revelation.

The gospel of intuition proved to be practically nothing more or less than this: a new manifesto of intellectual and spiritual independence. It was no great discovery that we see many things as truths which we cannot prove. But it was a great impulse to thought, a great

advance in the attitude of our thinking community, when the profoundly devout religious free-
thinker took the ground of the undevout and
irreligious free-thinker, and calmly asserted and
peaceably established the right and the duty of
the individual to weigh the universe, its laws
and its legends, in his own balance, without fear
of authority, or names, or institutions.

All this brought its dangers with it, like other
movements of emancipation. For the Fay *ce
que voudras* of the revellers of Medmenham
Abbey, was substituted the new motto, Pense *ce
que voudras*. There was an intoxication in this
newly proclaimed evangel which took hold of
some susceptible natures and betrayed itself in
prose and rhyme, occasionally of the Bedlam
sort. Emerson's disciples were never accused
of falling into the more perilous snares of antinomianism, but he himself distinctly recognizes
the danger of it, and the counterbalancing effect
of household life, with its curtain lectures and
other benign influences. Extravagances of opinion cure themselves. Time wore off the effects
of the harmless debauch, and restored the giddy
revellers to the regimen of sober thought, as re-
formed spiritual inebriates.

Such were some of the incidental effects of
the Emersonian declaration of independence.

It was followed by a revolutionary war of opinion not yet ended or at present like to be. A local outbreak, if you will, but so was throwing the tea overboard. A provincial affair, if the Bohemian press likes that term better, but so was the skirmish where the gun was fired the echo of which is heard in every battle for freedom all over the world.

Too much has been made of Emerson's mysticism. He was an intellectual rather than an emotional mystic, and withal a cautious one. He never let go the string of his balloon. He never threw over all his ballast of common sense so as to rise above an atmosphere in which a rational being could breathe. I found in his library William Law's edition of Jacob Behmen. There were all those wonderful diagrams over which the reader may have grown dizzy, — just such as one finds on the walls of lunatic asylums, — evidences to all sane minds of cerebral strabismus in the contrivers of them. Emerson liked to lose himself for a little while in the vagaries of this class of minds, the dangerous proximity of which to insanity he knew and has spoken of. He played with the incommunicable, the inconceivable, the absolute, the antinomies, as he would have played with a bundle of jack-straws. "Brahma," the poem which so mysti-

fied the readers of the " Atlantic Monthly," was
one of his spiritual divertisements. To the average Western mind it is the nearest approach to
a Torricellian vacuum of intelligibility that language can pump out of itself. If " Rejected
Addresses " had not been written half a century
before Emerson's poem, one would think these
lines were certainly meant to ridicule and par-
ody it.

> "The song of Braham is an Irish howl;
>   Thinking is but an idle waste of thought,
> And nought is everything and everything is nought."

Braham, Hazlitt might have said, is so obviously
the anagram of Brahma that dulness itself could
not mistake the object intended.

Of course no one can hold Emerson responsible for the "Yoga" doctrine of Brahmanism,
which he has amused himself with putting in
verse. The oriental side of Emerson's nature
delighted itself in these narcotic dreams, born
in the land of the poppy and of hashish. They
lend a peculiar charm to his poems, but it is not
worth while to try to construct a philosophy out
of them. The knowledge, if knowledge it be,
of the mystic is not transmissible. It is not
cumulative; it begins and ends with the solitary
dreamer, and the next who follows him has to
build his own cloud-castle as if it were the first
aerial edifice that a human soul had ever con-
structed.

Some passages of "Nature," "The Over-Soul," "The Sphinx," "Uriel," illustrate sufficiently this mood of spiritual exaltation. Emerson's calm temperament never allowed it to reach the condition he sometimes refers to, — that of ecstasy. The passage in "Nature" where he says "I become a transparent eyeball" is about as near it as he ever came. This was almost too much for some of his admirers and worshippers. One of his most ardent and faithful followers, whose gifts as an artist are well known, mounted the eyeball on legs, and with its cornea in front for a countenance and its optic nerve projecting behind as a queue, the spiritual cyclops was shown setting forth on his travels.

Emerson's reflections in the "transcendental" mood do beyond question sometimes irresistibly suggest the close neighborhood of the sublime to the ridiculous. But very near that precipitous border line there is a charmed region where, if the statelier growths of philosophy die out and disappear, the flowers of poetry next the very edge of the chasm have a peculiar and mysterious beauty. "Uriel" is a poem which finds itself perilously near to the gulf of unsounded obscurity, and has, I doubt not, provoked the mirth of profane readers; but read in a lucid moment, it is just obscure enough and just significant enough to give the voltaic thrill which comes from the sudden contacts of the highest imaginative conceptions.

Human personality presented itself to Emerson as a passing phase of universal being. Born of the Infinite, to the Infinite it was to return. Sometimes he treats his own personality as interchangeable with objects in nature, — he would put it off like a garment and clothe himself in the landscape. Here is a curious extract from " The Adirondacs," in which the reader need not stop to notice the parallelism with Byron's —

> " The sky is changed, — and such a change ! O night
> And storm and darkness, ye are wondrous strong." —

Now Emerson : —

> " And presently the sky is changed ; O world !
> What pictures and what harmonies are thine !
> The clouds are rich and dark, the air serene,
> *So like the soul of me, what if 't were me ?* "

We find this idea of confused personal identity also in a brief poem printed among the " Translations " in the Appendix to Emerson's Poems. These are the last two lines of " The Flute, from Hilali " : —

> " Saying, Sweetheart ! the old mystery remains,
> If I am I ; thou, thou, or thou art I ? "

The same transfer of personality is hinted in the line of Shelley's " Ode to the West Wind " :

> " Be thou, Spirit fierce,
> My spirit ! Be thou me, impetuous one ! "

Once more, how fearfully near the abyss of the ridiculous! A few drops of alcohol bring about a confusion of mind not unlike this poetical metempsychosis.

The laird of Balnamoon had been at a dinner where they gave him cherry-brandy instead of port wine. In driving home over a wild tract of land called Munrimmon Moor his hat and wig blew off, and his servant got out of the gig and brought them to him. The hat he recognized, but not the wig. "It's no my wig, Hairy [Harry], lad; it's no my wig," and he would not touch it. At last Harry lost his patience: "Ye'd better tak' it, sir, for there's nae waile [choice] o' wigs on Munrimmon Moor." And in our earlier days we used to read of the bewildered market-woman, whose *Ego* was so obscured when she awoke from her slumbers that she had to leave the question of her personal identity to the instinct of her four-footed companion: —

"If it be I, he'll wag his little tail;
And if it be not I, he'll loudly bark and wail."

I have not lost my reverence for Emerson in showing one of his fancies for a moment in the distorting mirror of the ridiculous. He would doubtless have smiled with me at the reflection, for he had a keen sense of humor. But I take the opportunity to disclaim a jesting remark

about "a foresmell of the Infinite" which Mr.
Conway has attributed to me, who am innocent
of all connection with it.

The mystic appeals to those only who have an
ear for the celestial concords, as the musician
only appeals to those who have the special endowment which enables them to understand his
compositions. It is not for organizations un-
tuned to earthly music to criticise the great
composers, or for those who are deaf to spiritual
harmonies to criticise the higher natures which
lose themselves in the strains of divine contemplation. The bewildered reader must not forget
that passage of arms, previously mentioned, between Plato and Diogenes.

Emerson looked rather askance at Science in
his early days. I remember that his brother
Charles had something to say in the "Harvard
Register" (1828) about its disenchantments.
I suspect the prejudice may have come partly
from Wordsworth. Compare this verse of his
with the lines of Emerson's which follow it.

> "Physician art thou, one all eyes ;
>   Philosopher, a fingering slave,
> One that would peep and botanize
>   Upon his mother's grave ? "

Emerson's lines are to be found near the end
of the Appendix in the new edition of his works.

> " Philosophers are lined with eyes within,
>   And, being so, the sage unmakes the man.
>   In love he cannot therefore cease his trade ;
>   Scarce the first blush has overspread his cheek,
>   He feels it, introverts his learned eye
>   To catch the unconscious heart in the very act.
>   His mother died, — the only friend he had, —
>   Some tears escaped, but his philosophy
>   Couched like a cat, sat watching close behind
>   And throttled all his passion.   Is 't not like
>   That devil-spider that devours her mate
>   Scarce freed from her embraces ? "

The same feeling comes out in the Poem
" Blight," where he says the " young scholars
who invade our hills "

> " Love not the flower they pluck, and know it not,
>   And all their botany is Latin names ; "

and in " The Walk," where the " learned men "
with their glasses are contrasted with the sons
of Nature, — the poets are no doubt meant, —
much to the disadvantage of the microscopic
observers. Emerson's mind was very far from
being of the scientific pattern. Science is quan-
titative, — loves the foot-rule and the balance,
— methodical, exhaustive, indifferent to the beautiful as such. The poet is curious, asks all manner of questions, and never thinks of waiting for
the answer, still less of torturing Nature to get
at it. Emerson wonders, for instance, —

> " Why Nature loves the number five,"

but leaves his note of interrogation without troubling himself any farther. He must have picked up some wood-craft and a little botany from Thoreau, and a few chemical notions from his brother-in-law, Dr. Jackson, whose name is associated with the discovery of artificial anæs-thesia. It seems probable that the genial companionship of Agassiz, who united with his scientific genius, learning, and renown, most delightful social qualities, gave him a kinder feeling to men of science and their pursuits than he had entertained before that great master came among us. At any rate he avails himself of the facts drawn from their specialties without scruple when they will serve his turn. But he loves the poet always better than the scientific student of nature. In his Preface to the Poems of Mr. W. E. Channing, he says: —

"Here is a naturalist who sees the flower and the bud with a poet's curiosity and awe, and does not count the stamens in the aster, nor the feathers in the wood-thrush, but rests in the surprise and affection they awake." —

This was Emerson's own instinctive attitude to all the phenomena of nature.

Emerson's style is epigrammatic, incisive, authoritative, sometimes quaint, never obscure, except when he is handling nebulous subjects.

His paragraphs are full of brittle sentences that break apart and are independent units, like the fragments of a coral colony. His imagery is frequently daring, leaping from the concrete to the abstract, from the special to the general and universal, and *vice versa*, with a bound that is like a flight. Here are a few specimens of his pleasing audacities : —

" There is plenty of wild azote and carbon unappropriated, but it is naught till we have made it up into loaves and soup." —

" He arrives at the sea-shore and a sumptuous ship has floored and carpeted for him the stormy Atlantic." —

" If we weave a yard of tape in all humility and as well as we can, long hereafter we shall see it was no cotton tape at all but some galaxy which we braided, and that the threads were Time and Nature." —

" Tapping the tempest for a little side wind." —

" The locomotive and the steamboat, like enormous shuttles, shoot every day across the thousand various threads of national descent and employment and bind them fast in one web." —

He is fond of certain archaisms and unusual phrases. He likes the expression " mother-wit," which he finds in Spenser, Marlowe, Shakespeare, and other old writers. He often uses the word " husband " in its earlier sense of economist. His use of the word " haughty " is so fitting, and it sounds so nobly from his lips, that we could wish its employment were forbidden henceforth to voices which vulgarize it. But his special, constitutional, word is " fine," meaning something like dainty, as Shakespeare uses it, — " my dainty Ariel," — " fine Ariel." It belongs to his habit of mind and body as " faint " and " swoon " belong to Keats. This word is one of the ear-marks by which Emerson's imitators are easily recognized. " Melioration " is another favorite word of Emerson's. A clairvoyant could spell out some of his most characteristic traits by the aid of his use of these three words; his inborn fastidiousness, subdued and kept out of sight by his large charity and his good breeding, showed itself in his liking for the word " haughty ; " his exquisite delicacy by his fondness for the word " fine," with a certain shade of meaning; his optimism in the frequent recurrence of the word " melioration."

We must not find fault with his semi-detached sentences until we quarrel with Solomon and criticise the Sermon on the Mount. The " point and surprise " which he speaks of as characterizing the style of Plutarch belong eminently to his own. His fertility of illustrative imagery is

very great. His images are noble, or, if borrowed from humble objects, ennobled by his
handling. He throws his royal robe over a
milking-stool and it becomes a throne. But
chiefly he chooses objects of comparison grand
in themselves. He deals with the elements at
first hand. Such delicacy of treatment, with
such breadth and force of effect, is hard to
match anywhere, and we know him by his style
at sight. It is as when the slight fingers of a
girl touch the keys of some mighty and many-
voiced organ, and send its thunders rolling along
the aisles and startling the stained windows of a
great cathedral. We have seen him as an unpretending lecturer. We follow him round as
he " peddles out all the wit he can gather from
Time or from Nature," and we find that " he has
changed his market cart into a chariot of the
sun," and is carrying about the morning light as
merchandise.

Emerson was as loyal an American, as thorough a New Englander, as home-loving a citizen,
as ever lived. He arraigned his countrymen
sharply for their faults. Mr. Arnold made one
string of his epithets familiar to all of us, —
" This great, intelligent, sensual, and avaricious
America." This was from a private letter to
Carlyle. In his Essay, " Works and Days," he

is quite as outspoken : "This mendicant America, this curious, peering, itinerant, imitative America." "I see plainly," he says, "that our society is as bigoted to the respectabilities of religion and education as yours." "The war," he says, "gave back integrity to this erring and immoral nation." All his life long he recognized the faults and errors of the new civilization. All his life long he labored diligently and lovingly to correct them. To the dark prophecies of Carlyle, which came wailing to him across the ocean, he answered with ever hopeful and cheerful anticipations. "Here," he said, in words I have already borrowed, "is the home of man — here is the promise of a new and more excellent social state than history has recorded."

Such a man as Emerson belongs to no one town or province or continent; he is the common property of mankind; and yet we love to think of him as breathing the same air and treading the same soil that we and our fathers and our children have breathed and trodden. So it pleases us to think how fondly he remembered his birthplace; and by the side of Franklin's bequest to his native city we treasure that golden verse of Emerson's : —

"A blessing through the ages thus
Shield all thy roofs and towers,

GOD WITH THE FATHERS, SO WITH US,
Thou darling town of ours ! ''

Emerson sympathized with all generous public movements, but he was not fond of working in associations, though he liked well enough to attend their meetings as a listener and looker-on. His study was his workshop, and he preferred to labor in solitude. When he became famous he paid the penalty of celebrity in frequent interruptions by those " devastators of the day " who sought him in his quiet retreat. His courtesy and kindness to his visitors were uniform and remarkable. Poets who come to recite their verses and reformers who come to explain their projects are among the most formidable of earthly visitations. Emerson accepted his martyrdom with meek submission ; it was a martyrdom in detail, but collectively its petty tortures might have satisfied a reasonable inquisitor as the punishment of a moderate heresy. Except in that one phrase above quoted he never complained of his social oppressors, so far as I remember, in his writings. His perfect amiability was one of his most striking characteristics, and in a nature fastidious as was his in its whole organization, it implied a self - command worthy of admiration.

The natural purity and elevation of Emer-

son's character show themselves in all that he
writes. His life corresponded to the ideal we
form of him from his writings. This it was
which made him invulnerable amidst all the
fierce conflicts his gentle words excited. His
white shield was so spotless that the least scru-
pulous combatants did not like to leave their de-
facing marks upon it. One would think he was
protected by some superstition like that which
Voltaire refers to as existing about Boileau, —

"Ne disons pas mal de Nicolas, — cela porte malheur."

(Don't let us abuse Nicolas, — it brings ill luck.)
The cooped-up dogmatists whose very citadel of
belief he was attacking, and who had their
hot water and boiling pitch and flaming brim-
stone ready for the assailants of their outer de-
fences, withheld their missiles from him, and even
sometimes, in a movement of involuntary human
sympathy, sprinkled him with rose-water. His
position in our Puritan New England was in
some respects like that of Burns in Presbyterian
Scotland. The *dour* Scotch ministers and elders
could not cage their minstrel, and they could not
clip his wings; and so they let this morning lark
rise above their theological mists, and sing to
them at heaven's gate, until he had softened all
their hearts and might nestle in their bosoms
and find his perch on " the big ha' bible," if he

would, — and as he did. So did the music of
Emerson's words and life steal into the hearts
of our stern New England theologians, and soften
them to a temper which would have seemed trea-
sonable weakness to their stiff-kneed forefathers.
When a man lives a life commended by all the
Christian virtues, enlightened persons are not so
apt to cavil at his particular beliefs or unbeliefs
as in former generations. We do, however, wish
to know what are the convictions of any such
persons in matters of highest interest about
which there is so much honest difference of
opinion in this age of deep and anxious and devout religious scepticism.

It was a very wise and a very prudent course
which was taken by Simonides, when he was
asked by his imperial master to give him his
ideas about the Deity. He begged for a day to
consider the question, but when the time came
for his answer he wanted two days more, and at
the end of these, four days. In short, the more
he thought about it, the more he found himself
perplexed.

The name most frequently applied to Emerson's form of belief is Pantheism. How many
persons who shudder at the sound of this word
can tell the difference between that doctrine and
their own professed belief in the omnipresence
of the Deity?

Theodore Parker explained Emerson's position, as he understood it, in an article in the "Massachusetts Quarterly Review." I borrow this quotation from Mr. Cooke : —

"He has an absolute confidence in God. He has been foolishly accused of Pantheism, which sinks God in nature, but no man is further from it. He never sinks God in man; he does not stop with the law, in matter or morals, but goes to the Law-giver; yet probably it would not be so easy for him to give his definition of God, as it would be for most graduates at Andover or Cambridge."

We read in his Essay, "Self-Reliance": "This is the ultimate fact which we so quickly reach on this, as on every topic, the resolution of all into the ever-blessed ONE. Self-existence is the attribute of the Supreme Cause, and it constitutes the measure of good by the degree in which it enters into all lower forms."

The "ever-blessed ONE" of Emerson corresponds to the Father in the doctrine of the Trinity. The "Over-Soul" of Emerson is that aspect of Deity which is known to theology as the Holy Spirit. Jesus was for him a divine manifestation, but only as other great human souls have been in all ages and are to-day. He was willing to be called a Christian just as he was willing to be called a Platonist.

Explanations are apt not to explain much in dealing with subjects like this. " Canst thou by searching find out God ? Canst thou find out the Almighty unto perfection? " But on certain great points nothing could be clearer than the teaching of Emerson. He believed in the doctrine of spiritual influx as sincerely as any Calvinist or Swedenborgian. His views as to fate, or the determining conditions of the character, brought him near enough to the doctrine of predestination to make him afraid of its consequences, and led him to enter a caveat against any denial of the self-governing power of the will.

His creed was a brief one, but he carried it everywhere with him. In all he did, in all he said, and so far as all outward signs could show, in all his thoughts, the indwelling Spirit was his light and guide ; through all nature he looked up to nature's God ; and if he did not worship the " man Christ Jesus " as the churches of Christendom have done, he followed his footsteps so nearly that our good Methodist, Father Taylor, spoke of him as more like Christ than any man he had known.

Emerson was in friendly relations with many clergymen of the church from which he had parted. Since he left the pulpit, the lesson, not of tolerance, for that word is an insult as applied by one set of well-behaved people to another, not of charity, for that implies an impertinent assumption, but of good feeling on the part of divergent sects and their ministers has been taught and learned as never before. Their official Confessions of Faith make far less difference in their human sentiments and relations than they did even half a century ago. These ancient creeds are handed along down, to be kept in their phials with their stoppers fast, as attar of rose is kept in its little bottles ; they are not to be opened and exposed to the atmosphere so long as their perfume, — the odor of sanctity, — is diffused from the carefully treasured receptacles, — perhaps even longer than that.

Out of the endless opinions as to the significance and final outcome of Emerson's religious teachings I will select two as typical.

Dr. William Hague, long the honored minister of a Baptist church in Boston, where I had the pleasure of friendly acquaintance with him, has written a thoughtful, amiable paper on Emerson, which he read before the New York Genealogical and Biographical Society. This Essay closes with the following sentence : —

" Thus, to-day, while musing, as at the beginning, over the works of Ralph Waldo Emerson, we recognize now as ever his imperial genius as

one of the greatest of writers; at the same time,
his life work, as a whole, tested by its supreme
ideal, its method and its fruitage, shows also a
great waste of power, verifying the saying of
Jesus touching the harvest of human life: ' HE
THAT GATHERETH NOT WITH ME SCATTERETH
ABROAD.' "

"But when Dean Stanley returned from
America, it was to report," says Mr. Conway
"('Macmillan,' June, 1879), that religion had
there passed through an evolution from Edwards
to Emerson, and that 'the genial atmosphere
which Emerson has done so much to promote is
shared by all the churches equally.'"

What is this "genial atmosphere" but the
very spirit of Christianity? The good Baptist
minister's Essay is full of it. He comes asking
what has become of Emerson's "wasted power"
and lamenting his lack of "fruitage," and lo!
he himself has so ripened and mellowed in that
same Emersonian air that the tree to which he
belongs would hardly know him. The close-
communion clergyman handles the arch-heretic
as tenderly as if he were the nursing mother of
a new infant Messiah. A few generations ago
this preacher of a new gospel would have been
burned; a little later he would been tried and imprisoned; less than fifty years ago he was called
infidel and atheist; names which are fast becom-

ing relinquished to the intellectual half-breeds
who sometimes find their way into pulpits and
the so-called religious periodicals.

It is not within our best-fenced churches and
creeds that the self-governing American is like
to find the religious freedom which the Concord
prophet asserted with the strength of Luther
and the sweetness of Melancthon, and which the
sovereign in his shirt-sleeves will surely claim.
Milton was only the precursor of Emerson when
he wrote : —

"Neither is God appointed and confined, where
and out of what place these his chosen shall be
first heard to speak ; for he sees not as man sees,
chooses not as man chooses, lest we should devote
ourselves again to set places and assemblies, and
outward callings of men, planting our faith one
while in the old convocation house, and another
while in the Chapel at Westminster, when all
the faith and religion that shall be there canon-
ized is not sufficient without plain convincement,
and the charity of patient instruction, to supple
the least bruise of conscience, to edify the meanest Christian who desires to walk in the spirit
and not in the letter of human trust, for all the
number of voices that can be there made; no,
though Harry the Seventh himself there, with
all his liege tombs about him, should lend their
voices from the dead, to swell their number."

The best evidence of the effect produced by
Emerson's writings and life is to be found in the
attention he has received from biographers and
critics. The ground upon which I have ventured
was already occupied by three considerable
Memoirs. Mr. George Willis Cooke's elaborate
work is remarkable for its careful and thorough
analysis of Emerson's teachings. Mr. Moncure
Daniel Conway's "Emerson at Home and
Abroad" is a lively picture of its subject by one
long and well acquainted with him. Mr. Alexander Ireland's "Biographical Sketch" brings
together, from a great variety of sources, as well
as from his own recollections, the facts of Emerson's history and the comments of those whose
opinions were best worth reproducing. I must
refer to this volume for a bibliography of the
various works and Essays of which Emerson
furnished the subject.

From the days when Mr. Whipple attracted
the attention of our intelligent, but unawakened
reading community, by his discriminating and
appreciative criticisms of Emerson's Lectures,
and Mr. Lowell drew the portrait of the New
England "Plotinus-Montaigne" in his brilliant
"Fable for Critics," to the recent essays of Mr.
Matthew Arnold, Mr. John Morley, Mr. Henry
Norman, and Mr. Edmund Clarence Stedman,
Emerson's writings have furnished one of the

most enduring *pièces de résistance* at the critical tables of the old and the new world.

He early won the admiration of distinguished European thinkers and writers : Carlyle accepted his friendship and his disinterested services ; Miss Martineau fully recognized his genius and sounded his praises ; Miss Bremer fixed her sharp eyes on him and pronounced him " a noble man." Professor Tyndall found the inspiration of his life in Emerson's fresh thought ; and Mr. Arnold, who clipped his medals reverently but unsparingly, confessed them to be of pure gold, even while he questioned whether they would pass current with posterity. He found discerning critics in France, Germany, and Holland. Better than all is the testimony of those who knew him best. They who repeat the saying that " a prophet is not without honor save in his own country," will find an exception to its truth in the case of Emerson. Read the impressive words spoken at his funeral by his fellow-townsman, Judge Hoar ; read the glowing tributes of three of Concord's poets, — Mr. Alcott, Mr. Channing, and Mr. Sanborn, — and it will appear plainly enough that he, whose fame had gone out into all the earth, was most of all believed in, honored, beloved, lamented, in the little village circle that centred about his own fireside.

27

It is a not uninteresting question whether Emerson has bequeathed to the language any essay or poem which will resist the flow of time like "the adamant of Shakespeare," and remain a classic like the Essays of Addison or Gray's Elegy. It is a far more important question whether his thought entered into the spirit of his day and generation, so that it modified the higher intellectual, moral, and religious life of his time, and, as a necessary consequence, those of succeeding ages. *Corpora non agunt nisi soluta*, and ideas must be dissolved and taken up as well as material substances before they can act. "That which thou sowest is not quickened except it die," or rather lose the form with which it was sown. Eight stanzas of four lines each have made the author of "The Burial of Sir John Moore" an immortal, and endowed the language with a classic, perfect as the most finished cameo. But what is the gift of a mourning ring to the bequest of a perpetual annuity? How many lives have melted into the history of their time, as the gold was lost in Corinthian brass, leaving no separate monumental trace of their influence, but adding weight and color and worth to the age of which they formed a part and the generations that came after them! We can dare to predict of Emerson, in the words of his old friend and disciple, Mr. Cranch : —

" The wise will know thee and the good will love,
 The age to come will feel thy impress given
  In all that lifts the race a step above
   Itself, and stamps it with the seal of heaven."

It seems to us, to-day, that Emerson's best literary work in prose and verse must live as long
as the language lasts; but whether it live or fade
from memory, the influence of his great and
noble life and the spoken and written words
which were its exponents, blends, indestructible,
with the enduring elements of civilization.

It is not irreverent, but eminently fitting, to
compare any singularly pure and virtuous life
with that of the great exemplar in whose footsteps Christendom professes to follow. The time
was when the divine authority of his gospel
rested chiefly upon the miracles he is reported
to have wrought. As the faith in these exceptions to the general laws of the universe dimin-
ished, the teachings of the Master, of whom it
was said that he spoke as never man spoke,
were more largely relied upon as evidence of his
divine mission. Now, when a comparison of
these teachings with those of other religious
leaders is thought by many to have somewhat
lessened the force of this argument, the life of
the sinless and self-devoted servant of God and
friend of man is appealed to as the last and con-

vincing proof that he was an immediate manifestation of the Divinity.

Judged by his life Emerson comes very near our best ideal of humanity. He was born too late for the trial of the cross or the stake, or even the jail. But the penalty of having an opinion of his own and expressing it was a serious one, and he accepted it as cheerfully as any of Queen Mary's martyrs accepted his fiery baptism. His faith was too large and too deep for the formulæ he found built into the pulpit, and he was too honest to cover up his doubts under the flowing vestments of a sacred calling. His writings, whether in prose or verse, are worthy of admiration, but his manhood was the underlying quality which gave them their true value. It was in virtue of this that his rare genius acted on so many minds as a trumpet call to awaken them to the meaning and the privileges of this earthly existence with all its infinite promise. No matter of what he wrote or spoke, his words, his tones, his looks, carried the evidence of a sincerity which pervaded them all and was to his eloquence and poetry like the water of crystallization ; without which they would effloresce into mere rhetoric. He shaped an ideal for the commonest life, he proposed an object to the humblest seeker after truth. Look for beauty in the world around you, he said, and you shall see it everywhere. Look within, with pure eyes and simple trust, and you shall find the Deity mirrored in your own soul. Trust yourself because you trust the voice of God in your inmost consciousness.

There are living organisms so transparent that we can see their hearts beating and their blood flowing through their glassy tissues. So transparent was the life of Emerson; so clearly did the true nature of the man show through it. What he taught others to be, he was himself. His deep and sweet humanity won him love and reverence everywhere among those whose natures were capable of responding to the highest manifestations of character. Here and there a narrow-eyed sectary may have avoided or spoken ill of him; but if He who knew what was in man had wandered from door to door in New England as of old in Palestine, we can well believe that one of the thresholds which "those blessed feet" would have crossed, to hallow and receive its welcome, would have been that of the lovely and quiet home of Emerson.

INDEX.

[For many references, not found elsewhere, see under the general headings of *Emerson's Books, Essays, Poems.*]

Haughty, a characteristic expression, 405.

Hawthorne, Nathaniel : his Mosses, 70 ; "dream-peopled solitude," 86 ; at the club, 223 ; view of English life, 335 ; grave, 356 ; biography, 368.

Hazlitt, William : British Poets, 21.

Health, inspiration, 289.

Hebrew Language, study, 48. (See *Bible*.)

Hedge, Frederic Henry : at a party, 149 ; quoted, 383.

Henry VII., tombs, 415.

Herbert, George : Poem on Man, 102 ; parallel, 170 ; poetry, 281 ; a line quoted, 345.

Herder, Johann Gottfried, allusion, 16.

Heredity : Emerson's belief, 1, 2 ; in Emerson family, 4, 19 ; Whipple on, 389 ; Jonson, 393.

Herrick, Robert, poetry, 281.

Higginson, Thomas Wentworth. (See *Emerson's Books, — Nature.*)

Hilali, The Flute, 399.

Hillard, George Stillman : in college, 24, 25 ; his literary place, 33 ; aid, 276.

Hindoo Scriptures, 199, 200. (See *Bible, India,* etc.)

History, how it should be written, 168.

Hoar, Ebenezer Rockwood : reference to, 223 ; on the Burns speech, 225 ; kindness, 273, 274, 276–279 ; at Emerson's death-bed, 349 ; funeral address, 351–353.

Hoar, Samuel : statesman, 72 ; tribute, 213, 214.

Holland, description of the Dutch, 217.

Holley, Horace, prayer, 267.

Holmes, John, a pupil of Emerson, 50.

Holmes, Oliver Wendell : memories of Dr. Ripley, 15 ; of C. C. Emerson, 20, 21 ; familiarity with Cambridge and its college, 45 ; erroneous quotation from, 251, 252 ; jest erroneously attributed to, 400, 401.

Holy Ghost, "a new born bard of the," 123. (See *Christ, God, Religion,* etc.)

Homer : poetic rank, 202, 320 ; plagiarism, 205 ; Iliad, 253 ; allusion, 315 ; tin pans, 325 ; times quoted, 382. (See *Greek,* etc.)

Homer, Jonathan, minister of Newton, 15.

Hooper, Mrs. Ellen, The Dial, 159, 160.

Hope : lacking in America, 143 ; in every essay, 284.

Horace : allusion, 22 ; Ars Poetica, 316.

Horses, Flora Temple's time, 388.

Howard University, speech, 263.

Howe, Samuel Gridley, the philanthropist, 223.

Hunt, Leigh, meeting Emerson, 195.

Hunt, William, the painter, 223.

IDEALISM, 98–100, 146, 150.

Idealists : Ark full, 191 ; Platonic sense, 391.

Imagination : the faculty, 141 ; defined, 237, 238 ; essay, 283 ; coloring life, 324.

Imbecility, 231.

Immortality, 262. (See *God, Religion,* etc.)

Incompleteness, in poetry, 339.

India : poetic models, 338 ; idea of preëxistence, 391 ; Brahmanism, 397. (See *Emerson's Poems, — Brahma.*)

Indians : in history of Concord, 71 ; Algonquins, 72.

Inebriation, subject in Monthly Anthology, 30.

Insects, defended, 190.

Inspiration : of Nature, 22, 96, 141 ; urged, 146.

Instinct, from God or Devil, 393.

Intellect, confidence in, 134.

Intuition, 394.

Ipswich, Mass., 3, 4, 8.

Ireland, Alexander : glimpses of Emerson, 44, 64, 65 ; reception, 193, 194 ; on Carlyle, 196 ; letter from Miss Peabody, 317 ; quoting Whitman, 344 ; quoted, 350.

Irving, Washington, 33.

Italy : Emerson's first visit, 62, 63 ; Naples, 113.

JACKSON, CHARLES, garden, 38.

Jackson, Dr. Charles Thomas, anæsthesia, 403.

Jackson, Miss Lydia, reading Carlyle, 81. (See *Mrs. Emerson.*)

Jahn, Johann, studied at Andover, 48.

Jameson, Anna, new book, 131.

Jesus : times mentioned, 382 ; a divine manifestation, 411 ; followers, 417 ; and Emerson, 419. (See *Bible, Christ, Church, Religion,* etc.)

WORKS OF
OLIVER WENDELL HOLMES.

———◆———

As he is everybody's favorite, there is no occasion for critics to meddle
with him, either to censure or to praise. He can afford to laugh at the
whole reviewing fraternity. His wit is all his own, so sly and tingling,
but without a drop of ill-nature in it, and never leaving a sting behind.
His humor is so grotesque and queer that it reminds one of the frolics of
Puck; and deep pathos mingles with it so naturally that when the reader's eyes are brimming with tears he knows not whether they have their
source in sorrow or in laughter. — *North American Review.*

PROSE WORKS.

THE AUTOCRAT OF THE BREAKFAST-TABLE. New Edition, revised, and containing a new Preface and Bibliographical Notes. Crown 8vo, gilt top,
$2.00.

Handy Volume Edition. 32mo, $1.25; half calf, $2.50; morocco, tree
calf, or seal, $4.00.

THE PROFESSOR AT THE BREAKFAST-TABLE. New Edition, revised, and
with a new Preface. Crown 8vo, gilt top, $2.00.

THE POET AT THE BREAKFAST-TABLE. New Edition, revised, and with a
new Preface. Crown 8vo, gilt top, $2.00.

THE BREAKFAST-TABLE SERIES, containing "The Autocrat," "The Professor," and "The Poet." 3 vols. crown 8vo, $6.00; half calf, $12.00;
morocco, $15.00.

ELSIE VENNER. A Romance of Destiny. New Edition. Crown 8vo, gilt
top, $2.00.

THE GUARDIAN ANGEL. New Edition. Crown 8vo, gilt top, $2.00.

PAGES FROM AN OLD VOLUME OF LIFE, including "Soundings from the
Atlantic" and "Mechanism in Thought and Morals," etc. Crown 8vo,
gilt top, $2.00.

THE BREAKFAST-TABLE SERIES, ELSIE VENNER, THE GUARDIAN ANGEL,
PAGES FROM AN OLD VOLUME OF LIFE, and POEMS (*Household Edition*).
The set, 7 vols gilt top, uniform in box, $12.00; half calf, $24.00.

A MORTAL ANTIPATHY. Crown 8vo, $1.50.

MEDICAL ESSAYS (including the volumes published under the titles,
"Currents and Counter-Currents in Medical Science," and "Border
Lines," etc.) Crown 8vo, gilt top, $2.00.

CURRENTS AND COUNTER-CURRENTS in Medical Science, with other Essays.
New Edition. Uniform with New Edition of Dr. Holmes's Works
Crown 8vo, gilt top, $2.00.

BORDER LINES IN SOME PROVINCES OF MEDICAL SCIENCE. 16mo, $1.00

SOUNDINGS FROM THE ATLANTIC. 16mo, $1.75.

MECHANISM IN THOUGHT AND MORALS. 16mo, $1.00.

JOHN LOTHROP MOTLEY. A Memoir. *Popular Edition*. 16mo, gilt top, $1.50.

RALPH WALDO EMERSON. In "American Men of Letters" Series With Portrait. 16mo, gilt top, $1.25.

THE STORY OF IRIS (together with Favorite Poems). "Modern Classics" No. 30. Illustrated. 32mo, orange edges, 75 cents.

SELECTIONS FROM "BREAKFAST-TABLE SERIES," and "PAGES FROM AN OLD VOLUME OF LIFE." "Modern Classics" No. 33. Illustrated. 32mo, orange edges, 75 cents. *School Edition*. 32mo, 40 cents.

POETICAL WORKS.

POEMS. *Household Edition*. Illustrated. 12mo, $2.00; cr. 8vo, full gilt, $2.50; half calf, $4.00; morocco, or tree calf, $5.00.

Handy Volume Edition. With Portrait. 2 vols. 32mo, gilt top, $2.50; half calf, $5.00; morocco, tree calf, or seal, $8.00.

The Same. Together with *Handy Volume* "Autocrat." 3 vols. 32mo, $3.75; half calf, $7.50; tree calf, morocco, or seal, $12.00.

Illustrated Library Edition. With 32 full page Illustrations, and Portrait. 8vo, full gilt, $4.00; half calf, $7.00; morocco, or tree calf, $9.00

SONGS OF MANY SEASONS 16mo, $2.00.

SONGS IN MANY KEYS. 16mo, $1.50.

ASTRÆA. THE BALANCE OF ILLUSIONS. 16mo, 75 cents.

THE SCHOOL-BOY. Illustrated. 4to, full gilt, $3.00; morocco, or tree calf, $7.50.

GRANDMOTHER'S STORY, and other Poems. "Riverside Literature Series," No. 6. 16mo, paper covers, 15 cents.

THE IRON GATE, and other Poems. With Portrait. 12mo, gilt top, $1.25

FAVORITE POEMS (together with the Story of Iris). "Modern Classics." No. 30. Illustrated. 32mo, orange edges, 75 cents.

COMPILATIONS.

HOLMES LEAFLETS. Selections from the Writings of Holmes, for Home and School Use. With Biographical Sketch. Illustrated. 12mo, paper covers, 48 cents. Leaflets or pamphlet separately, each 24 cents.

HOLMES CALENDAR. Selections from the Writings of Holmes, for every Day in the Year. On decorated card. $1.00.

* *For sale by all Booksellers. Sent by mail, post-paid, on receipt of price by the Publishers,*

HOUGHTON, MIFFLIN & CO., PUBLISHERS, BOSTON, MASS.

WORKS OF
RALPH WALDO EMERSON.

—•—

There is no man living to whom, as a writer, so many of us feel and thankfully acknowledge so great an indebtedness for ennobling impulses. We look upon him as one of the few men of genius whom our age has produced; and there needs no better proof of it than his masculine faculty of fecundating other minds. — JAMES RUSSELL LOWELL.

In doing homage to that sweet nature, we do it to the highest type of our common humanity. Emerson was a splendid manifestation of reason in its most comprehensive form, and with all its most godlike aspirations. — JOHN TYNDALL.

COMPLETE WORKS.

Riverside Edition. With two Portraits. In 11 volumes, 12mo, gilt top, each, $1.75. The set, $19.25; half calf, $38.50; half crushed levant, $49.50.

An entirely new library edition of the works of Mr. Emerson, printed from new electrotype plates. It includes the prose and poetical writings of Mr. Emerson hitherto published in book form, and, in addition, two new volumes of essays, lectures, and speeches. The order of the volumes is as follows: —

   I. NATURE, ADDRESSES, AND LECTURES (formerly known as Miscellanies).

  II. ESSAYS. First Series.

 III. ESSAYS. Second Series.

 IV. REPRESENTATIVE MEN.

  V. ENGLISH TRAITS.

 VI. CONDUCT OF LIFE.

VII. SOCIETY AND SOLITUDE.

VIII. LETTERS AND SOCIAL AIMS.

 IX. POEMS.

  X. LECTURES AND BIOGRAPHICAL SKETCHES. (A new volume.)

 XI. MISCELLANIES. (A new volume.)

The workmanship of this elegantly simple edition is what we expect from the taste that presides over the publications of the Riverside Press. — *New York Evening Post.*

" Little Classic" Edition. In 11 volumes, 18mo, each, $1.50. The set, 11 volumes, $16.50; half calf, or half morocco, $32.00; tree calf, $40.00.

"WASHINGTON IRVING."

Mr. Warner has not only written with sympathy, minute knowledge of his subject, fine literary taste, and that easy, fascinating style which always puts him on such good terms with his readers, but he has shown a tact, critical sagacity, and sense of proportion full of promise for the rest of the series which is to pass under his supervision. — *New York Tribune.*

It is a very charming piece of literary work, and presents the reader with an excellent picture of Irving as a man and of his methods as an author, together with an accurate and discriminating characterization of his works. — *Boston Journal.*

It would hardly be possible to produce a fairer or more candid book of its kind. — *Literary World* (London).

"NOAH WEBSTER."

Mr. Scudder's biography of Webster is alike honorable to himself and its subject. Finely discriminating in all that relates to personal and intellectual character, scholarly and just in its literary criticisms, analyses, and estimates, it is besides so kindly and manly in its tone, its narrative is so spirited and enthralling, its descriptions are so quaintly graphic, so varied and cheerful in their coloring, and its pictures so teem with the bustle, the movement, and the activities of the real life of a by-gone but most interesting age, that the attention of the reader is never tempted to wander, and he lays down the book with a sigh of regret for its brevity. — *Harper's Monthly Magazine.*

It fills completely its place in the purpose of this series of volumes. — *The Critic* (New York).

"HENRY D. THOREAU."

Mr. Sanborn's book is thoroughly American and truly fascinating. Its literary skill is exceptionally good, and there is a racy flavor in its pages and an amount of exact knowledge of interesting people that one seldom meets with in current literature. Mr. Sanborn has done Thoreau's genius an imperishable service. — *American Church Review* (New York).

Mr. Sanborn has written a careful book about a curious man, whom he has studied as impartially as possible; whom he admires warmly but with discretion; and the story of whose life he has told with commendable frankness and simplicity. — *New York Mail and Express.*

It is undoubtedly the best life of Thoreau extant. — *Christian Advocate* (New York).

"GEORGE RIPLEY."

Mr. Frothingham's memoir is a calm and thoughtful and tender tribute. It is marked by rare discrimination, and good taste and simplicity. The biographer keeps himself in the background, and lets his subject speak. And the result is one of the best examples of personal portraiture that we have met with in a long time. — *The Churchman* (New York).

He has fulfilled his responsible task with admirable fidelity, frank earnestness, justice, fine feeling, balanced moderation, delicate taste, and finished literary skill. It is a beautiful tribute to the high-bred scholar and generous-hearted man, whose friend he has so worthily portrayed. — *Rev. William H. Channing* (London).

"JAMES FENIMORE COOPER."

We have here a model biography. The book is charmingly written, with a felicity and vigor of diction that are notable, and with a humor sparkling, racy, and never obtrusive. The story of the life will have something of the fascination of one of the author's own romances. — *New York Tribune.*

Prof. Lounsbury's book is an admirable specimen of literary biography. . . . We can recall no recent addition to American biography in any department which is superior to it. It gives the reader not merely a full account of Cooper's literary career, but there is mingled with this a sufficient account of the man himself apart from his books, and of the period in which he lived, to keep alive the interest from the first word to the last. — *New York Evening Post.*

"MARGARET FULLER OSSOLI."

Here at last we have a biography of one of the noblest and the most intellectual of American women, which does full justice to its subject. The author has had ample material for his work, — all the material now available, perhaps, — and has shown the skill of a master in his use of it. . . . It is a fresh view of the subject, and adds important information to that already given to the public. — Rev. Dr. F. H. Hedge, in *Boston Advertiser.*

He has filled a gap in our literary history with excellent taste, with sound judgment, and with that literary skill which is preëminently his own. — *Christian Union* (New York).

Mr. Higginson writes with both enthusiasm and sympathy, and makes a volume of surpassing interest. — *Commercial Advertiser* (New York).

"RALPH WALDO EMERSON."

A biography of Emerson by Holmes is a real event in American literature. . . . He has brought Emerson himself so near, and painted him for us with a pencil so loving and yet so just, that it will remain with many of us a question which shall be hereafter most dear to us, the man whom the artist thus reveals, or the artist himself. — *Standard* (Chicago).

Dr. Holmes has written one of the most delightful biographies that has ever appeared. Every page sparkles with genius. His criticisms are trenchant, his analysis clear, his sense of proportion delicate, and his sympathies broad and deep. — *Philadelphia Press.*

"EDGAR ALLAN POE."

Mr. Woodberry has contrived with vast labor to construct what must hereafter be called the authoritative biography of Poe — a biography which corrects all others, supplements all others, and supersedes all others. — *The Critic* (New York).

The best life of Poe that has yet been written, and no better one is likely to be written hereafter. This is high praise, but it is deserved. Mr. Woodberry has spared no pains in exploring sources of information ; he has shown rare judgment and discretion in the interpretation of what he has found; he has set forth everything frankly and fairly; and he has brought to bear upon the critical part of his work a keen instinct, a well-informed mind, a sound judgment, and the utmost catholicity of spirit. —*Commercial Advertiser* (New York).

"NATHANIEL PARKER WILLIS."

Prof. Beers has done his work sympathetically yet candidly and fairly and in a philosophic manner, indicating the status occupied by Willis in the republic of letters, and sketching graphically his literary environment and the main springs of his success. It is one of the best books of an excellent series. — *Buffalo Times.*

The work is sober, frank, honest, trustworthy, and eminently readable. — *The Beacon* (Boston).

A delightful biographical study. — *Brooklyn Union.*

⁎ *For sale by all Booksellers. Sent, post-paid, on receipt of price by the Publishers,*

HOUGHTON, MIFFLIN AND COMPANY,
BOSTON AND NEW YORK.

American Statesmen.

A Series of Biographies of Men conspicuous in the Political History of the United States.

EDITED BY

JOHN T. MORSE, Jr.

———•———

The object of this series is not merely to give a number of unconnected narratives of men in American political life, but to produce books which shall, when taken together, indicate the lines of political thought and development in American history, — books embodying in compact form the result of extensive study of the many and diverse influences which have combined to shape the political history of our country.

The series is under the editorship of Mr. JOHN T. MORSE, Jr., whose historical and biographical writings give ample assurance of his special fitness for this task. The volumes now ready are as follows : —

John Quincy Adams. By JOHN T. MORSE, Jr.
Alexander Hamilton. By HENRY CABOT LODGE.
John C. Calhoun. By DR. H. VON HOLST.
Andrew Jackson. By PROF. W. G. SUMNER.
John Randolph. By HENRY ADAMS.
James Monroe. By PRES. DANIEL C. GILMAN.
Thomas Jefferson. By JOHN T. MORSE, Jr.
Daniel Webster. By HENRY CABOT LODGE.
Albert Gallatin. By JOHN AUSTIN STEVENS.
James Madison. By SYDNEY HOWARD GAY.
John Adams. By JOHN T. MORSE, Jr.
John Marshall. By A. B. MAGRUDER.
Samuel Adams. By JAMES K. HOSMER.

IN PREPARATION.

Henry Clay. By Hon. CARL SCHURZ.
Martin Van Buren. By HON. WM. DORSHEIMER.

Others to be announced hereafter. Each biography occupies a single volume, 16mo, gilt top. Price $1.25.

ESTIMATES OF THE PRESS

—◆—

"JOHN QUINCY ADAMS."

That Mr. Morse's conclusions will in the main be those of posterity we have very little doubt, and he has set an admirable example to his coadjutors in respect of interesting narrative, just proportion, and judicial candor. — *New York Evening Post.*

Mr. Morse has written closely, compactly, intelligently, fearlessly, honestly. — *New York Times.*

"ALEXANDER HAMILTON."

The biography of Mr. Lodge is calm and dignified throughout. He has the virtue — rare indeed among biographers — of impartiality. He has done his work with conscientious care, and the biography of Hamilton is a book which cannot have too many readers. It is more than a biography; it is a study in the science of government. — *St. Paul Pioneer-Press.*

"JOHN C. CALHOUN."

Nothing can exceed the skill with which the political career of the great South Carolinian is portrayed in these pages. The work is superior to any other number of the series thus far, and we do not think it can be surpassed by any of those that are to come. The whole discussion in relation to Calhoun's position is eminently philosophical and just. — *The Dial* (Chicago).

"ANDREW JACKSON."

Prof. Sumner has, . . . all in all, made the justest long estimate of Jackson that has had itself put between the covers of a book. — *New York Times.*

One of the most masterly monographs that we have ever had the pleasure of reading. It is calm and clear. — *Providence Journal.*

"JOHN RANDOLPH."

The book has been to me intensely interesting . . . It is rich in new facts and side lights, and is worthy of its place in the already brilliant series of monographs on American Statesmen. — Prof. MOSES COIT TYLER.

Remarkably interesting. . . . The biography has all the elements of popularity, and cannot fail to be widely read. — *Hartford Courant.*

"JAMES MONROE."

In clearness of style, and in all points of literary workmanship, from cover to cover, the volume is well-nigh perfect. There is also a calmness of judgment, a correctness of taste, and an absence of partisanship which are too frequently wanting in biographies, and especially in political biographies. — *American Literary Churchman* (Baltimore).

The most readable of all the lives that have ever been written of the great jurist. — *San Francisco Bulletin.*

"THOMAS JEFFERSON."

The book is exceedingly interesting and readable. The attention of the reader is strongly seized at once, and he is carried along in spite of himself, sometimes protesting, sometimes doubting, yet unable to lay the book down. — *Chicago Standard.*

The requirements of political biography have rarely been met so satisfactorily as in this memoir of Jefferson. — *Boston Journal.*

"DANIEL WEBSTER."

It will be read by students of history ; it will be invaluable as a work of reference ; it will be an authority as regards matters of fact and criticism ; it hits the key-note of Webster's durable and ever-growing fame ; it is adequate, calm, impartial ; it is admirable. — *Philadelphia Press.*

The task has been achieved ably, admirably, and faithfully. — *Boston Transcript.*

"ALBERT GALLATIN."

It is one of the most carefully prepared of these very valuable volumes, . . . abounding in information not so readily accessible as is that pertaining to men more often treated by the biographer. . . . The whole work covers a ground which the political student cannot afford to neglect. — *Boston Correspondent Hartford Courant.*

Frank, simple, and straightforward. — *New York Tribune.*

"JAMES MADISON."

The execution of the work deserves the highest praise. It is very readable, in a bright and vigorous style, and is marked by unity and consecutiveness of plan. — *The Nation* (New York).

An able book. . . . Mr. Gay writes with an eye single to truth. — *The Critic* (New York).

"JOHN ADAMS."

A good piece of literary work. . . . It covers the ground thoroughly, and gives just the sort of simple and succinct account that is wanted. — *Evening Post* (New York).

A model of condensation and selection, as well as of graphic portraiture and clear and interesting historical narrative. — *Christian Intelligencer* (New York).

"JOHN MARSHALL."

Well done, with simplicity, clearness, precision, and judgment, and in a spirit of moderation and equity. A valuable addition to the series. — *New York Tribune.*

"SAMUEL ADAMS."

Thoroughly appreciative and sympathetic, yet fair and critical. . . . This biography is a piece of good work — a clear and simple presentation of a noble man and pure patriot; it is written in a spirit of candor and humanity. — *Worcester Spy.*

A brilliant and enthusiastic book, which it will do every American much good to read. — *The Beacon* (Boston).

****** *For sale by all booksellers. Sent, post-paid, on receipt of price by the Publishers,*

HOUGHTON, MIFFLIN & COMPANY,

BOSTON AND NEW YORK.

American Commonwealths,

EDITED BY

HORACE E. SCUDDER.

A series of volumes narrating the history of such States of the Union as have exerted a positive influence in the shaping of the national government, or have a striking political, social, or economical history.

The commonwealth has always been a positive force in American history, and it is believed that no better time could be found for a statement of the life inherent in the States than when the unity of the nation has been assured; and it is hoped by this means to throw new light upon the development of the country, and to give a fresh point of view for the study of American history.

This series is under the editorial care of Mr. Horace E. Scudder, who is well known both as a student of American history and as a writer.

The aim of the Editor will be to secure trustworthy and graphic narratives, which shall have substantial value as historical monographs and at the same time do full justice to the picturesque elements of the subjects. The volumes are uniform in size and general style with the series of "American Statesmen" and "American Men of Letters," and are furnished with maps, indexes, and such brief critical apparatus as add to the thoroughness of the work.

Speaking of the series, the *Boston Journal* says: "It is clear that this series will occupy an entirely new place in our historical literature. Written by competent and aptly chosen authors, from fresh materials, in convenient form, and with a due regard to proportion and proper emphasis, they promise to supply most satisfactorily a positive want."

The series, so far as arranged, comprises the following volumes : —

NOW READY.

Virginia. A History of the People. By JOHN ESTEN COOKE, author of "The Virginia Comedians," "Life of Stonewall Jackson," "Life of General Robert E. Lee," etc.

Oregon. The Struggle for Possession. By WILLIAM BARROWS, D. D.

Maryland. By WILLIAM HAND BROWNE, Associate of Johns Hopkins University.

Kentucky. By NATHANIEL SOUTHGATE SHALER, S. D., Professor of Palæontology, Harvard University, recently Director of the Kentucky State Survey.

Michigan. By Hon. T. M. COOLEY, LL. D.

Kansas. By LEVERETT W. SPRING, Professor of English Literature in the University of Kansas.

California. By JOSIAH ROYCE, Instructor in Philosophy in Harvard University.

IN PREPARATION.

Tennessee. By JAMES PHELAN, Ph. D. (Leipsic).

Connecticut. By ALEXANDER JOHNSTON, author of a "Handbook of American Politics," Professor of Jurisprudence and Political Economy in the College of New Jersey.

Pennsylvania. By Hon. WAYNE MCVEAGH, late Attorney-General of the United States.

South Carolina. By Hon. WILLIAM H. TRESCOT, author of "The Diplomacy of the American Revolution."

New York. By Hon. ELLIS H. ROBERTS.

Missouri. By LUCIEN CARR, M. A., Assistant Curator of the Peabody Museum of Archæology.

Massachusetts. By BROOKS ADAMS.

Others to be announced hereafter. Each volume, with Maps, 16mo, gilt top, $1.25.